Aviation Weather Services *Explained*

by John Holley

Making the most of the government weather services book

Second Edition

Aviation Supplies & Academics, Inc.
Newcastle, Washington

Aviation Weather Services Explained
Second Edition
John Holley

© 1996–2001 ASA, Inc.

ASA-WX-EX2

ISBN 1-56027-386-0

Aviation Supplies
& Academics, Inc. (ASA)
7005 132nd Place SE
Newcastle, Washington
98059-3153

Printed in the United States
of America

05   04   03

9   8   7   6   5   4   3   2

Important: **This book should be used in conjunction with *Aviation Weather Services, Advisory Circular 00-45E,* by the Federal Aviation Administration.** ASA reprints the FAA's AC 00-45E; it is sold separately and is available from aviation retailers nationwide. Order #ASA-AC00-45E.

Acknowledgments for illustrations

Information for creation of the following figures came from NWS (National Weather Service) and FAA (Federal Aviation Administration) websites: Figure 2-1, 2-3, 4-1, 6-1, 7-2, 9-1, 10-1, 11-1, 11-2, 12-3, 19-1. (NWS material used in this book is in the public domain and therefore not subject to copyright protection.) Cartesia software was used to create maps for Figures 4-1, 6-1, 6-2, 9-1, 11-1, 19-1, and Appendix B Page 164. Information and charts from the AWC (Aviation Weather Center, NWS) website were used in Figures 6-1, 7-2, 10-1, 10-2, and Appendix C Pages 169–171. Figure 3-2 satellite photo: NOAA GOES (Geostationary Orbiting Environmental Satellite) website. Canadian weather charts in Chapter 18, and Appendix C Page 176, are excerpted from charts available on the NavCanada website. Alaskan weather charts (Chapter 18, and Appendix C) are from the AAWU (Alaska Aviation Weather Unit, NWS) website. Thanks to Greg Thompson for permission to use weather analysis chart examples from the RAP/UCAR website reprinted on Appendix C Pages 170–171 (copyright UCAR); and thanks to Dave Dempsey at the San Francisco State University Department of Geosciences, for use of the jet stream chart analyses from the California Regional Weather Server at SFSU (Appendix C Pages 172–173). All the internet addresses for websites mentioned above can be found in Appendix E (Pages 185–187).

Editor's Note

On each chapter's initial page in a shaded box in the top right column, you'll find the AC 00-45E page reference for the main topics and charts covered in that chapter. Throughout the author's discussion in the text, this column calls out additional notes regarding or pages for further study reference for a subject in the main text discussion across from the note. Common icons for "book-reference," "take-a-closer-look" hints, and notes are used to highlight the supplemental tips and references. Terms for memorization are defined in this outside column in order to reinforce recall of the many acronyms and abbreviations associated with aviation weather services.

Page numbers that refer to the AC 00-45E are easily identified by their format: *hyphenated* page numbers refer to the *section–page* in the AC 00-45E. Single (no hyphen) page numbers refer to pages in this book.

Contents

	Covers material in Section of AC 00-45E:	
Chapter 13 *Weather Depiction Chart*	Section 6 pp. 6-1 through 6-5	**87**
Chapter 14 *Composite Moisture Stability Chart*	Section 9 pp. 9-1 through 9-15	**91**
Chapter 15 *Constant Pressure Charts and the Four-Dimensional Weather Picture*	Section 8 pp. 8-1 through 8-12	**97**
Chapter 16 *Significant Weather Progs*	Section 11 pp. 11-1 through 11-14	**105**
Chapter 17 *The Tropopause, Jet Stream, and Clear Air Turbulence*	Section 14 pp. 14-1, 14-2	**111**
Chapter 18 *North American Weather Services North of 48° Latitude*	Section 1 p. 1-3	**119**

Chapter 19
Aviation Weather Services of Mexico **131**

Chapter 20
Weather Decisions and The Weather Briefing **135**

Appendix A
Surface Chart Symbology Explained **147**

Appendix B
Handy Weather Information Tables **153**

Appendix C
Color Illustrations: Weather Maps and Analyses **165**

Appendix D
Glossary **177**

Appendix E
Weather Websites **185**

Appendix F
Answers to Practice Questions **189**

Suggested Reading List **197**

Preface

Recently, AOPA's Nall Report 2000 came out with their analysis of the 1999 aircraft accidents. The good news is that the number of fatal fixed-wing general aviation accidents decreased from 1998's figure of 341 to 320. The total number of fixed-wing accidents increased from 1998's 1,679 to 1,701 in 1999; as is always the case, the most common accident cause is the pilot.

Weather-related accidents, which are more likely to be fatal than any other factor, showed a slight drop in 1999. But they still are the highest probability of fatalities in the statistics. In single-engine fixed-gear aircraft, 65 percent of weather-related accidents were fatal. The numbers made a large jump for single-engine retractable-gear aircraft: 88.9 percent, with 85.7 percent fatalities involving multi-engine aircraft.

Seventy-five percent of all weather-related accidents involved fatalities.

It is a sad commentary on general aviation, as well as commercial aviation, that many pilots still have very little knowledge of aviation weather, and how to read and interpret the aviation weather services that are available to all. Even sadder is the fact that pilots can successfully complete all of their flight certifications—but miss a significant number of the weather and weather-related questions on those exams!

With the emphasis upon more and more high-tech, computer-generated weather and data retrieval/display, pilots simply must have a broader as well as a more in-depth knowledge of the weather, and the available weather services and products. In fact, if you don't have this knowledge you are in violation of one of the many federal aviation regulations!

This book was first introduced in 1996 to serve as a companion to the FAA's Advisory Circular 00-45D. This new edition serves the same role as a companion to the FAA's new AC 00-45E which was published in the fall of 1999. Its purpose, like its predecessor, is to help the pilot understand and utilize the National Weather Service and FAA services described in the AC 00-45E.

I would like to respectfully dedicate this book to two wonderful people: My wife, Darthula, who has given me such wonderful support and encouragement; and Jennie Trerise, my editor, encourager, and spelling, syntax and grammar coach.

John M. ("Stormy") Holley
Professor Emeritus — Meteorology
Embry-Riddle Aeronautical University

The Big Picture of Aviation Weather Services

Products	What are they?	What do they tell you?
Surface Weather Reports		
Surface weather observations (METAR/SPECI)	Surface weather reports collected from airports and cities around the world	Current weather information at specific locations.
Pilot Reports (PIREPs) (UAs)	Reports by pilots en route of significant weather changes	Verification of forecast weather or new weather information reported.
Radar Observations (ROBs)	Radar observations taken at 05 and 35 minutes past the hour	Current location of radar echoes, their intensity, type of precipitation, intensity changes and echo movement.
Satellite Observations	Visible, infrared and water vapor images of the Earth's cloud cover; taken every 30 minutes	Through imagery looping, images indicate large-scale cloud movement, and from infrared, infer cloud top temperatures.
Current Weather Charts		
Radar Summary Chart	Summarizes U.S. Doppler radar weather reports every hour at 35 minutes past the hour	Gives the pilot information on extent and intensity of convective and nonconvective precipitation, how it is changing as well as direction and speed of movement.
Surface Analysis	Analysis of METAR reports every 3 hours (00, 03 GMT, etc.)	Gives the pilot location of pressure systems as well as frontal and trough positions. Pilots can also easily determine the general flow of air over the U.S. or a region.
Weather Depiction	Partial analysis of METARs—sky condition, visibility, obstructions to visibility and/or precipitation. Chart prepared every 3 hours (01, 04 GMT, etc.)	A pictorial display of VFR, marginal VFR and IFR conditions at map time over the U.S. and southern Canada. Frontal and trough positions are plotted from previous-hour surface analysis chart.
Composite Moisture Stability Chart	Partial analysis of U.S. radiosonde data every 12 hours (0000, 1200 GMT)	Analysis of atmosphere for potential instability/stability; also, vertical distribution of water vapor and relative humidity.
Constant Pressure Charts	Plotted from radiosonde data for selected levels of the atmosphere	General flow pattern of air across the U.S. and much of Canada with location of troughs and ridges, and the isothermal pattern.
Forecast Messages		
Convective Outlook (AC)	Describes where convective activity might occur in a 24-hour time period	General description of where non-severe and severe thunderstorm activity might be anticipated in a 24-hour period.
Aerodrome Forecast (TAF)	Forecast prepared and disseminated 4 times a day	Forecast of wind, weather and sky conditions at an airport over a 24-hour period.
Area Forecast (FA)	Forecast of weather conditions for a large geographical region	Information concerning enroute weather conditions and interpretation of weather at airports that don't have a TAF.
In-Flight Advisories (WAs) AIRMETs	In-flight advisory of significant weather phenomena for general aviation aircraft	Scheduled 6-hour forecast for moderate turbulence, moderate icing, sustained surface winds of 30 knots or more, and ceilings of 1,000 feet, visibility less than 3 miles.

Products	What are they?	What do they tell you?
SIGMET (WS)	Nonscheduled advisory for significant weather phenomena which would affect all aircraft	Advises pilots of nonconvective weather that is potentially hazardous to all aircraft: severe icing, turbulence, volcanic ash and dust/sand storms.
Convective SIGMET (WST)	Nonscheduled 2-hour forecast for severe thunderstorm and/or tornadic activity	Synopsis describing the cause of severe activity; where it is currently located, its intensity and movement, and where it is expected to be in the future.
Transcribed Weather Enroute Bulletin (TWEB)	A 15-hour weather forecast which is route-specific	Forecast for a number of specific U.S. cross-country routes for sky condition, cloud tops, visibility, weather and obstructions to vision; for a flight corridor 25 NM each side of the flight route.
Forecast Winds/Temperatures Aloft (FD)	Forecast values for specific locations in the U.S.	Prepared twice daily, pilots use these for cross-country flight planning.
Center Weather Service Products (CWA & MIS)	Meteorological Impact Statements (MIS) and Center Weather Advisory (CWA), nonscheduled, for weather conditions in the en route and terminal areas	Short range forecasts, for use by pilots and air traffic controllers, of possible adverse weather conditions anticipated in the center's area of responsibility.
Severe Weather Alert (AWW)	Preliminary alert to the public that a Severe Weather Watch will be issued shortly	A message which gives the location of the severe convective activity and what is expected over a 2- to 3-hour time period.
Severe Weather Watch (WW)	Not a warning. Forecasts for severe thunderstorms/tornadoes; issued at least 30 minutes before severe activity is forecast to occur, effective for 4-6 hours.	Forecasters are pretty sure severe weather will occur; one step further than an AWW.

Forecast Weather Charts

Products	What are they?	What do they tell you?
Volcanic Ash Chart (VAFTAD)	Nonscheduled forecast of volcanic ash dispersal	Experimental chart which graphically displays where volcanic plume is expected to be for three flight altitudes.
Convective Outlook Chart	A chart depiction of the Convective Outlook (AC) message	Preliminary look at where nonsevere and severe thunderstorms are expected to occur for a 24- and 48-hour period.
Significant Low-Level Prog chart	Forecast weather conditions for a 12- and 24-hour period from surface to a flight level 24,000 feet (400 mb)	Forecast location of turbulence, freezing levels, MVFR and IFR conditions, frontal location, and significant precipitation coverage.
Surface Weather Prog (36 – 48 hour)	A continuation of the low-level prog	No MVFR or IFR, but areas of overcast clouds are depicted along with forecast location of fronts and pressure systems. Freezing precip is not forecast.
Significant High-Level Weather Prog	For domestic and international flights at Flight Levels 25,000 – 60,000 feet	Depicts active thunderstorms and cloud layers that are associated with the activity, moderate to severe turbulence, moderate to severe icing and surface positions of frontal systems and their direction of movement and speed.
Forecast Winds and Temperatures Aloft	A graphical display of the FD message	Shows the wind direction, speed and temperatures for different levels. Difficult to pick specific wind direction/speeds, but shows the overall pattern forecast over the U.S.
Collaborative Convection Forecast Product (CCFP)	Extended forecast for thunderstorm activity, for up to 6 hours.	Charts thunderstorm activity throughout contiguous U.S., and what is expected for thunderstorm intensity, growth, area coverage, and movement.

Chapter 1: *Decisions, Decisions, and More Decisions*

Flying is a wonderful, exhilarating experience that can enrapture those who fly. The sheer pleasure and joy of mimicking the maneuvers of the creatures of the sky is something special for most of us. But flying is also a very demanding taskmaster, quite unforgiving of a rushed decision or a wrong action at the wrong time.

While flight training is generally relentless in the learning of the subjects, the number of nonfatal and fatal accidents in general aviation strongly suggests that pilot training, education, and decision making could be improved. And in the area of pilot weather education, we could do better—much better. Weather is one of the most important subjects in the pilot training/education curriculum and unfortunately, many pilots are only exposed to enough of it to "pass the FAA knowledge test." This is not education, it is rote learning—which is superficial, and really has very little to do with flying and the decision making processes of flight.

I consider the well-educated pilot is one who would endeavor to take additional course work in the subject of weather/meteorology. He or she would also have flight time and instruction in unusual attitude flight as well as personal experience in "weather flying." It's true that the FAA knowledge tests do not delve as deeply into the subject of weather as is needed for a *full understanding* of aviation weather and its dynamics. Realize that the FAA *is* "on your side," but it is not an educational body per se. Obviously it does encourage all pilots to learn.

The knowledge tests may leave a lot to be desired, but the truth is that learning is *your* responsibility. Whether you take advanced aerodynamics (and that's a good thing to do!), or pay someone qualified to take you up so you can experience IFR weather; either way, you will become more knowledgeable about this inexact science we call the weather. The whole point is that it is your personal responsibility and obligation to learn, and learn as much as you can!

Situational Awareness and Decision Making

With the exhortation to learn more in mind, let's take a look at a current buzzword—"aeronautical decision making (ADM)"—especially with respect to weather. This is not about teaching you how to make decisions. You must realize that good decisions are based on knowledge and information—the more you know, the better off you are going to be. Flying is really a series of informed decisions from your preliminary flight planning, to shutdown at your destination. In planning a flight and en route you make informed decisions, as well as in the approach and landing phase. These decisions are based on input from many sources—weather services being no exception. You need to survey all your sources, decide which

> *In subsequent chapters, watch this space at the beginning for the AC 00-45E reading assignment for that chapter.*

situational awareness: "What's going on?"…always knowing what is happening that could affect any flight decision.

 ADM is covered in the FAA publication, "Aeronautical Decision Making," AC 60-22.

ones are the best to use in which situations, and use the information to derive your flight and cockpit decisions. Read more about ADM in the FAA's Advisory Circular 60-22, "Aeronautical Decision Making" a common-sense approach to improving pilot performance for every aspect of flight.

If you haven't had the opportunity to read the 1999 Nall Report on aircraft accidents, you might want to pull it up from the AOPA website (www.aopa.org) or check to see if your local FBO has a copy available. According to the 1999 Nall Report, "Seventy-two percent of the fatal "weather" accidents (39 accidents) in 1998 occurred when VFR pilots *failed to recognize* [emphasis mine] clouds or the loss of visual conditions." As the report points out, neophyte pilots are given very little, if any, instruction in cross-country flight and this is where those 39 accidents occurred—cross-country, where the weather is!

Frankly, the only way to get experience flying weather is to do exactly that—fly the weather! But we cannot easily change this shortcoming in flight training, so let's concentrate on the *recognition* factor which implies knowledge and education in the subject of weather to such a degree that you *know* what is out there and what it might do. Throughout this book you will learn more about the weather services designed to help you make decisions. You'll learn to recognize tough weather situations—and be aware of the possibilities.

Take This Flight

The day started off with a high cirrostratus overcast (remember your ten basic types of clouds?) which later thickened and lowered to about 12,000 feet. By mid-afternoon the east winds picked up a bit and the cloud bases, while still looking fairly high, are once again lower than before...The temperature–dewpoint spread is 6°.

Two hours later, you notice that very light drizzle is now occurring and the visibility, while still above 6 miles, is definitely lower then before.

It still looks like good weather, and your personal minimums are 1,000 feet and 5 miles, so you decide to take off and fly to a nearby uncontrolled airport some 30–40 nautical miles away for touch and go's (since the traffic at your home field is too heavy for your liking).

On the way out at 4,500 feet, you observe that the visibility is about 5 or 6 miles with intermittent light rain, and with some scud below you at about 2,000 feet AGL. The slant range visibility is probably about 5 miles. The "nearby airport" (uncontrolled with no AWOS or ASOS reporting station) is now only a few miles away; but in a quick check of your home-field frequency you hear that the latest weather observation indicates a heavy scattered layer at 1,800 feet, an overcast above 10,000 feet and a visibility of 6 miles with drizzle. Perhaps discretion is the better part of valor, you think—let's go home!

Good move!

Do you get the picture? Do you recognize what situation is probably developing? Did you check what the regional and/or national weather picture looked like before you left for your touch and go's?

These are some typical aviation weather scenarios, to get you started thinking in weather "real-time."

AWOS: Automated Weather Observing System

ASOS: Automated Surface Observing System

This situation could have been that of an approaching warm front; that scud could quickly become a broken or overcast condition—thanks to the evaporation of precipitation into the air below the cloud base. The increasing humidity can also play havoc with the visibility. If you have a good grasp of the current and forecast weather in your region (and nationally), then you have a good grasp of *situational awareness.*

Therefore, a cardinal rule about flight and weather is to always check to see what is *developing* in your local area and region. Watch the weather channel or make a phone call to the nearest FSS and get the latest PATWAS ... and use your eyes!

PATWAS: Pilot's Automatic Telephone Weather Answering System

Second rule: If you're planning a flight, start thinking about that flight about two days in advance, and look for evidence that the weather pattern over your region might change.

Third rule: Get as much weather information that you can concerning the proposed and current weather along and either side of your route (a corridor at least 60 nautical miles wide). Spot likely diversion and alternate airports en route and at destination. Check runway configurations as well as any special field information. Don't know much about geography? Well, take a good look at the terrain and consider what subtle (or not-so-subtle) changes the prevailing winds might bring into play across the route due to the topography of the ground.

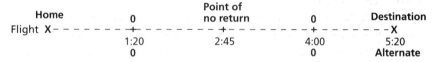

Times below the line of flight are times en route.

Draw this flight-line/time-line over your route on your sectional chart, it helps you keep track of your progress, when and where to call flight watch for the latest reports, and stay "situationally aware"!

Another "What If?" Flight Profile

To get back to our virtual flying:

Flight – 48 Hours: Your flight is two days away, but it appears there will be big-time weather changes occurring. Start *now* and get a good idea of what is across the country, *particularly* to the west of your area. Sketch a map of the surface fronts, highs and lows, areas of bad weather. If you have a computer, you can download a copy of the surface analysis chart (*see* examples in AC 00-45E Section 5, Page 5-3, and in this text, Page 80), as well as the constant pressure chart at or near your proposed flight altitude. You will download other charts later, but these will do for now.

Examples of constant pressure charts are in AC 00-45E Section 8.

Flight – 24 Hours: Same weather-seeking procedure as yesterday, but start examining the radar summary and weather depiction charts. Get your forecast winds and temps now, in order to do some serious pre-planning. Pick out possible diversion and alternate airports and start monitoring their weather and forecasts.

Do you have any rising terrain across the route? Are the winds blowing upslope or downslope across the route? This could give you additional cloud cover and lowering ceilings or decreasing clouds on the leeward side of the terrain.

outlook briefing: Received when estimated time to departure (ETD) is +6 hours or more.

TWEB: Transcribed Weather Enroute Broadcast

EFAS: Enroute Flight Advisory Service

See "Suggested Reading" (Page 197) for information on ordering your own copy of *Weatherwise*.

Do your homework: Go to the airport directory and find out as much as you can about these airports—it will save time later in the cockpit when you will have enough to do without worrying about runway configuration, etc. At this time you should also get an *outlook briefing*.

Flight Day: Get a standard weather briefing and check to see if the latest forecast winds and temps aloft are significantly different from the ones you obtained last night. Check all current weather (including PIREPs and radar reports) along your route, including all the "what if" diversion airports and alternates. Get the TWEB route information, if available. In short, *get current and stay current*.

Flight 1:20 En Route: Ask EFAS for current weather conditions at home base as well as en route and destination. Ask for any PIREPs, and then give PIREPs if anything is significantly different from what you were briefed on. (Do not ask EFAS for a complete weather briefing! These people are very busy and that is not what they are there for.)

Point of No Return: Contact EFAS and ask for current weather at the diversion, destination and alternate airports ahead of you. Again, ask for and give PIREPs. Based on what is going on currently, you might want to see if there is any change in the destination and alternate airports. Is weather starting to deteriorate en route and at destination? Start planning now for diverting to your alternate.

Remember that weather moves, and it moves with the winds aloft. The forecast winds you obtained in your briefing will give a good indication of the winds at flight level and these winds should be similar to the wind pattern on the constant pressure chart you checked that day. Remember from your flight planning phase and be alert to the rising terrain, and whether the winds are blowing upslope or downslope across the route.

This process requires diligence and organization to avoid a time-consuming task. This is why you begin 1–2 days in advance to start downloading data into that computer you call a brain. Repetitious? I like to think of it as thorough, which is especially important when learning weather.

More Weather Learning Strategies

Do you want to learn more about weather? You should do as many of the following things as you possibly can:

1. Check your local library and see if they have a subscription to a magazine called *Weatherwise* (if they don't have it, you might suggest they order a subscription). This magazine is written strictly for the weather enthusiast, and many of them are pilots! While the articles may not be written specifically for pilots, they are a very good way to learn more about weather—the why and how of it.

2. See if your local community college or university offers a basic meteorology class. These might not be geared specifically to aviation, but they will give you a good, solid course in the basics.

3. Start your own weather library. *See* "Suggested Reading" for several good basic books on weather and meteorology that would give you a good understanding of weather basics.

4. *Important:* If available, take a course in unusual attitude flight, or even a few hours in spin training and basic aerobatics. Too many pilots become spatially disoriented in inclement weather (for example, the recent Kennedy tragedy), and lose it.

5. Ask Questions! Too many pilots listen to the briefer with no more comment then an occasional "yeah." Remember, there are no dumb questions when you are getting a weather briefing!

6. Watch your attitude! I have read articles in flying magazines that suggest the NWS and FAA are a bunch of scared folk who paint a rather pessimistic picture because of liability concerns. Well, how negative can you get? Most pilots know but often forget that the FAA briefer is not a weather forecaster—he or she is a weather forecast *reader.* And the NWS people, many of whom are pilots, are well-trained professionals trying to predict what will happen to a very small portion of a massive envelope of air in a very short period of time. Now that is a very hard thing to do!

NWS: National Weather Service

Recognize that weather forecasts are just what they claim to be: a *forecast.* Learn how to read and comprehend them, and also understand their limitations.

Tailor Your Briefings and Reports

A good weather briefing and thorough planning is always important, but what about someone who just wants to go out to the practice area and do some turns about a point or touch and go's at a local airport—do they need to start planning two days in advance and view every weather product offered by the FAA and NWS?

No, good planning for a VFR local flight shouldn't include every aspect of planning I suggested for a MVFR or VFR cross-country. But consider this: If you practice *obtaining* the weather services, you are going to be ahead of your learning curve. So let's not pull out the stops and grab AIRMETs, SIGMETs, SWSTs, etc., for a local flight. But do start watching and observing the weather and don't be afraid to pick the brains of the FAA briefers—many of them are pilots as well.

For a good, quick weather check for around-the-pattern and practice area flight, I recommend the following:

1. Are there any other airports with weather equipment within a 60–70 mile radius of your field? If so get the current weather when obtaining a briefing and check if there are any NOTAMs on file for these fields. Why do this? Well, what if you had to divert to one of these fields?

2. Obtain the lower-level forecast winds and temps aloft. There may not be a forecast wind and temperature value in your specific area, so ask the briefer for an average value for your region.

3. Are there any AIRMETs or SIGMETs in effect that would impact your local flight? Probably not, but *ask* anyway.

4. What weather changes, if any, are anticipated for your home field? If you are going to be in radio range you can also keep a check on the local weather by dialing in your ATIS frequency.

WSI: Weather Services International

Note: This one is a true story!

Many FBOs now have their own or lease a weather terminal from a private vendor such as WSI. All FBOs usually have a telephone and/or a drop line to the FSS. Weather terminals are really neat and can give you anything and everything about the weather. But a word of caution on using them: *Always check the date and time of any weather data you receive for your request.* It just might be old data which could possibly be dangerous to your health!

Several years ago at airport KXZY, a student at a large FBO pulled up the terminal forecast for the field and was puzzled: the forecast looked remarkably like the one he had pulled up three days ago. A check by one of the flight instructors found that access to the vendor had been disrupted and the machine was spitting out data it had downloaded three days ago! Now this doesn't happen very often but the lesson is clear: *always* make sure you have current data and information.

You can tailor your flight weather needs to your type of flight, and the general weather scenario; then you select the weather messages and charts applicable for that situation. For example: for the past few days the weather in your region has been "severe clear" with little or no wind, above average temperatures, and The Weather Channel indicates very little if any change over the next couple of days. Okay, check the latest METARs/TAFs for your cross-country, obtain the forecast winds and temps for your planned altitude, ask the briefer for any valid PIREPs, and check for current NOTAMs. What weather scenario would most likely create the weather pattern just described?

I think some of you said high pressure, which would win a round of "Jeopardy" for you if "A.T." used that as the final question. In order to obtain the weather information needed to come to this conclusion in the quickest possible time, check these sources:

1. The TWEB message (described on AC 00-45E Page 1-3) is your best bet, but it doesn't furnish NOTAM information, so also check out the TIBS (Page 1-5). *See* the Airport/Facility Directory for TIBS telephone numbers.

2. Direct User Access Terminal Service (DUATS) is great for getting weather data, as well as filing flight plans. There are also a number of weather and flight services servers on the internet (but generally there is a charge for using them). The AC 00-45E introduces enroute weather services on Pages 1-6 through 1-8.

TIBS: Telephone Information Briefing Service

3. When asked by the briefer what type of briefing you want for this VFR high-pressure flight, request the abbreviated briefing (after all, you don't need to get a standard in-depth briefing for this type of flight). If you call 6–7 hours before your scheduled flight, just ask for an outlook briefing. Then, when filing, ask if there has been any significant changes since you received the outlook briefing.

We will be addressing other weather scenarios and how to *tailor* your weather needs. If you go through all the steps we will be covering in advance, briefers will appreciate your efficiency and they will know they're talking to a "professional."

Chapter 2: *Surface Weather Observations*

Introduction to METARs

All the weather information you receive in a weather briefing, via DUAT, computer, telephone, or briefer is based on observations and the analysis of those observations. Surface weather observations are taken routinely every hour at airports and other sites—these include the hourly routine reports, which are called METARs and SPECIs. Many of these sites are now automated (AUTO) while others are "augmented"—manned sites.

This chapter will cover the observing systems themselves (which are not mentioned in AC 00-45E), as well as further aspects of the METAR and SPECI reports from AC 00-45E Section 2.

Observations on AWOS and ASOS

There are two primary automated weather observing systems now deployed at airports and other sites in the U.S.: the ASOS and AWOS. The National Weather Service (NWS) operates ASOS-equipped weather sites, and the FAA utilizes the AWOS system. The U.S. military (especially the USAF's Air Weather Agency) also operates a version of the ASOS observing system. The pilot has access to the observations taken by all three major users since all use the same basic METAR format; the USAF, with its global commitments, does offer more weather information which may be of use to general or commercial aviation. There are several instrumentation options offered by both weather observing systems and other private vendors to non-federal users (municipalities, agricultural colleges, fire departments, etc.) who have need of a weather system.

Canada is now following suit with the same basic type of automated system; they expect to have their network complete in the near future. All these systems consist of electronic sensors, connected to a computer system, that measure and process weather observations every minute. They provide one minute, five minute, hourly and special (SPECI) observations, 24 hours a day.

AC 00-45E Reading Assignment
Section 2
Pages 2-1 through 2-20

METAR: Aviation routine weather report

SPECI: Special weather report

 The Aviation Weather Center (AWC) website is very helpful for finding surface weather observation information quickly—*see* the web address at the bottom of the page.

http://www.awc-kc.noaa.gov (Aviation Weather Center)

http://weather.noaa.gov/ (NWS Internet Weather Source)

http://www.faa.gov/asos/asos.htm (Automated Weather Sensors homepage)

http://www.nws.noaa.gov/oso/oso1/oso12/metar.htm (NWS METAR/TAF information page)

The Electronic Weather Observation

All automated systems measure only that weather that the sensors can scan. Therefore the siting of these sensors becomes crucial; many of these electronic observers are located at airports near the touchdown zone of the main instrument runway. Large airport complexes may have as many as three different weather-observing sites; this also can apply to sites that contain significant variation in terrain and geographical features.

Basically, mathematical logic (algorithms) is applied to the collected information in order to extrapolate the weather over a wider area than the instrument site itself. Table 2-1 gives a general summary of the area around an ASOS site. It was determined that 30 minutes was sufficient time to observe clouds passing over the station to obtain an accurate picture of the sky condition. The last ten minutes of the data is doubly weighed to give more credence to the latest sky condition.

Weather element	Processing interval (Minutes)	Radius validity (Miles)
Sky condition	30	3 – 5
Visibility	10	2 – 3
Precipitation	10	1 – 2
Freezing rain	15	2 – 3

Table 2-1. *Weather sensor processing*

The ASOS Sensor Group

The weather sensors used by the ASOS units are similar to those used by the AWOS units. The ASOS home page has an explanation of the sensors—the information below was taken from this site (and there is a link to a page that has photographs of an ASOS installation):

http://www.nws.noaa.gov/asos/index.html

1. Tipping bucket (rain gauge). Many of these have a 48-inch diameter windshield which reduces updrafts over the gauge.

2. Temperature-dewpoint sensor (hygrothermometer). The sensor uses a chilled mirror method to measure the dew point.

3. Precipitation identification sensor. Detects precipitation type and measures intensity. This sensor reports 3 precip conditions to the acquisition control unit—rain, snow, and "precipitation undetermined."

4. Wind sensor. A rotating 3-cup anemometer and wind vane mounted on a tipping 10-meter tower. Information is fed to the data collection package.

5. Data collection package (DCP). These are usually placed at different locations at an airport. Communication between them is controlled by the acquisition control unit (ACU).

6. Cloud height sensor (ceilometer). This determines cloud height and levels in the atmosphere. This unit uses a laser beam to detect cloud layers. Data is collected and then sent to the DCP.

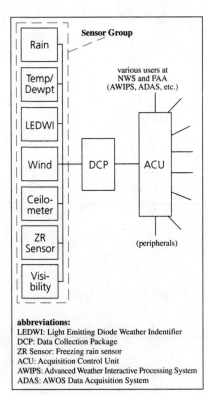

abbreviations:
LEDWI: Light Emitting Diode Weather Indentifier
DCP: Data Collection Package
ZR Sensor: Freezing rain sensor
ACU: Acquisition Control Unit
AWIPS: Advanced Weather Interactive Processing System
ADAS: AWOS Data Acquisition System

*ASOS hardware configuration
(from NWS website)*

7. Freezing rain sensor. This detects when rain freezes. The DCP polls the sensor every minute, and then the DCP relays the data to the ACU.

8. Visibility and day/night sensor. This uses "forward scatter technique" to measure ambient visibility.

9. Acquisition control unit (ACU). Receives all the data from the DCP. The ground-to-air (GTA) radio is installed in the ACU, and this continuously broadcasts updated weather to pilots and other listeners on an automatic mode. There is also a speech processor with digitized human speech. Hourly and SPECI reports are continuously broadcast to pilots (ATIS).

 The normal range of GTA radio is 25 miles at 10,000' altitude.

ATIS: Automatic Terminal Information Service

Caution! Handle with Care

As with any electronic system where data has to be collected, analyzed, and logic applied, there is some "lag" time in getting the final data out to the user. In rapidly changing conditions, the automated systems will lag the actual weather with its changes by several minutes. For example, if skies are scattered and then this rapidly changes to an overcast condition (according to the sensors), the ASOS/AWOS will take about 2 minutes to report a scattered deck of clouds. Then within ten minutes the sensors will indicate a broken deck of clouds.

Visibility sensors show a similar pattern: if visibility drops suddenly (1 minute) from 7 miles to 1 mile, the system needs about 4 minutes before the ACU will report a visibility of 3 miles (these readings are an average of the past 10 minutes). This 3-mile value is a criteria threshold that tells the ACU to issue a SPECI observation, which alerts potential users of this significant change in visibility. It will take the unit a total of nine minutes before the ACU reports the current visibility as one mile. Therefore, if a rapidly-changing fog condition (forming or dissipating) occurs, the observation might not be very representative of the airport and its immediate environs.

Conversely, when the visibility improves from 1 to 7 miles, a SPECI is generated 4 minutes after the 1.5-mile threshold is reached. In about 10–12 minutes, the unit will report 7 miles. Why the time difference? The algorithms are so designed that the visibility values will raise more slowly than when they are lowered. This serves as a buffer, a safety margin for rapidly changing visibility conditions over a short time interval.

In inclement weather, the AWOS may generate quite a few SPECI observations—many of which will only appear at uncontrolled airports where pilots can receive weather updates every minute via land-line telephone or radio. With good VFR, the pilot should listen to at least the past ten minutes of observations, when contacting these weather updates. With IFR conditions, the pilot should listen for 20–25 minutes to determine if there is any trend occurring at that airport.

When IFR, listen to the radio and telephone weather reports for at least 20 minutes to determine the trend.

The automated weather sites are not perfect. In some instances both the AWOS and ASOS may report lower cloud layers than what is actually encountered. There will be times that precipitation, scud, or fog aloft will cause the sky sensor to mistakenly report a cloud layer or layers. A pilot receiving an erroneous low sky condition may then have to divert to his or her alternate. Therefore pilots should also be aware there are some weather phenomena not detected or reported by the automated weather stations. Only a trained observer can report such phenomena as a funnel cloud, tornado or waterspout (location and possible movement), hail size and frozen precipitation. Bottom line: get all the reports you can, and realize they need to be carefully evaluated to see if a trend is being established. Always take these automated reports with a grain of salt, and see what other stations in the vicinity are reporting. Is there a USAF base nearby? Check their reports, as they are always augmented.

In the old days, BA (before automation), it was decided that a layer of clouds or an obscuration that was transparent and covering 5/10 or more of the sky did not constitute a ceiling—it was reported as a thin layer in the sky condition portion of the observation. Now the ASOS/AWOS sensing equipment picks up a smoke or fog layer aloft and reports it as: 15 BKN. Along comes Captain Midnight (who suffers terribly from insomnia), who wants to fly to a field reporting a sky condition of 15 BKN. If this was an augmented station, there no doubt would be a remark such as this: FU BKN 015…

FU: smoke (*See* AC 00-45E Page 2-9.)

ASOS or AWOS?

Why have two separate weather-reporting systems—ASOS *and* AWOS? The FAA, NWS, and the Department of Defense (DOD) all utilize the ASOS system which is primarily for use by the aviation community. The basic ASOS observation unit may or may not be equipped with a precipitation discriminator, which distinguishes between liquid and frozen precipitation. The ASOS AO2 is equipped with this sensor; the basic ASOS AO1 is not.

 A guide to ASOS for pilots is available at:
http://www.nws.noaa.gov/om/ asosbook.htm

The AWOS system is similar to the ASOS and can be configured to suit various federal and non-federal users. All federal AWOS units, which are designated as AWOS III units, are maintained by the FAA. The non-federal units that are purchased and maintained by state, local or private organizations have custom designed instrumentation. The AWOS III units broadcast the following information primarily for the aviation community and the word AUTO is usually attached to the METAR report:

 For ASOS units, wind data is averaged at 2-minute intervals.

1. Airport 4-letter ID
2. Zulu time, and date
3. Wind direction and speed
4. Visibility
5. Sky condition

6. Temperature–dewpoint
7. Altimeter setting
8. Remarks
9. Density altitude
10. Wind gusts

Remember that wind direction given in METARs is true north … ATIS and airport advisories give wind direction in magnetic north.

Notice that the AWOS III does not report present weather or precipitation. But the AWOS III can be equipped with a present weather and precipitation detector. This model would be classed as an AWOS III-P. AWOS units equipped with a lightning (thunderstorm) detector are identified as AWOS III-T. If the unit is equipped with the precipitation and thunderstorm/lightning detector, it is designated as an AWOS III-P-T.

AWOS III-P: This is the same package as ASOS, with added FZRA and TS (freezing rain and thunderstorm) sensors.

There is more information on these systems at: http://www.faa.gov/ asos/asos.htm. For example, an excerpt of this website's information (Figure 2-1) shows stations mapped and a table displaying the ASOS/AWOS network on a state-by-state basis. The weather stations listed for Arizona

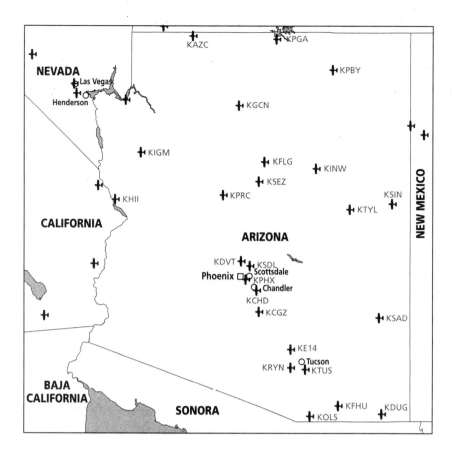

ASOS-AWOS Sites— Arizona, 25 stations (excerpt)

City	Site ID	Freq.	Telephone	Type	Commis.
Avra Valley	KE14	245/NDB	520-682-4104	AWOS III	Yes
Bedard Field (Kayenta)	KPBY	259/NDB	520-677-5165	AWOS III	Yes
Casa Grande	KCGZ	132.175	520-836-3392	AWOS III	Yes
Douglas	KDUG	119.275	520-364-7208	ASOS	No

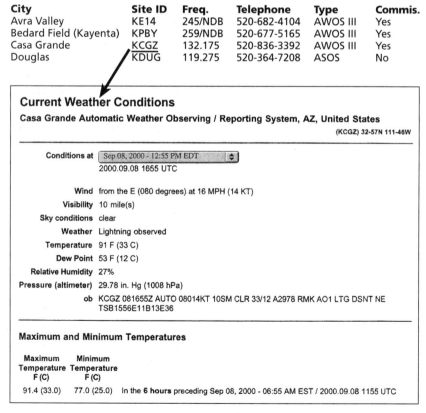

Figure 2-1. *ASOS/AWOS explained on this website—underlined links take you straight to current weather reports for that station.*

http://www.nws.noaa.gov

More METAR details:
On these reports, wind shifts are a change in direction of 45 degrees or more in less than 15 minutes, with speeds of 10 kts or more.

Cloud layer heights are reported as follows—

When clouds are from	Report bases to nearest
Surface to 5,000'	100' AGL
5,000 to 10,000'	500' AGL
10,000' and above	1,000' AGL

Appendix A in this book, "Surface Chart Symbology Explained" contains diagrams and tables that further describe what the METARs, and the charts that are created from them, say about the weather at the observation stations.

For an easier way to *visualize* the pressure changes over time, *see* the Appendix C example of a chart series* plotted from surface observations—including a "3-Hour Pressure Tendency" chart showing the values mapped out in full color (Pages 170–171).

(*From the National Center for Atmospheric Research (NCAR) website.)

---

are either state-owned or FAA-owned. The ASOS units with ATIS given as the frequency are FAA sites. Military installations such as Davis Monthan AFB, Tucson, or Luke AFB, Phoenix are not listed in this particular website. The military weather can be obtained from the briefer or by visiting the NWS home webpage and clicking "Current Conditions."

You can also call up "http://weather.noaa.gov" and get a 24-hour summary of weather conditions at each station across your route and at destination. You'll find maps of ASOS/AWOS stations by state when you explore the NWS "Interactive Weather Information Network" at "http://iwin.nws.noaa.gov/iwin/main.html"—click on the station and it takes you to the reports for that area. It's helpful to see if there is any sort of trend going on at the route stations, and this is a good way to get that information quickly.

Visibility may be manually determined at either the surface, from the tower cab or both. Where no visibility is being reported from the surface, the tower visibility will be the one used in the body of the METAR. Where both the surface and tower readings are taken, the tower visibility will be reported in remarks.

Where the visibility is electronically and automatically determined by either the ASOS or AWOS units, the visibility algorithm calculates a mean visibility which is the electronic sensor's *equivalent of prevailing visibility*. Actually, the electronically-derived visibility value is what I would call a "sector visibility" (the visibility in a specified direction that represents at least a 45° arc of the horizon circle).

The METAR Remarks Section (RMK)

The "Remarks" table on AC 00-45E Page 2-21 is lacking some examples of METAR remarks, and some explanation of each entry would also be helpful for quick reference. Read through Figure 2-2 for a more complete list of the remarks you may encounter in METAR and SPECI reports. Remember to *always* read the observational material in the remarks—there will be times this information will be just as important as the body of the weather report.

Additive and Automated Data

In this section of Figure 2-2, notice the "3-Hourly Pressure Tendency/Change." Every three hours, METARs are required to include the sea-level pressure change and how it changed over this time period. While originally intended for weather personnel, this pressure tendency and amount of pressure change (given in hectopascals–millibars) can furnish pilots with some information as well. See further explanation of how to read these pressure groups in Appendix A of this book (Page 149).

Consider a reported group (pressure tendency) of 53018: the pressure tendency "3" could indicate the passage of a cold frontal system—"pressure falling or steady, then increasing." If the pressure increases at a rapid rate of 0.06 inches of mercury or more per hour, for a total of 0.02 inches or more, the Remarks section would also include "PRESRR"—"pressure rising rapidly."

Automated, Manual, and Plain Language Remarks

Sample METAR:
METAR KXYZ 211154Z AUTO 21016G24KT 180V240 1SM R11/P6000FT -RA BR BKN015 OVC070 06/04 A2992 RMK AO2 PK WND
  20036/28 WSHFT 15 FROPA VIS 3/4V1 3/4 VIS 3/4 RWY11 RAB08 CIG 013V018 CIG 017 RWY11 PRESFR SLP125 P0003
  60009 70067 8/72/ T00640036 58033 TSNO $.

REMARKS (with interpretation)	EXAMPLE (from the sample METAR)
VOLCANIC ERUPTION Name of volcano/Latitude-longitude. Date/ Time of eruption/Height and direction of movement of ash cloud.	MT. HICCUP ERUPTED 2141. ASH CLOUD TO APRX 6000 FEET MOVG SW (Example only.)
TORNADIC ACTIVITY, FUNNEL CLOUDS or WATER SPOUTS B/E(hh)mm LOC/DIR_(MOV) Begin, End time.	TORNADO B13 6 NE. WATERSPOUT & NW OVR BAY B22 E52 (Example only.)
TYPE OF AUTOMATED STATION AO1 or AO2. Station without precipitation discriminator is identified as AO1.	AO2
PEAK WIND (PK WND) ddaff(f)/(hh)mm Data coded and transmitted in the next METAR report. Example: A peak wind of 200/36 occurred at 28 minutes past the hour.	PK WND 20036/28 (d=direction, f=force)
WIND SHIFT (WSHFT) (hh)mm. Time of wind shift in hours and minutes if the hour cannot be inferred from the report. The term CD FROPA will be entered if wind shift is due to cold frontal passage. Note: WRM = Warm, OCLDD= Occluded	WSHFT 15 CD FROPA
TOWER or SURFACE VISIBILITY (TWR or SFC VIS) vvvv. Example: Tower visibility of 1-3/4 miles.	TWR VIS 3/4 (Example only—not found in sample METAR above.)
VARIABLE PREVAILING VISIBILITY When the prevailing visibility is less then 3 miles and considered variable. Example: visibility variable between 3/4 and 1-3/4 miles. (Manual or augmented stations only.)	VIS 3/4V 1 3/4
SECTOR VISIBILITY (VIS, DIR, VSBY) Direction to 8 cardinal points of the compass. Visibility in miles. Used only when prevailing visibility is 3 miles or less and the sector visibility differs from that value by 1 or more reportable values. (Manual or augmented stations only.)	VIS SW 3/4 (Example only—not found in sample METAR above.)
VISIBILITY (at Second Location) Designated airports with more than one automated observing site. Only reported when value is less than the VIS value in the body of the METAR. Example: visibility at runway 11 is 3/4 mile.	VIS 3/4 RWY11
LIGHTNING LTG (frequency, type and location) For manual stations, the observer. In-cloud (IC), Cloud-Cloud (CC), Cloud-Air (CA), Cloud-Ground (CG). Auto stations will report TS if lightning is detected within 5 miles of station. If LTG is detected 5-10 miles of station, VCTS will be reported in body of METAR.	OCNL LTGICCCCG W-NW (Example only—not found in sample METAR above.)
PRECIPITATION (type, beginning-ending) Time in minutes only if the hour can be inferred from METAR.	RAB08
THUNDERSTORMS (TS) (location, movement and direction) Example: A storm located SW of station moving to the northeast. (Manual or augmented stations only.)	TS SW MOVG NE (Example only—not found in sample METAR above.)

Figure 2-2. *Automated, manual, and plain language remarks in the METAR (continued on next two pages).*

REMARKS	EXAMPLE
HAILSTONE SIZE (GR) (size, plain language) Small hail would be reported in body of METAR as GS; no remark is needed. Largest stone size reported. (Manual or augmented stations.)	GR 2" (Example only—not found in sample METAR above.)
VIRGA (VIRGA) Direction. (Manual or augmented stations only.)	VIRGA SW-NW (Example only—not found in sample METAR above.)
VARIABLE CEILING HEIGHT Ceiling variable from 1,300 feet to 1,800 feet.	CIG 013V018
OBSCURATIONS Surface-based or aloft. Type of obscuration, amount of sky obscured and height.	FG BKN 002 (Example only—not found in sample METAR above.)
VARIABLE SKY CONDITION Example: The ceiling of 1,500 feet is variable from scattered to broken.	BKN015 V SCT (Example only—not found in sample METAR above.)
SIGNIFICANT CLOUD TYPES TCU, CB, CBMAM, ACC, SCSL, ACSL, CCSL, ROTOR CLD These must always be reported if observed. See AC 00-45E for examples of these. (Manual or augmented stations only.)	LN CB SW-NE MOVG E (Example only—not found in sample METAR above.)
CEILING HEIGHT at Second Location (CIG, height, location) Only reported if the value at second location is lower then the reported ceiling value in METAR.	CIG 017 RWY11
PRESSURE RISING/FALLING RAPIDLY Only if the pressure changes rapidly at the time of observation. Pressure change must be at least 0.06 inches per hour and the amount of change totals 0.02 inches.	PRESFR
SEA LEVEL PRESSURE (SLP) Coded in hectopascals (millibars). Example: Sea level pressure of 1012.5	SLP125
AIRCRAFT MISHAP (ACFT) Plain Language. This information is NOT transmitted, it is strictly for NTSB use.	
SPECIAL REPORTS (NO SPECI) At manual stations where Specials (SPECI) are not taken, this remark will be entered to indicate that no changes in the weather will be reported until the next METAR.	
ADDITIVE AND AUTOMATED DATA	
HOURLY PRECIPITATION (Prrrr) P is the indicator, rainfall of 00.03 is coded as P0003; rainfall less than 00.01" fell in the past hour. This group omitted if there is no precipitation.	P0003
3- and 6-HOUR PRECIPITATION (6RRRR) 6 is the indicator. The 3 hour amounts are reported .00.09. 12 inches recorded in the past 6 hours would be coded 61200. 6///... indeterminate amount of precipitation (water equivalent).	60009
24-HOUR PRECIPITATION AMOUNT (7RRRR) At designated stations, the 1200Z observation will report the 24-hour precipitation. Indeterminate amount is recorded as 7//// Example: 1.12 inches	70112 (Example only.) (Sample METAR shows 70067.)

Figure 2-2. *Automated, manual, and plain language remarks in the METAR (continued).*

REMARKS	EXAMPLE
CLOUD TYPES This data is reported and coded on the 3- and 6-hour observations (00,03,06,09, etc). 8 is the indicator, followed by a solidus; then CL, CM and CH indicate low, middle and high clouds respectively (see Cloud Symbols, AC 00-45E Page 5-10). In the METAR, they are reporting low cloud 7 and middle cloud 2. High clouds are not visible (/).	8/72/ (*See also* Appendix A of this book. A good website for cloud type information is: http://ww2010.atmos.uiuc.edu/(Gh)/home.rxml, the "Weather World 2010" project.)
HOURLY TEMPERATURES Temperature and dew point values to nearest 0.10 Celsius. Temp is +06.4, dew point is +03.6 Celsius. The number following the T is an indicator for positive or negative values: 0 for +, 1 for below freezing values.	T00640036
3-HOURLY PRESSURE TENDENCY/CHANGE Reported on the 3- and 6-hour observations. 5 = indicator for this data group; 8 = pressure is decreasing, then decreasing rapidly; the next number = character or tendency and amount of pressure change in hectopascals (millibars). A 3.3 change is coded as 033.	58033 (*See also* Appendixes A and C of this book.)
SENSOR STATUS INDICATORS. If the following sensors are not working, the following status indicators should be coded/sent: 1. If the lightning detection system at an automated site is inoperative.. 2. If the runway visual range is not reported.................................... 3. If the present weather identifier/sensor is inoperative.............. 4. If the tipping bucket rain gauge/sensor is inoperative............... 5. If the freezing rain sensor is inoperative.................................... 6. If the site's secondary visibility sensor is inoperative...................	TSNO (in sample METAR) RVRNO PWINO PNO FZRANO VSNO LOC
MAINTENANCE INDICATOR. This is coded and sent when an automated system detects that maintenance is needed on the system.	$

Figure 2-2. *Automated, manual, and plain language remarks in the METAR.*

For a reported group of 58021: Pressure decreasing, then decreasing more rapidly—this indicates 2.1 mb of change over the last three hours. Anytime the pressure is falling, then falling more rapidly, or steady, then decreasing, alarm bells should go off in your head. The pressure doesn't just fall for no reason; something is going on, so you need to start asking questions. It is a good clue that you need to check further into the weather picture on your route.

Falling pressure changes are also predictive of the direction of movement of frontal lows. These lows tend to move towards the area with the largest pressure falls, and they usually move to that location within 12–18 hours.

One final note about the remarks section of a METAR: You will occasionally see the word LAST. This means that this is the last observation from a manual station or an automated station with augmentation. (AWOS units installed before the changeover to the METAR format are still manually operated, and some still report in the old format). As a rule, all the automatic AWOS and ASOS units (FAA, NWS and DOD) operate continuously at all flight facilities/airports. Augmented stations will normally close at the same time the tower goes off duty for the night. Information regarding the hours of operation at uncontrolled airports can be found in the A/FD.

More METAR details:
- Automatic stations only report up to 3 cloud layers; augmented stations report up to 6.
- A gust is a speed variation of 10 kts or more, between low and high values in the last ten minutes of the hour.

A/FD: Airport/Facility Directory

Get Them All, Including Military METARs

Military flight facilities are automated as well, but they are also augmented by highly-trained weather observers—while the FAA and NWS ASOS/AWOS automated stations are not augmented (except at AFSS sites). This is a good reason to try to get all the different METAR station reports you can for the areas you'll be flying in. Table 2-2 is a list of U.S. military-base flight facilities and their four-letter identifiers.

The FSS briefers will not mention these military reports—you have to ask for them. A DUAT briefing will give you *all* available METARs. But you can easily find all the METAR stations by going to the "Interactive Weather Information Network" website (run by NWS—*see* the web address in the sidebar). This is another way, with slightly differing maps (*see* Figure 2-3), of getting to the same place as shown in Figure 2-1. This page not only has site location maps by state, but you can click on the map location of an airport or base and get the latest METAR report. If you do not have access to a computer, ask the briefer for *all* METAR reports along and within a 60 NM corridor of your route. Why not 50 NM like with the TWEBs? Simply that the number of bases along your route is low especially in the western states, so with 60 NM you will probably gather in a better picture of the enroute weather.

http://iwin.nws.noaa.gov/iwin/iwdspg1.html

Mountain pass weather is difficult to obtain due to few stations situated in these areas. But Colorado is installing six new AWOS units at two ski lodges and four mountain passes, due to be in by late 2001.

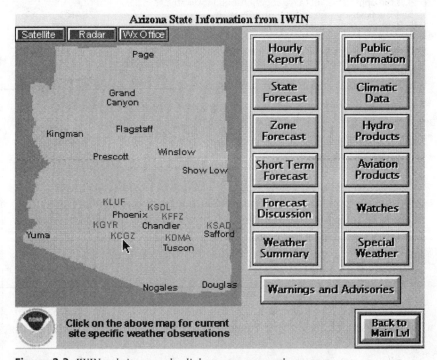

Figure 2-3. *IWIN website map also links to current weather reports.*

State	ICAO ID	City	Latitude / Longitude	State	ICAO ID	City	Latitude / Longitude
Alabama				**Kentucky**			
Cairns Army Airfield	KOZR	Ozark	31°17'N / 85°43'W	Fort Campbell Army Airfield	KHOP	Hopkinsville	36°40'N / 87°30'W
Maxwell AFB	KMXF	Montgomery	32°23'N / 86°22'W				
Alaska				**Louisiana**			
Elmondorf AFB	PAED	Anchorage	61°15'N / 149°48'W	Barksdale AFB	KBAD	Bossier City	32°30'N / 93°40'W
Eielson AFB	PAEI	Fairbanks	64°39'N / 147°04'W	Fort Polk Army Airfield	KPOE	Leesville	31°02'N / 93°02'W
Allen Army Airfield	PABI	Fort Greely	64°00'N / 145°44'W	**Maine**			
Wainwright Army Airfield	PAFB		64°50'N / 147°37'W	Brunswick NAS	KNHZ	Brunswick	43°54'01"N / 69°56'06"W
Arizona				**Maryland**			
Davis-Monthan AFB	KDMA	Tucson	32°10'N / 110°53'W	Andrews AFB	KADW	Camp Springs	38°49'N / 76°51'W
Fort Huachuca Libby Field	KFHU		31°35'N / 110°20'W	Patuxent River NAS	KNHK	Lexington Park	38°16'43"N / 76°24'50"W
Gila Bend Army Airfield	KGBN	Gila Bend	32°26'N / 112°41'W	Phillips Army Airfield	KAPG	Aberdeen	39°28'N / 76°10'W
Luke AFB	KLUF	Phoenix	33°32'N / 112°23'W	**Massachusetts**			
USMC Air Station	KNYL	Yuma	32°37'25"N / 113°45'50"W	Westover AFB	KCEF	Chicopee Falls	42°12'N / 72°32'W
Arkansas				**Mississippi**			
Eaker AFB	KBYH	Blytheville	35°58'N / 89°57'W	Columbus AFB	KCBM	Columbus	33°39'N / 88°27'W
Little Rock AFB	KLRF	Little Rock	34°55'N / 92°09'W	Keesler AFB	KBIX	Biloxi	30°25'N / 88°55'W
California				Meridian NAS	KNMM	Meridian	32°32'47"N / 88°32'35"W
Beale AFB	KBAB	Marysville	39°08'N / 121°26'W	**Missouri**			
China Lake Naval Air Facility	KNID	China Lake	35°41'11"N / 117°41'24"W	Fort Leonard Wood	KTBN	St. Robert	37°44'N / 92°08'W
Edwards AFB	KEDW		34°55'N / 117°54'W	Whiteman AFB	KSZL	Knob Noster	38°44'N / 93°33'W
El Centro Naval Air Facility	KNJK	El Centro	32°49'30"N / 115°39'38"W	**Montana**			
Fairfield/Travis AFB	KSUU	Fairfield	38°16'N / 121°57'W	Malmstrom AFB	KGFA	Great Falls	47°30'N / 111°11'W
Lemoore NAS	KNLC		36°18'N / 119°56'W	**Nebraska**			
Los Alamitos Army Airfield	KSLI		33°47'N / 118°03'W	Offutt AFB	KOFF	Omaha	41°07'N / 95°54'W
McClellan AFB	KMCC		38°40'N / 121°24'W	**Nevada**			
March AFB	KRIV	Riverside	33°54'N / 117°15'W	Nellis AFB	KLSV	Las Vegas	36°14'N / 115°02'W
Miramar NAS	KNKX	San Diego	32°51'52"N / 107°07'51"W	Fallon NAS	KNFL	Fallon	39°25'56"N / 118°41'08"W
Colorado				**New Hampshire**			
USAF Academy	KAFF	Colorado Springs	38°58'N / 104°49'W	Pease AFB	KPSM	Portsmouth	43°05'N / 70°49'W
Buckley Air National Guard Base	KBKF	Denver	39°43'N / 104°45'W	**New Jersey**			
Delaware				Lakehurst NAS	KNEL	Lakehurst	40°02'N / 74°19'W
Dover AFB	KDOV	Dover	39°08'N / 75°28'W	McGuire AFB	KWRI	Wrightstown	40°01'N / 74°36'W
Florida				**New Mexico**			
Patrick AFB	KCOF	Cocoa Beach	28°14'N / 80°36'W	Cannon AFB	KCVS	Clovis	34°23'N / 103°19'W
Homestead AFB	KHST	Homestead	25°29'N / 80°23'W	Holloman AFB	KHMN	Alamogordo	32°51'N / 106°06'W
Key West NAS	KNQX	Key West	24°34'46"N / 81°41'02"W	Kirtland AFB (Albuquerque Int'l)	KABQ	Albuquerque	35°02'N / 106°36'W
Jacksonville NAS	KNIP	Jacksonville	30°14'03"N / 81°40'29"W	**New York**			
MacDill AFB	KMCF	Tampa Bay	27°51'N / 82°30'W	Fort Drum Army Airfield	KGTB	Watertown	44°03'N / 75°44'W
Pensacola NAS	KNPA	Pensacola	30°21'22"N / 87°19'24"W	**North Carolina**			
Tyndall AFB	KPAM	Panama City	30°04'N / 85°35'W	Cherry Point USMC Air Station	KNKT	Havelock	34°53'52"N / 76°52'51"W
Eglin AFB	KVPS	Valparaiso	30°29'N / 86°31'W	Fort Bragg Army Airfield	KFBG	Fayetteville*	35°08'N / 78°56'W
Georgia				New River USMC Air Station	KNCA	Jacksonville	34°42'21"N / 77°26'27"W
Fort Benning Army Airfield	KLSF	Columbus	32°20'N / 84°50'W	Pope AFB	KPOB	Fayetteville*	35°10'N / 79°02'W
Hunter Army Airfield	KSVN	Savannah	32°01'N / 81°09'W	Seymour-Johnson AFB	KGSB	Goldsboro	35°20'N / 77°58'W
Dobbins AFB	KMGE	Marietta	33°55'N / 84°31'W	* bases are colocated, 15 miles NW of Fayetteville			
Moody AFB	KVAD	Valdosta	30°58'N / 83°12'W	**North Dakota**			
Warner Robins AFB	KWRB	Warner Robins	32°38'N / 83°36'W	Grand Forks AFB	KRDR	Grand Forks	47°58'N / 97°24'W
Idaho				Minot AFB	KMIB	Minot	48°25'N / 101°21'W
Mountain Home AFB	KMUO	Mountain Home	43°03'N / 115°52'W	**Ohio**			
Illinois				Wright-Patterson AFB	KFFO	Dayton	39°50'N / 84°03'W
Scott AFB	KBLV	Belleville	38°33'N / 89°51'W	**Oklahoma**			
Indiana				Altus AFB	KLTS	Altus	34°39'N / 99°16'W
Grissom AFB	KGUS	Peru	40°39'N / 86°09'W	Tinker AFB	KTIK	Oklahoma City	35°25'N / 97°23'W
Kansas				Vance AFB	KEND	Enid	36°20'N / 97°55'W
McConnell AFB	KIAB	Wichita	37°37'N / 97°16'W	**Pennsylvania**			
				Muir Army Airfield	KMUI	Indiantown	40°26'N / 76°34'W
				Willow Grove NAS	KNXX	Montgomeryville	40°11'35"N / 75°08'40"W

Table 2-2. *U.S. military bases with ICAO identifiers (continued on next page)*

State	ICAO ID	City	Latitude / Longitude	State	ICAO ID	City	Latitude / Longitude
South Carolina				**Utah**			
Charleston AFB	KCHS	Charleston	32°53'56"N / 80°02'26"W	Hill AFB	KHIF	Ogden	41°07'N / 111°58'W
Myrtle Beach AFB	KMYR	Myrtle Beach	33°41'N / 78°56'W	**Virginia**			
Shaw AFB	KSSC	Sumter	33°58'N / 80°29'W	Langley AFB	KLFI	Hampton	37°05'N / 76°21'W
South Dakota				Norfolk NAS	KNGU	Norfolk	36°56'01"N / 76°17'45"W
Ellsworth AFB	KRCA	Rapid City	44°09'N / 103°06'W	Virginia Beach NAS	KNTU	Oceana	36°49'16"N / 76°01'42"W
Texas				**Washington**			
Corpus Christi NAS	KNGP	Corpus Christi	27°41'19"N / 97°17'30"W	Fairchild AFB	KSKA	Spokane	47°37'N / 117°39'W
Dyess AFB	KDYS	Abilene	32°25'12"N / 99°51'25"W	Fort Lewis			
Fort Hood				Army Airfield	KGRF	Tacoma	47°07'N / 122°33'W
Army Airfield	KGRK	Killeen	31°04'N / 97°50'W	McChord AFB	KTCM	Tacoma	47°09'N / 122°29'W
Kelly AFB	KSKF	San Antonio	29°23'N / 98°35'W	**Wyoming**			
Kingsville NAS	KNQI	Kingsville	27°30'11"N / 97°48'42"W	Warren AFB			
Laughlin AFB	KDLF	Del Rio	29°07'00"N / 100°28'00"W	(Cheyenne Int'l)	KCYS	Cheyenne	41°09'N / 104°48'W
Randolph AFB	KRND	San Antonio	29°32'N / 98°17'W				

Table 2-2. *U.S. military bases with ICAO identifiers (continued from previous page)*

Practice METARs

Below are four METAR observations for practice. Determine the location of these stations using the Inflight Advisory Plotting Chart on Page 49 in this book*. Whiteman AFB (KSZL) is located approximately 65 NM east–southeast of KMKC. Offutt AFB (KOFF) is colocated at Omaha, NE.

```
METAR KFCM 180253Z 06008KT 4SM BR OVC026 M04/M06 A3019 RMK A02
    SLP239 LAST AUGMENTED OBSERVATION 60000 T10441056 57001

SPECI KOFF 180304Z 07010KT 5SM -FZDZ BR OVC007 00/00 A2996 RMK

METAR KMCW 180250Z 09011KT 2SM -SN BR BRKN012 OVC023 M03/M05 A3013
    RMK SLP223 60002 T10291046 56007

METAR KSZL 180255Z VRB06KT 3SM -TSRA BR OVC005CB 02/01 A2986 RMK TWR
    VIS 2 OCNL LTGICCG TS OHD AND 8 W MOV NE SLP119 60012 8/9// 56029
```

1. If SPECI criteria are met at the time of a routine METAR observation, the report transmitted will be:
   a. METAR-SPECI KXYZ
   b. SPECI KXYZ
   c. METAR KXYZ

2. What report modifier identifies an observation from a fully automated system with no human augmentation?
   a. AWOS
   b. ASOS
   c. AUTO
   d. AWIP

3. Encode the following wind observations:

Direction	Speed	Gusts	
063	14		_____
241	35	52	_____
Calm			_____

4. The wind direction is observed to be variable between 320–040 degrees, with an average speed of 12 knots, wind gusts to 24 kts. How would you code this wind condition?

---

* Table 2-2 is also helpful for finding identifiers for the military base airfields, when using this Advisory Plotting Chart.

5. Let's work with the first METAR KFCM (Flying Cloud Airport, Minneapolis, MN):

    a. What visibility range is implied when BR is reported?

    b. T10441056 57001. Decode this supplemental information.

6. **SPECI KOFF 180304Z -FZDZ BR**.

    Decipher the present weather at KOFF.

7. Decode the METAR for KSZL.

8. Encode the runway visual range data:

Runway	RVR Value	
060	700 feet	_____
120 Left	1200 feet	_____
240 Right	2400 feet	_____

9. Weather occurring at the point of observation or in the vicinity of the station shall be coded

    a. Before the observed wind data.

    b. In the body of the report.

    c. After the visibility data.

    d. In the remarks section of the report.

10. Present weather obscuration shall be coded into the report if the prevailing visibility is less than

    a. 1-1/2 statute miles.

    b. 3 nautical miles.

    c. 7 statute miles.

    d. 3 statute miles.

11. What description terms are used with fog?

12. The precipitation at a station is reported as +RASHSN. The use of the plus sign is used to denote the intensity of both the RASH and the SN. (True / False)

Also, decipher the +RASHSN _____

13. A station observer observes a volcanic eruption and a tornado 10 miles east of the airport moving to the southwest at 2152 GMT (UTC). Which entry should be entered first in the RMK's section?

a. Both!

b. The volcano

c. The tornado

14. How would you code the above tornado remark? (No, evacuating the tower is not a good phrase to use!)

15. Encode a peak wind remark for a wind of 280 degrees at 46 knots that occurred at 22 minutes past the current hour.

16. What two cloud types can be reported in the sky condition section of a METAR report?

17. CLR will be used at a station when no clouds are detected below what level?

_____ feet

18. "Clear" is used at both automated and non-automated stations. (True / False)

19. Now let's try something different! Go back and examine the four METARs and note that the first three reports are reporting what kind of winds? What type of weather and temps do these three report? How about Whiteman AFB—what type of winds, weather, and temps is this station reporting? It is fairly obvious that something is taking place between Whiteman AFB and the other three northerly stations. What kind of frontal system could be doing all of this?

a. Cold Front

b. Warm Front

c. Occluded Front

d. Cold or Occluded

e. Warm or Occluded

Chapter 3: *Pilot and Radar Reports, Satellite Imagery, and Radiosondes*

Pilot Weather Reports (UAs, PIREPs)

PIREPs, along with the METARs, radar reports, and satellite imagery, all work together to give you a picture of weather for a given location and time. Pilot reports are especially valuable in that rather than being scheduled, they represent reports specific to a location, timeframe, or weather occurrence. Also they are the only verifiers of turbulence and icing conditions. The only way to become familiar with PIREPs is to practice, practice, and practice some more.

Timely PIREPs will be included in your briefing (FSS or DUAT). There is now a website where PIREPs are displayed as to type (icing, turbulence, sky, and weather conditions): *see* http://www.adds.awc-kc.gov, the "Aviation Digital Data Service," for plenty of graphically displayed PIREPs. This site also has information on icing and turbulence forecasts— which is still largely experimental but worth a look.

There is a new guide to the "contractions" used in these and other types of reports in the back section of AC 00-45E (Page 14-6). But here is a contraction that none of the PIREP examples in AC 00-45E used: /TB LGT-MDT DURC. Nothing hard about this one: "light to moderate turbulence on climb out."

Notice the two different codes used—UUAs and UAs. Usually the first warning about severe icing or turbulence is an urgent PIREP and this is coded "UUA." A "routine" PIREP is coded as "UA." When that PIREP is first broadcast as a UUA, at the tail end of the report will be a four-letter group, for example, KZAB. This alerts aircraft traffic that the ARTCC at Albuquerque, NM has issued either an MIS or CWA message about the severe phenomena.

Radar Weather Observations (ROBs)

While the AC 00-45E refers to the radar observations as SDs, they are easier to obtain if you use their new acronym, ROB. These are gathered from individual radar stations and then put into a collective by the Aviation Weather Center (AWC). You can easily pull them up from the Aviation Weather Center's website (*see* Page 7, bottom of page).

AC 00-45E Reading Assignment
Section 3
Pages 3-1 through 3-18

UA: A routine pilot report
UUA: An urgent pilot report
MIS: Meteorological impact statement
CWA: Center weather advisory

"SD" is an older designation for what most weather stations are now calling ROBs.

http://adds.awc-kc.noaa.gov/ (Aviation Digital Data Service)

http://www.awc-kc.noaa.gov/awc/radar_obs_text.html (ROBs homepage)

http://www.rap.ucar.edu/weather/radar.html (NEXRAD images from RAP/NCAR)

http://www.goes.noaa.gov (Geostationary Satellite Server)

http://iwin.nws.noaa.gov/iwin/images/rcmloop.gif (IWIN's NEXRAD looped image)

Polar coordinate graph paper may be purchased at most stationery stores.

ROBs are well explained in AC 00-45E, Pages 3-6 through 3-9. After reviewing this section along with the "PPI" (plotted precipitation intensity) chart on Page 3-10, practice plotting some ROBs. Included on the next two pages are polar coordinate graphs for this purpose (Figure 3-1), which have been labeled in degrees and the concentric circles labeled in nautical miles. The radar unit is located at the center of the chart. Therefore, an echo reported as **TRW+ 180/60 C2435 MTS 450** would be interpreted as a heavy thunderstorm located south (180 degrees) of the radar at a distance of 60 nautical miles with max echo tops at 45,000 feet MSL; the cell is moving to the east northeast (060 degrees) at 35 knots.

These reports are nice in that by getting the latest reports and quickly mentally or physically plotting them, you will have your own personal radar summary chart, ahead of the NWS-prepared charts. But then why not just use the U.S. national radar summary chart? Well, which radar summary has the smaller scale and the greater detail? Obviously your paper graph version. Also consider that for the radar summary chart (made up of the combined individual radar reports from all over the country), they only use the reports taken at 35 minutes past the hour. Then, the complete chart reached the AFSS's (or, the internet) about 40 minutes later.

Radar observations are taken at 5 minutes and at 35 minutes past the hour, then speedily transmitted to AWC where they are arranged by state. (AWC doesn't have Hawaii or Alaska online yet but these can be obtained from the Alaskan Aviation Weather Unit (AAWU) or the Aviation Weather Unit of the NWS.) Therefore, the ROBs are much more *timely* than the radar summary chart (which should be used for flight planning only).

But to save yourself plotting time and still be able to observe the latest radar pictures in living color and motion, there are several sites on the internet for real-time radar data. An excellent example is at one of the National Center for Atmospheric Research (NCAR) websites. (If you don't have a fast enough computer at home for this type of website, perhaps your FBO has a weather drop.)

Satellite Weather Imagery

We have all seen the satellite imagery on The Weather Channel or on our local TV station's weather news. Usually these images are looped and animated so it is easy to see the movement of storm systems and the clouds associated with them. Pilots planning a cross-country should start monitoring the weather "big picture" at least two days before flight time. Watching the radar and satellite imagery is a very good way to gain additional insight into what is occurring across the U.S. and your region.

While the AC 00-45E gives a nice concise overview of the weather satellites and the visible and infrared (IR) imagery, for some reason they neglected to mention a third method of depicting weather information from the satellites—water vapor imagery. Admittedly these valuable and interesting displays are important for the operational meteorologist and the research "think-tank" folks, but they can also be useful to the pilot. You should learn more about what the water vapor images can show you.

See Chapter 18 for more on the AAWU.

www.rap.ucar.edu: This full web address is shown at the bottom of Page 23.

Also see color radar image example in Appendix C (Page 169). This is from the AWC "Product Overlay" webpage, where you can combine many kinds of weather data onto one chart.

weather drop: At an FBO, computer or other connection to a weather subscription service provider, such as DUAT or WSI.

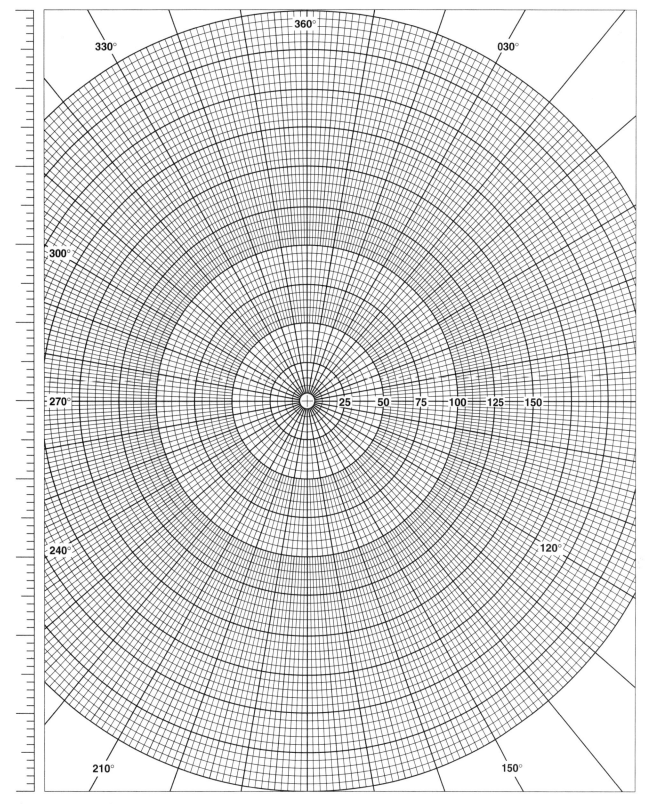

Figure 3-1. *Blank polar-coordinate graphs for practicing ROBs.*

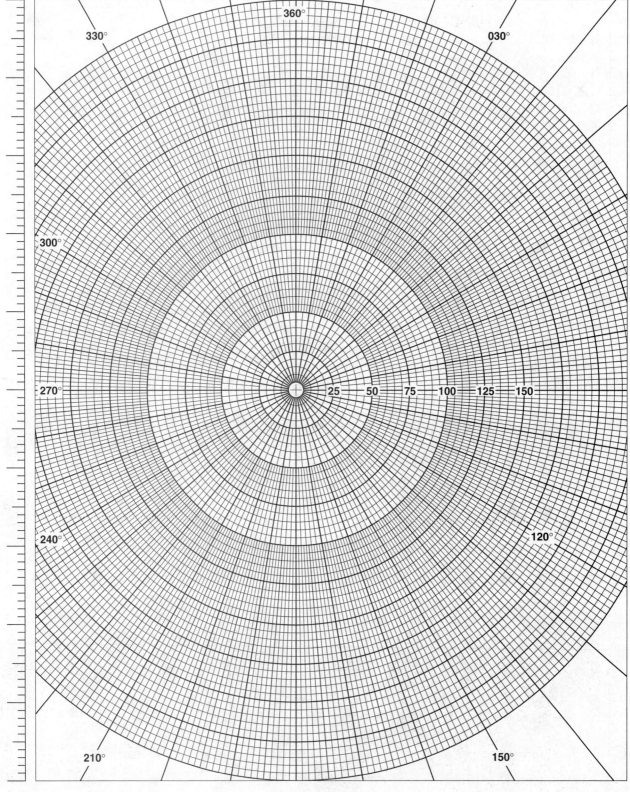

Figure 3-1. *Blank polar-coordinate graphs for practicing ROBs (continued).*

Aviation Weather Services *Explained*

Water vapor absorbs and re-radiates electromagnetic radiation in different wavelengths, the *infrared* 6.7 to 7.3 micron range. The GOES and TIROS satellites are equipped with radiometer instrumentation that records and transmits the data to ground receiving stations. On these images each pixel is given a "gray shade" according to the measured brightness temperature. White is for very cold brightness temperature (radiation from a moist layer or clouds in the upper troposphere), whereas black indicates a warm brightness temperature (radiation from the earth or from a dry layer in the middle troposphere).

The features seen on the water vapor imagery are the result of such factors as vertical motion, horizontal deformation in the wind and pressure fields, and moisture advection. In other words, water vapor can be used as a tracer to determine three-dimensional atmospheric motions.

Figure 3-2 shows one example of the GOES-9, which is situated over the equator at 135 degrees west longitude. GOES-8 is parked at 75 west longitude over the equator. GOES-10 is on standby or storage at 105 west longitude. One drawback of the GOES satellites is the distortion of images pole-ward of 30–40 degrees north and south of the equator. In order to cover this rather large area of the earth's surface, NOAA has launched polar orbiting satellites (TIROS). These circle the globe from north to

 Water vapor images are viewable at the GOES website: **www.goes.noaa.gov**

GOES: Geostationary Operational Environmental Satellite

TIROS: Television InfraRed Observation Satellite

 The NCDC has a website with more information on TIROS: go to **http://perigee.ncdc.noaa.gov/** and click on their "documentation" page.

Figure 3-2. *GOES-9 water vapor image*

south and the earth rotates beneath them. They are very nice for watching the storm tracks of the middle and high latitudes, since movement is quite pronounced from each successive north-south pass.

See also Appendix E in this book, "Weather Websites" (Page 177).

All these images are easily called up from a variety of websites (*see* Page 23), but one easy place to start is "Landings" (www.landings.com). There's a wealth of weather web-addresses on their weather links page.

The water vapor image shown in Figure 3-2 is from September 11, 2000 at 0030 UTC. One outstanding part of the image is the eye and spiral bands of Hurricane Lane, located south of the lower Baja California peninsula. The short arrows indicate the airflow while the longer arrows north and northeast of the hurricane indicate the outflow which is streaming into Texas. The white puffy areas (indicated by the letter "A" and short arrows) are thunderstorms.

West of south-central California is a small *cut-off low* which is aloft; the surface reports do not indicate this feature at all (because stations in the area are sparse and scattered, so reporting isn't as consistent). South of the cut-off low is the subtropical jet stream—the moisture stream with the jet weakens as the airflow turns southeastwards into the drier subsiding air found west of the hurricane.

Another low is also indicated north-northwest of the low aloft, and the long arrows over the ocean and the northwestern U.S. indicate the upper-air pattern with a trough of low pressure over central Washington State, southwards over western Nevada. There is a weak jet stream of 75–80 knots lying southwest–northeast along the arrow that extends from southeast Idaho to eastern Montana, to North Dakota.

You don't have a computer? You can still view these, as the water vapor chart is one of the TV meteorologist's pet images. Why? Because when you put the images together into a loop, the motion of the upper atmosphere becomes quite obvious—which makes a nice razzle dazzle for their presentation. (Too bad they do not share the information on the images with the viewers—a classic case of using the KISS principle in doing the weather!)

Radiosonde Additional Data

See AC 00-45E Page 9-5, and Chapter 14.

The NWS defines radiosonde as a contraction for "radio-sounding device."

The freezing level data is now collected, plotted, and disseminated in chart form on the composite moisture and stability chart's freezing level panel. This data is collected by "radiosonde" instruments sent aloft via weather balloons. The AC 00-45E still refers to the text message received from the radiosonde as a RADAT, but this term is phasing out of use for pilots, as more products now available are the result of plotting the RADATs themselves.

If you're looking for *forecast* freezing level information, this can be found on the significant weather prognostic charts. You should know, however, that if a radiosonde run identifies two or more freezing levels, only the *highest* observed freezing level will be used in determining the forecast freezing level for that station.

Take a closer look at the plotted RADAT on AC 00-45E Page 3-16, Figure 3-5: notice that from 2,400 feet MSL to 10,000 feet MSL that the temperature profile is above freezing. This area is called a "Warm Nose" and is usually a signature for one big bad airplane killer: FZRA or FZDZ. If there are sufficient clouds and moisture present, frozen precipitation—snow—might fall into the warm above-freezing air and melt. Then the cold liquid drops will fall into the lower below-freezing air and become colder. If they freeze again, we call this cold hard stuff "sleet." If they remain liquid they could then freeze on impact with a cold object—an airplane.

Therefore, instead of stopping after you scan the area forecast for the forecast freezing levels, check out the four-panel moisture and stability chart as well. If there are multiple freezing levels along or near your route be sure to make a mental or written note about it.

To learn more about how the NWS obtains and uses data from the radiosonde instrument packages, go to the websites below and you will find a nice introduction to the upper-air sounding product called the "Skew T":

http://weather.unisys.com/upper_air/skew/details.html

http://www-das.uwyo.edu/upperair/sounding.html

Vertical Wind Profilers

The AC 00-45E doesn't get into an explanation of this experimental data service. But again, the more you know about weather the better off you will be—you should at least know that this service is out there. All of the Vertical Profiler sites, with a few exceptions, are located in the central U.S.—which is also known as "Tornado Alley." The vertical wind profilers are experimental and used almost exclusively for research. But this data gives you another view of what weather is about.

The VP equipment resembles huge bed-springs with spindly "birds" peering down at the springs. These vertically measure wind direction and speed from about 500 meters AGL to 9.25 kilometers. Winds at each level are averaged every 6 minutes for an hour, then displayed on a chart as a vertical profile of what wind is doing at each level. At the bottom of the display chart is a timeline for each hour. Another part of this equipment is the Radio Acoustic Sounding System (RASS), which measures air temperature in the vertical.

These profilers are still very much in the experimental stage of development; yet they have already shown they have a future potential to furnish winds and temperatures aloft, as well as information on the vertical structure of frontal systems, cold and warm air advection aloft, and wind shear.

Consider a vertical wind profile at a vertical profiler station:

    Surface winds .... 300/12 kts, T = 5°C

    500 meters .... 240/21 kts, T = 8°C

    10 Kilometer .... 250/85 kts, T = -15°C

(I have not indicated the data for every layer of air—just these three levels, in order to illustrate the information below.)

- Between the surface and 500 meters there has been a wind shift (wind shear), which may be due to a frontal system that passed the profiler station earlier. Note the temperature increase (inversion) from the sur-

FZRA: Freezing rain

FZDZ: Freezing drizzle

The current NWS weather balloon network (U.S.) is gradually being replaced by a new "GPS Radiosonde" network. *See* Appendix B (Page 163) for a diagram and explanation of the new system.

On the web, this is a good place to start:

http://weather.cod.edu/profiler

advection: The movement of heat, cold, or moisture by the wind. (*See* Appendix D, Glossary.)

face to 500 meters. (Fronts aloft are always marked by the presence of an inversion.)

- From the data gathered by the radar at 10 Km, approximately 32,000 feet, it appears that the jet stream is active over the station.

- When the wind direction changes in the vertical in a veering manner (clockwise), this change suggests that warm air advection is occurring. This also implies that the air is becoming warmer and more stable.
- If the wind direction changes in a backing manner (counterclockwise), cold air advection is occurring.

It appears from the data above that the winds are changing from the surface upwards through 500 meters in a backing manner—this implies cold air advection, or cold air moving in. This is very typical at an airport that has recently had a cold frontal passage.

Practice PIREPs and ROBs

1. Decode the UA:

   ```
   UUA /OVSEA 060045/TM 2018/FL140 /TPBE55/SK BKN 080-TOP 132 /TA MO4 /
      TB SVR CAT /IC LGT RIME 080-120 DURC KZSE
   ```

2. Figure 3-1 on AC 00-45E Page 3-10 is an example of how to plot on paper the digitized radar informa-tion given at the end of an SD (or, ROB)—*see also* Page 3-8. Using the polar-coordinate graphs on Pages 25–26, plot the coded information for the ICT and MAF ROB messages on AC 00-45E Page 3-8. The ICT report also explains how to plot the data and draw a short arrow in order to indicate cell move-ment, with the speed written in next to the arrowhead.

3. You are at 9,500 feet cruise altitude on instruments and approximately 40 NM west of the Oklahoma City VOR, when you encounter light-to-moderate turbulence as well as a light buildup of mixed ice on the leading edges of your C-172's wing struts. The OAT is registering a plus 01 Celsius. Naturally, you would not be sitting there coding up a PIREP, but how would this report be coded up for transmittal? Hmm, maybe we are neglecting to let EFAS* know a piece of important information—what has been left out of the PIREP?

4. Decipher and translate the following PIREPs.

   ```
   KGFK UUA/OV GFK/TM 1705/FL DURD/TP DC9/ TB LLWS 200AGL ON APCH RNWY
      21 ±15KTS
   ```

   ```
   KSEE UA/OVOCN060040/TM 1727/FL 060/TP C152/SK 035 SCT 060/WX FV 6HK
      SFC TO 035/TB OCNL LGT AT 060
   ```

   ```
   KTVL UA/OV TVL-SCK/TM 0040/FL 125/TP C210/SK IN CLDS/TA-01C/IC LGT
      RIME/RM DURC TVL MVFR CONDS MDT-STG UDDFS
   ```

   ```
   KDTW UA/OV DTW210030/TM 1901/FL DURC/TP B727/SK OVC 070 150 BKN 210/
      TB LGT OCNL MDT 100 TO 150
   ```

   ```
   UUA/OV PUB 200035/TM 2219/FL 135/TP C182/ SK ACSL NW/TB MDT OCNL
      SVR/RM STG UDDFS ± 900 FEET ZDV
   ```

---

* *See* Chapter 7 for **EFAS: Enroute Flight Advisory Service**

Chapter 4: *Aviation Terminal Forecasts (TAFs)*

TAF Locations

Figure 4-1 shows the NWS regional forecast offices; this is similar to an "interactive" map you can find via links on the website for NWS regional headquarters. If you click on the cities shown, you can get TAF information for your area *geographically*—a handy aviation weather aid. Each click leads to the regional NWS office's website, which usually will have a link to the specific aviation weather products they provide—mostly TAFs and METARs, but some give TWEB routes and other information. The AC 00-45E has maps with TAF locations given by station identifier, Pages 4-13 through 4-16.

Are TAFs available for all airports, you may ask, and if not, why not? All airports do not have a TAF, nor do all airports have an AUTO or augmented AWOS or ASOS observation site. All NWS and FAA sites do operate observation sites; the regional Weather Forecast Offices (WFOs) issue TAFs for these stations.

Uncontrolled airports may or may not have AWOS- or ASOS-equipped weather observation sites. These usually do not have TAFs issued for them—which is one major reason the area forecast was created. Why doesn't the federal government equip these airports with AWOS or ASOS equipment? I believe you already know the answer…MONEY. It is up to the municipality, county, and/or state to come up with funds to accomplish this herculean task and it is fiscally impossible to equip every small uncontrolled airport with a weather observation site. But even if every small airport from Podunk Corner, IA to U-Katchem Fish Camp, FL was so equipped, it doesn't necessarily follow that there will be an individual TAF issued for each little airport; this would create another huge workload for the NWS forecasters.

The final chapter in this book (Chapter 20) brings together all the elements of a thorough and in-depth weather briefing. Obviously no *one* weather message or forecast can stand alone—although there will be flights where it is not necessary to check every message or forecast product that the NWS puts out. However there is a companion message to the TAF and that is the METAR which gives you the current weather at a location.

AC 00-45E Reading Assignment
Section 4
Pages 4-1 through 4-16

 This NWS regional headquarters map is the second web address listed below.

TAF: Acronym for the French term that translates roughly to "terminal aerodrome forecast."

WFOs: NWS field offices designed to take advantage of WSR-88D and other new technologies, when they replaced the old NWS "WSFO/WSO" system.

See Chapter 5 for area forecasts (FAs).

---

http://weather.noaa.gov/weather/coded.html (NWS "Current Weather")

http://www.wrh.noaa.gov/wrhq/nwspage.html (NWS Offices and Forecast Office home pages)

http://www.nws.noaa.gov/oso/oso1/oso12/metar.htm (NWS METAR/TAF information page)

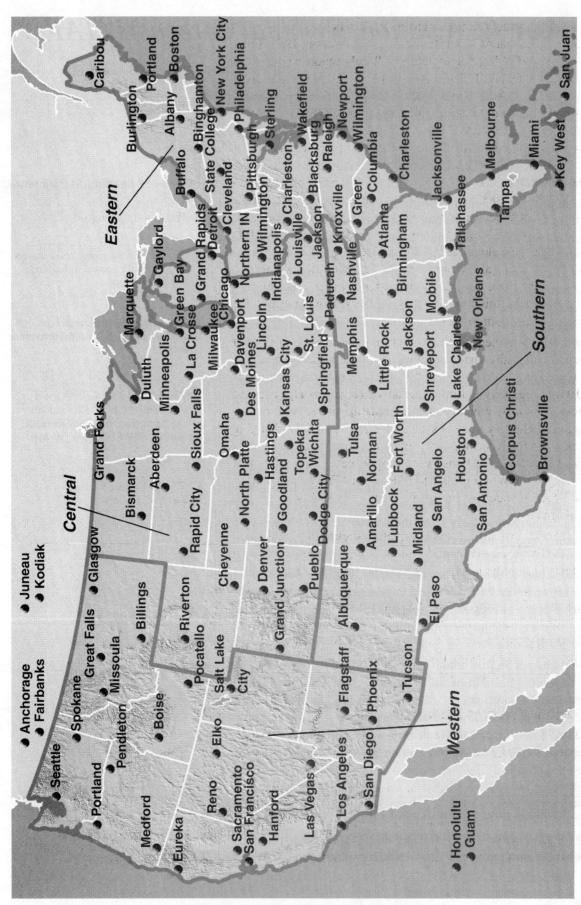

Figure 4-1. *National Weather Service regional forecast offices, showing regional boundaries.*

Aviation Weather Services *Explained*

More on Automated Observation Stations

There are some things that AC 00-45E doesn't mention about TAFs. First, consider that the AWOS laser ceilometers will only report clouds from the surface to 12,000 feet AGL. Older AUTOB units can only report from the surface to 6,000 feet AGL, and if there is a heavy surface based obscuration (thick fog), there could be multiple layers to 12,000 feet and you would never know it! The forecast for an AWOS location will only forecast a sky condition based on two-thirds of the reporting range height of the ceilometer. While the AWOS and ASOS ceilometers are able to detect clouds from surface to 12,000 feet AGL, the TAF will only consider from the surface upwards to 8,000 feet AGL. If the WFO issues a forecast for this location, it might conceivably forecast "CLR BLO 80." Well, 8,000 feet is good VFR! So what's the problem? Let's say this location is 2,000 feet MSL, which puts the clouds at 10,000 feet MSL. Since most sites are at airports in valleys, let's also assume that around the valley the terrain rises to 9,000–11,000 feet. Get the picture? In the eastern relatively flat half of the United States, this would be no problem. But in the west, CLR BLO 080 could mean big problems.

Fog is a fickle phenomenon. When it is forming or dissipating, it will frequently create a rapidly-changing situation at the airport where one minute the visibility is virtually nil, and the next minute the visibility is unrestricted. Once fog has fully formed, usually there are no large changes in the restricted visibility. When it starts to break up, due to wind or surface heating, the field may once again be plagued by rapidly-changing conditions until the fog has completely either evaporated or lifted into a stratus layer of clouds. A good observer can spot these—the automated stations cannot. So when you use a METAR or a TAF, you also need to add to it the larger, broader picture of the weather in your en route and destination/alternate areas.

Several years ago an airport was completely socked in with the visibility, as reported by an observer, at 3/4-miles with an indefinite obscured sky of 100 feet. Across the field at an FBO the visibility was even less than the value reported by the observer on the other side of the field—but the *departure end* of the runway complex probably had a visibility of 7 miles! A C-172 taxied down the taxiway and after run up, took off. The aircraft had not yet rotated when it disappeared in the fog bank which was blanketing the rest of the airport. The pilot caught a lot of flak when he returned to the airport two hours later!

TAFs from Military Sources

As is true with METARs from military observation installations, an advantage with military TAFs is that every operational USAF base has its own staff of meteorologists *and* observers as well as access to the USAF Global Weather Center. Their weather information is open to and usable by everyone, but the observations and forecasts by the FAA and NWS don't include these stations. Remember that when you talk to a briefer, you are not talking to a meteorologist, but to a well-trained FAA weather briefer who *reads* the forecasts. The NWS makes all the forecasts you normally receive, but does not do pilot briefings.

AC 00-45E, top of Page 4-2: Note the list of elements included in international and military TAFs which are *not* included in NWS-prepared TAFs.

DUAT: Direct User Access Terminal service

Many pilots use DUAT to obtain their weather briefings. DUAT will give you both observations and forecasts of military installations along your intended route. If you are getting a telephone briefing, you will have to request these reports/forecasts from the briefer.

```
TAF GSB 091818 24012G20 9999 10SM SCT 040
    BKN100 QNH 3011 INS
```

Obviously very nice weather is anticipated for Seymour-Johnson AFB, SC. The TAFs follow the same format as the METARs. The mystic-looking 9999 means "unrestricted visibility" and the rest is virtually self-explanatory.

If TAFs are issued in a collective (more than one TAF), the contraction "TAF" will not repeat for each individual forecast:

```
TAF COLLECTIVE
TAF 071320Z
ADW 1414 21010KT 9000 HZ SCT035 SCT250 QNH
    2992INS
BECMG 2021 19012KT 9000 HZ BKN035 BKN120
    BKN250 QNH2988INS CIG035
BECMG 0102 16006KT 8000 HZ SCT035 SCT100
    BKN250 QNH2988INS CIG250
BECMG 0809 14006KT 4800 BR SCT015 SCT120
    QNH2990INS SKY-X T35/20
T26/10=

TIK 1414 20014G21KT...
```

Note that only military TAFs give forecast QNH values.

QNH: Atmospheric pressure (Q) at nautical height

ADW is Andrews AFB and the TAF is valid from the 7th of July, 1995 at 1400Z to the 8th of July, 1400Z. This looks very much like the METAR format except for the use of 9000 which is the forecast visibility of 9 km (5 miles). A forecast value of 9999 means 10 km or more. Notice the last line of the ADW TAF, SKY-X: the NWS/FAA METARs cannot report or forecast partial obscurations, but the U.S. Air Force can forecast them.

SKY-X: Sky partially obscured

What about **T35/20** and **T26/10**? These are the anticipated maximum and minimum temperatures and dew points for the forecast period.

Here is an example TAF from Monterey, Mexico:

```
TAF MMMY 271051Z 1212 00000KT 6SM HZ SCT015
    SCT230 FM18 22010KT 6SM HZ SCT030 BKN230
    PROB40 2103 5SM TSRA BKN025CB FM04 00000KT
    6SM HZ SCT080 SCT230=
```

This looks similar to the ADW TAF with a couple of exceptions. PROB40 2103 simply means that there is a 40% probability that a TSRA with 5 miles visibility and a ceiling of 2,500 feet (cumulonimbus) will occur and last less than an hour (*see* AC 00-45E, Page 4-7). Absent on the MMY TAF are forecast altimeter settings—only the U.S. military forecasts QNH values. *Note:* BKN025CB is underlined to draw your attention to the fact that while all other countries will identify CB or TCU cloud types, the U.S. (and possibly Canada) will only identify CB cloud types.

TSRA: Thunderstorm with rain

Practice TAFs

Below are three TAFs to be used in answering the following questions.

Minneapolis, Minnesota

```
KMSP 251605Z 251612 12015KT 4SM DZ BR OVC005
    TEMPO 1619 2SM -SHRA BR OVC009
    FM1900 13015G23KT 5SM BR OVC018
    FM0000 140115G25 5SM BR BKN015 OVC040 PROB40 0006 3SM BR OVC15
    FM0600 15015G20KT 5SM BR BKN020 OVC040 PROB30 0612 -TRSA BR OVC020CB
```

Bismarck, North Dakota

```
KBIS 252340Z 260024 35012KT 2SM RA BR SCT 060 OVC010
    TEMPO 0004 4SM -RA BR OVC005
    FM0400 34016G26KT 3SM -RASN OVC007
    TEMPO 0408 1SM SN BLSN OVC003
    FM0800 32020G35KT 1/2SM SN BLSN OVC003
    BECMG 0911 32025G40KT 1/4SM +SN VV001
    FM1800 31025G35KT 3SM -SN BLSN OVC010
```

Mason City, Iowa

```
KMCW 252356Z 260024 16022G28KT 5SM BR SCT020 BKN100
    TEMPO 0004 2SM TSRA BR BKN030CB
    FM0400 16013G23KT P6SM SCT040 SCT100
    TEMPO 0407 4SM-SHRA BR BKN025 BKN080
    FM1200 18017G26KT P6SM SCT040
    BECMG 1517 21017G27 BKN03O
    FM2100 25020G28KT P6SM OVC030
    TEMPO 2124 -SHRA BKN025CB
```

1. You are filing into MSP with an estimated arrival time of 0330Z. What will you use for a forecast landing condition?

2. The MSP TAF is valid for what date and period of time?

3. Is the MSP TAF a federal (NWS/FAA) site or a military site? What did you base your answer on?

4. The first TEMPO conditions forecast for the Bismarck (BIS) TAF is valid for what time interval? What wind condition and weather is forecast for that interval?

Continued

5. Using the Mason City (MCW) TAF, what can you say about the probability of TSRA occurring during the 0000–0400Z time period?

   a. Less than 30%

   b. Less than 40%

   c. Greater than 50%

   d. 40% to 50%

   e. Probability not used for first 6 hours

   When can the term NSW be used in a TAF?

6. What is the definition of the term "P6SM" used in as TAF message?

7. You want to fly into Hogwarts (KHQT) airport and when you ask for the KHQT TAF, you receive: KOKO 252300Z NIL. What does this message mean, and how/when can you receive a TAF for Hogwarts airport?

Chapter 5: *Aviation Area Forecast (FA)*

Get to Know FAs

As AC 00-45E describes on Page 4-17, when there isn't a TAF available for your route, checking the FAs together with SIGMETs and AIRMETs is a good alternate method for obtaining forecasts and conditions. The FA deals with the VFR side of things; for IMC you go to the inflight advisories (SIGMET, AIRMET, convective SIGMET—all covered in Chapter 6). *All* airports are "covered" by one of the three types of FAs (continental U.S. and AK/HI, plus two "specialized" FAs), whereas TAFs are issued only to select stations (usually FAA or NWS observation sites). There are many internet sources for obtaining FAs, but probably the easiest to use is the Aviation Weather Center's page at the "www.awc-kc.noaa.gov" address shown below.

There's more to the FA than that, however, which will be covered later in this chapter. Also, there is a statement that could be misleading about inflight advisories in this section of the AC 00-45E: under "Precautionary Statements" (Page 4-18) it states, "The user shall always check the latest AIRMET Sierra for the FA area." This does not mean that the only AIRMET that could be in effect would be "Sierra"; remember, the AIRMETs are scheduled inflight advisories and there will also be an AIRMET issued for turbulence (AIRMET TANGO), or icing and freezing levels (AIRMET ZULU) as well.

Probably the biggest problem pilots have with the FA is deciphering the contractions in the SYNOPSIS section of the message, because of the numerous *contractions* of words. Many contractions can be easily decoded, since they simply remove most or all of the original vowels and still *resemble* the original word phonetically. But what about, for example, "OTRW"? We all recognize TRW, it's the old contraction for a thunderstorm and rain shower, right? However, OTRW stands for "otherwise." You'll get the knack of the contractions used in these reports if you practice a few:

Practice Deciphering Contractions

The list of contractions and acronyms in AC 00-45E Section 14 is extensive and helpful. Given the contractions on the next page, write out their original words/meanings.

AC 00-45E Reading Assignment
Section 4
Pages 4-17 through 4-22, and
Pages 4-27 through 4-31; also,
Section 14
Pages 14-6 through 14-19

These two "specialized" FAs are:
FAGX—Gulf of Mexico FA
International FA—such as for the Atlantic or Caribbean.

The Aviation Weather Center (AWC) prepares and issues FAs and inflight weather advisories.

---

http://www.awc-kc.noaa.gov/awc/awc-fa.html (Aviation Area Forecasts—by the Aviation Weather Center)

http://iwin.nws.noaa.gov/iwin/aviationframe.html (IWIN's Weather Links)

Intensity Contractions

(e.g., LiGhT rain)

LGT _____, MDT _____, HVY _____,

SVR _____, WK _____, XTRM

_____,

VLNT _____.

Speed Contractions

Give the contractions for the word or phrase.

RAPIDLY _____, SLOWLY _____,

INCREASING _____, DECREASING _____,

MOVING RAPIDLY _____.

Terrain — Geographical Contractions

VLY_____, MTNS _____,

LK _____, GLF _____,

GLFMEX _____, CSTL WTRS _____,

RVR _____, MTN SLPS_____,

GRTLKS _____,

SRN RCKYS _____.

Location Qualifiers

(e.g., Near Coastal Mountains: NR CSTL MTNS)

NR _____, OVR _____, Vicinity of _____,

Below _____, Along _____.

Fronts and Weather (FNTS, WX)

CDFNT _____, WMFNT _____,

SQ LN _____. OCFNT _____.

Trough _____, Stationary _____.

Thunder _____, Thunderstorm _____,

CD FNTL PSG _____.

Direction (DRCTN) Contractions

North _____, SW _____, Eastward _____,

Southwesterly _____.

Having trouble with the geographical contractions? A knowledge of geography is helpful in studying weather as it has an effect on climate and pattern—*see* Appendix B, Page 164 for a topographical map of the U.S. showing typical yearly storm tracks, and some of the relationship of climate to landforms.

PNHDL = Panhandle, i.e. of Texas, Oklahoma, and Florida

FROPA = Frontal passage

Precipitation

What are the new contractions for the following precipitation types? (*See* Section 14.)

Rain _____, _____. Snow Shower _____, _____.

Freezing Rain _____, _____. Ice Pellets _____, _____.

Blowing Snow _____, _____.

Thunderstorm _____, _____.

Potpourri of Contractions

Surface _____, Aloft _____, Cold _____,

Visibility _____, Layer(s) _____.

IR STLT IMGRY_____

...Surprise! You cannot find this in the contractions listed in Section 14. "IR STLT" is "infra-red satellite" imagery.

For the Synopsis section of the FA, you can decipher most of it by using the list of contractions in Section 14. After practice, you'll get used to how the contractions are used in this part of the FA. But there are a few contractions which are a little confusing: **MS** is Mississippi, but it also stands for "minus." **M6** is "minus 6 degrees Celsius."

The Broader Perspective

Let's do a recap at this point: You know that the METAR gives you the current as well as earlier weather conditions at the airport. The TAF gives you a detailed look at what the NWS folks at the Aviation Weather Center think the weather will be at selected airports at some time in the future. The area forecast along with its sister messages (AIRMETs and SIGMETs) were designed to give the pilot a broader and in-depth weather picture over a much larger region. So it simply isn't enough to check only the current weather METARs and the TAF(s) for most flights. After all, the METAR and TAF cannot tell you what to expect with respect to icing, turbulence, wind shear, or severe weather.

```
FAUS6 KCHI 260245
CHIC FA 260245
SYNOPSIS AND VFR CLDS/WX
SYNOPSIS VALID UNTIL 262100
CLDS/WX VALID UNTIL 261500...OTLK VALID
  261500-262100
ND SD KS MN IA MO WI LM LS MI LH IL IN KY


SEE AIRMET SIERRA FOR IFR CONDS AND MTN OBSCN
TS IMPLY SEV OR GTR TURBC SEV ICE LLWS AND
  IFR CONDS
NON MSL HGTS DENOTED BY AGL OR CIG.
```

Correlate this FA (which continues on the next page) with the TAFs that follow and see how much more weather-picture emerges from the FA.

Continued

```
SYNOPSIS...STRONG AREA OF LO PRES CNTRD OVR
    ERN SD AT 03Z WILL MOV OVR WRN AND CNTRL MN
    BY 15Z AND INTO CAN BY 21Z. ASSOCD CDFNT AT
    03Z FM ERN SD WRN IA WRN MO. BY 21Z FNTL
    BNDRY FM LS ERN WI WRN IL ACRS SERN MO.


ND
WRN ND...CIGS OVC010 TOPS FL300. OCNL VIS
    3-5SM SN. 13-15Z BECMG CIGS BKN030-050 OCNL
    -SN. OTLK...VFR. CNTRL AND ERN ND...CIGS
    OVC010-020 TOPS FL300. -RA/WDLY SCT EMBD -
    TSRA. CB TOPS FL400. 15Z BECMG VSBY 3-5SM.
    -SN. CIGS 025BKN 060OVC TOPS 150. CNTRL ND
    ARND 05Z BECMG -SN. OTLK...IFR CIG RASN.
    CNTRL ND 19-21Z VFR.


IA
WRN IA...CIGS BKN020-030 TOPS 100. WINDS NWLY
    020G30KT 04-05Z BECMG SCT020-030 TOPS 060.
    CNTRL IA CIGS BKN-OVC015 OVC040 TOPS FL350.
    SCT -TSRA CB TOPS 450 TS PSBLY SVR. 06-08Z
    BECMG BKN-OVC030 TOPS FL180 ISLTD CB. GD
    VFR AFTR 09Z. OTLK...VFR WINDS NWLY.
```

Correlating TAFs and FAs

Let's say we want to get a good idea of what is forecast to occur across the region of North Dakota to Iowa on the 26th day of the month between 0400 and 1000Z. Take another look at a couple of TAFs from the previous chapter:

```
KBIS 252340Z 260024 35012KT 2SM RA BR SCT 060
    OVC010
      TEMPO 0004 4SM -RA BR OVC005
      FM0400 34016G26KT 3SM -RASN OVC007
      TEMPO 0408 1SM SN BLSN OVC003
      FM0800 32020G35KT 1/2SM SN BLSN OVC003
      BECMG 0911 32025G40KT 1/4SM +SN VV001
      FM1800 31025G35KT 3SM -SN BLSN OVC010


KMCW 252356Z 260024 16022G28KT 5SM BR SCT020
    BKN100
      TEMPO 0004 2SM TSRA BR BKN030CB
      FM0400 16013G23KT P6SM SCT040 SCT100
      TEMPO 0407 4SM -SHRA BR BKN025 BKN080
      FM1200 18017G26KT P6SM SCT040
      BECMG 1517 21017G27 BKN030
      FM2100 25020G28KT P6SM OVC030
      TEMPO 2124 -SHRA BKN025CB
```

KBIS TAF called for TEMPO conditions from 0400–0800Z of 1 mile visibility in moderate snow and blowing snow with a 300-foot overcast. Winds are from 340 degrees at 16 knots with gusts to 26 knots.

From 0800–1100Z, they are forecasting 1/2-mile visibility in moderate snow and blowing snow with a 300-foot covercast; winds will be from

320 degrees at 20 knots, gusting to 35 knots. Conditions by 1100Z will drop to 100-foot obscured (vertical visibility 01) in heavy snow with winds from 320 degrees at 25 knots, gusting to 40 knots.

KMCW TAF in Iowa: at 0400Z, 6 miles VSBY, 4,000-foot and 10,000-foot scattered layers. Winds from 160 at 13 kts, gusts to 23 kts. MCW is also expecting 4 miles with scattered light rain showers from 0400–0700Z.

Now read the synopsis from the CHI FA at top of Page 42: Strong low pressure with a cold front to the south through eastern Kansas. The low pressure is expected to move northeastward from eastern South Dakota into Minnesota and then into Canada. The cold front will move eastward to a position through western Illinois/eastern Missouri by 2100Z on the 26th.

This certainly gives us a larger weather picture then the two TAFs! More importantly, now you have information on cloud tops (see the outlooks that follow the synopsis). Now follow the advice given right below the synopsis valid time period: "SEE AIRMET SIERRA FOR IFR CONDS AND MTN OBSCN"—and naturally, also check AIRMET TANGO (turbulence) and AIRMET ZULU (icing and freezing level).

In the FA above, and in the one on AC 00-45E Page 4-17, do you see any forecast wind information? No, because the FA will not include wind information unless they are forecasting sustained wind in excess of 25 knots. Should you then assume that the winds are not significant? No, you should check the current reports (if available) for wind information (*see* the TAFs above), and/or look at a surface analysis chart to give you a clue as to wind direction and possible strength.

The surface analysis chart is discussed in Chapter 12 of this book, and AC 00-45E Section 5.

If the forecast calls for **SCT-BKN** conditions, opt for the "pessimistic" side and assume it will be broken. The same pessimistic rationale also applies for **BKN-OVC.**

Continue to next page for Practice Session.

Area Forecast Practice

1. *See* the KCHI FA starting on Page 41. You are scheduled to fly into northeastern North Dakota with a arrival time of 261245Z at Devils Lake. Yes, there really is an airport at Devils Lake and no, there is no TAF for this location. Determine what will be your landing forecast and write it here.

   Weather/Obstructions _____

   Ceilings/Clouds _____

   Wind Condition _____ ...Hmmm, there is no wind forecast (no speeds of 25 knots or greater expected). But you have some FA messages to work with (*see* Pages 41-42), plus you can check the forecast condition on the KBIS TAF for your arrival time at Devils Lake and arrive at a good estimate.

2. How many times a day is the area forecast issued?

3. Sustained surface winds are forecast when the forecast wind speeds equal or exceed:
   a. 6 knots
   b. 12 knots
   c. 20 knots

4. Decipher this part of an FA:

   ```
   TX
   WRN TX N OF A MAF-SJT LN. CIGS 15-25 BKN-OVC 150 SCTD -SHRA. 03Z
       30-50 SCT 120 SCT. OTLK...VFR
   ```

5. Are cloud top heights (HGTS) given in feet AGL or MSL?

6. Decipher this into plain English:

   ```
   SYNOPSIS...SFC FNTL BNDRY FRM GRTLKS SWWD INTO SWRN TX WILL MOV
       SEWRD TO SERN ONT TO LWR MS RVR VLY BY 15Z.
   ```

7. Why would a pilot use the Area Forecast?

8. The term OCNL…How is this defined and used in the FA message?

Chapter 6: *In-Flight Advisories (WA, WS, WST)*

AIRMETs (WA)

An AIRMET is a 6-hour forecast issued every 6 hours. Distances are given in NM (visibility, if given, is in statute miles) and heights are in feet MSL, except for ceilings (CIG). As the AC 00-45E points out, these cover significant weather, but of an intensity lower than that forecast in the SIGMET. Let's take a look at part of an AIRMET which has occurred on the same date as the METARs, TAFs and FAs used so far in this book:

```
AIRMET TANGO UPDT 4 FOR TURBC AND LLWS VALID
   UNTIL 130200
ND SD NE KS MN IA MO WI
TURBC DUE TO STG WNDS ASSOCD WITH LO PRES
   SYS. ISOLD SVR TURBC UNTIL 1600Z
```

Severe turbulence being forecasted on an AIRMET? Mistake? No, as long as the turbulence is forecast to be *isolated*, an AIRMET can forecast this adverse condition. The AC 00-45E has a good example of a TANGO AIRMET (Page 4-25), but the example above is included to illustrate something. AIRMETs (TANGO) are issued for moderate turbulence, but this message has been issued for isolated severe turbulence below 10,000 feet MSL. This is perfectly legitimate as long as the severe turbulence is isolated; a SIGMET is issued if the turbulence is occasional or persistent.

```
WAUSI KBOS 042145
BOSZ WA 042145 AMD
AIRMET ZULU UPDT 2 FOR ICG...VALID UNTIL 050400
ME NH VT NY CT RI MA AND CSTL WTRS
FROM CAR TO YSJ TO 150E ACK TO BDR TO YOW TO
   CAR
OCNL MDT RIME OR MXD ICGICIP FRM FRZLVL TO
   140. CONDS CONTG BYD 04Z.
SEE SIGMET OSCAR1
```

Note that this is an example of an AIRMET (ZULU) which lets you know a SIGMET has been issued. Currently, SIGMETs are still not broadcast routinely like the AIRMETs. The three-letter VOR IDs that start with

AC 00-45E Reading Assignment
Section 4
Pages 4-23 through 4-27

WA: AIRMET

WS: SIGMET

WST: Convective SIGMET

U.S. AIRMETs are always identified by the phonetic letters **S** (SIERRA), **T** (TANGO), and **Z** (ZULU).

The 4th line of this AIRMET shows the states affected.

---

http://www.awc-kc.noaa.gov/awc/aviation_weather_center.html (AWC's "Standard Briefing" page)

http://iwin.nws.noaa.gov/iwin/main.html (Interactive Weather Information Network)

http://www.awc-kc.noaa.gov/overlay/prod-olay.html (AWC Product Overlay page)

a Y (YSJ) are Canadian locations. Canadian AIRMETs do not have reserved or "fixed" phonetic letters like U.S. AIRMETs do, and may last for two hours or possibly eight hours; they are in effect until canceled or superseded.

The "adds.awc-kc.gov" web address (bottom of Page 23) is for the Aviation Digital Data Service, an experimental forecast website where you can pull up a nice map with combined and plotted AIRMETs and SIGMETs for the contiguous U.S., as well as radar information and many other aviation weather products. Also, at the AWC website you can link to a page ("Product Overlay") where a radar image can be plotted along with convective SIGMETs, outlooks, and other weather warnings and forecasts—it's interactive, so you have a choice of weather messages to layer together into one chart.

SIGMETs (WS)

The first issuance of a SIGMET is always identified as an Urgent Weather SIGMET (UWS), and at this point the ARTCC affected by this information has probably already issued a CWA and/or an MIS message (*see* Chapter 9) for the affected area. Figure 6-1 (at right) is a chart that can help you locate and geographically pinpoint the advisory information: the Inflight Advisory Plotting Chart.

Route-planning hint: It is helpful to make photocopies of the Inflight Advisory chart—it is handy for working with the FA messages and the WA, WS, and WST, as well as the CWA/MIS messages to follow this chapter.

Convective SIGMETs (WST)

AC 00-45E Pages 4-26 and 4-27 have excellent WST bulletins to study, but also take a look at this WST message:

```
WKCE WST 101355
CONVECTIVE SIGMET 6E
VALID UNTIL 1555Z
FL GA CSTL WTRS

FROM 100SE CHS-60E VRB
LINE EMBDD TSTMS 30 MI WIDE MOVG FRM 2520.
  TOPS ABV 480.

OUTLOOK VALID 10155-101955
FROM ILM-140SSE ILM-190E VRB-90WSW
  PIE-CEW-ILM

LINES/CLUSTERS OF TSTMS EXPCD TO DVLP OVR FL
  AND SRN ATLC/CSTL WTRS. LARGE AREA OF STG
  LIFT WITH LIFTED INDEX OF -8 AND -9 ASSOCD
  WITH UPR LVL CRCLN AND STG PVA OVER NERN
  GLFMEX. E-W STNRY FNT WILL ALSO AID GOOD
  CNVCTN IN VERY MOIST AIR MASS.

  ...HUDSON
```

See Appendix C, Page 169 for an example of a "product overlay" image.

See also the map of ARTCC boundaries in Chapter 9, Page 64.

AC 00-45E has an Advisory Chart (Page 4-46), but the one in Figure 6-1 is more up-to-date and easier to read.

Appendix B (Pages 157–158) contains a list of all the station identifiers shown on the Advisory Plotting Chart.

2520: Direction and speed of movement, of a line of thunderstorms—from 250 degrees at 20 knots.

Aviation Weather Services *Explained*

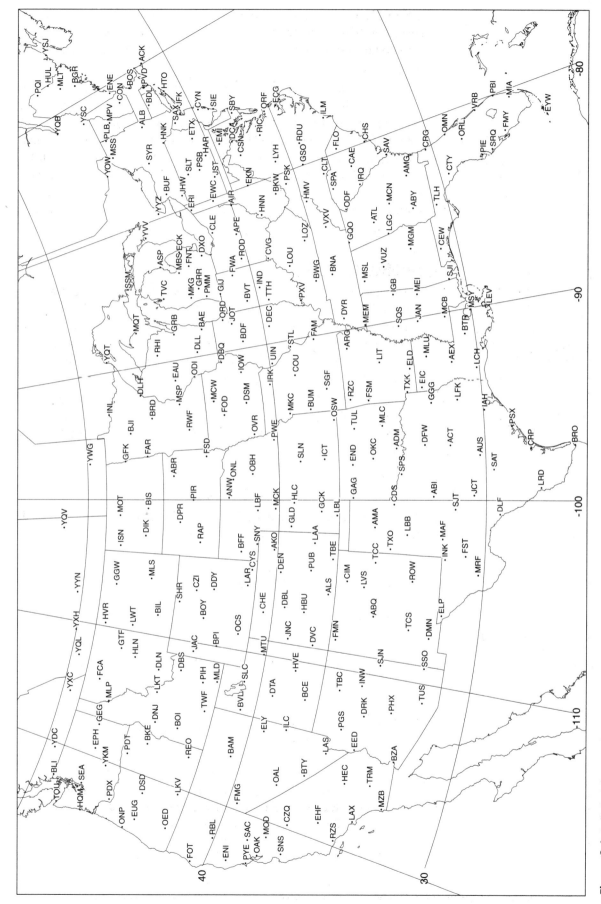

Figure 6-1. *Inflight Advisory Plotting Chart (Dec. 2000)*

This example is included mainly to explain the last section (translated): "...lifted index of -8 and -9 associated with upper level low cell, and strong positive vorticity advection (pva) over the northeastern Gulf of Mexico."

The Lifted Index is an index or measure of the atmosphere's stability or instability, and this will be covered in Chapter 14. Vorticity and vorticity advection is an important factor in atmospheric vertical motion; some basic college texts will cover this concept. It is particularly important to understand messages like the WST outlook, the FA synopsis or other messages in which the *why*, *what*, *when* and *where* of weather is discussed.

Study the WST on AC 00-45E Pages 4-26 and 4-27 and try to decipher it. You can use the list of contractions in AC 00-45E Section 14, just as with the FAs. For example, in the first convective SIGMET: (this is a pretty simple one)...there is a diminishing line of thunderstorms 15 NM wide, and moving from 300 degrees at a speed of 25 knots. "POSS" at the end of this message means that 50-knot wind gusts are possible.

Now look at the "OUTLOOK" portion at the bottom of the page. "Connect the dots" on the Inflight Advisory Plotting Chart to get a picture of where this is happening (*see* the chart excerpt in Figure 6-2). As a rule, the included area starts with the northernmost points working clockwise. If you see any three-letter station IDs that start with a "Y"— that is a Canadian station. A helpful hint for this one: the first point, "ISN" is in North Dakota.

See "Suggested Reading," Page 197, for some titles of some basic weather textbooks.

See AC 00-45E, Page 4-26, about mid-page.

If you can't find a station given in the advisory on the Inflight Advisory Plotting Chart, try the TAF locations maps in AC 00-45E (Page 4-13 to 4-14), or other lists of VORs and other stations such as the one in Appendix B (Page 157). In the excerpt below, for example, SBN and BRL were added after consulting AC 00-45E's Figure 4-2.

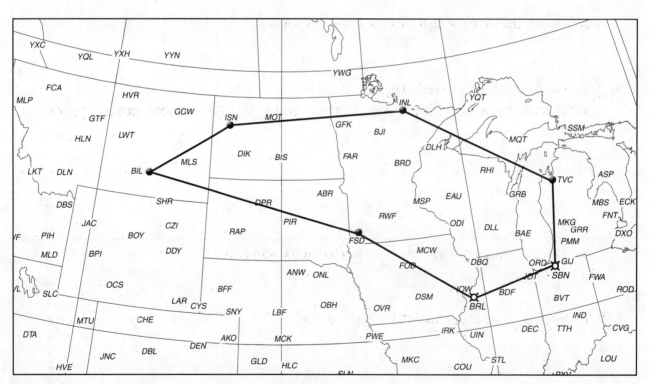

Figure 6-2. *How to find the area covered by the convective SIGMET.*

Aviation Weather Services *Explained*

Practice Reading Advisories

1. Decipher the convective SIGMET 56C at the bottom of AC 00-45E Page 4-26 (concluding at top of 4-27). Refer to the map in Figure 6-2 (at left) for area to be considered.

2. A WST forecast is valid for up to _____ hours. (12, 8, 6, 4, or 2)

3. True or False: The WST forecast is issued only for severe thunderstorms and associated phenomena.

4. WST bulletins are issued
   a. Only as required.
   b. Every three hours.
   c. Every hour.

5. What phenomena are associated with severe thunderstorms?

6. Translate this AIRMET into plain English:

   ```
   ISOLD SVR TSTM D30 MOVG FROM 2420. TOPS ABV 500. WIND GUSTS TO 65
   KTS PSBL
   ```

7. What forecast center are WSTs issued from? (*See* AC 00-45E Page 1-2.)

8. What forecast center issues SIGMET inflight advisories?

Continued

9. Translate this SIGMET into plain English:

```
SFOR WS 100130
SIGMET ROMEO 2 VALID UNTIL 100530
OR WA
FROM SEA TO PDT TO EUG TO SEA
OCNL MOGR CAT BTWN 280 AND 350 EXPCD DUE TO JTSTR.
CONDS BGNG AFT 0200Z CONTG BYD 0530Z AND SPRDG
OVR CNTRL OR BY 0400Z.
```

10. Translate this message into plain English. Include in your answer the following features of the message: forecast is valid for _____ hours, states affected.

```
DFWP UWS 051700
SIGMET PAPA1 VALID UNTIL 052100
AR LA MS
FROM MEM TO 30N MEI TO BTR TO MLU TO MEM
MDT TO OCNL SVR ICG BTWN FRZLVL AND 150. FRZLVL 80 E TO 120 W.
```

11. What is the maximum valid period for SIGMETs?

12. What is the maximum valid period for AIRMETs?

13. For freezing levels and icing, heights are given in
    a. AGL
    b. MSL

14. WAs are prepared and transmitted every _____ hours.

Chapter 7: *Transcribed Weather Enroute Bulletin (TWEB)*

A Route Forecast

This message has had a major overhaul during the past two years with a lot of the TWEB routes dropped and changed. See the new route chart shown on AC 00-45E Page 4-34. (We've included a cleaner version of this same chart for better legibility on Page 56.) The AWC website has a link to keep pilots informed of new or canceled routes.

The TWEB from a briefer, as well as the recorded information from an FAA telephone briefing, will follow this format when you use a touch-tone telephone:

200	Menu
201	Fast File (IFR only)
300	Synopsis of weather over area
301	Flight Precautions
302	Hourly weather reports within the area
303	TAFs for those airports that report weather observations
304	Forecast winds and temperatures aloft for 6,000, 9,000 and 12,000 feet MSL
305	Route forecasts, cross-country
3XX	Additional flight precautions. PIREPs, NOTAMs, etc.
400	IFR departure. 30 minutes to 1 hour prior to proposed ETD
401	IFR departure. More than 1 hour prior to proposed ETD

PATWAS: Pilot's automatic telephone weather answering service

TIBS: Telephone information briefing service

```
037 TWEB 191910 DCA-ROA-TRI. ALL HGTS MSL XCP
    CIGS. DCA-ROA TIL 23Z CLR...AFT 23Z BCMG 40
    SCT-BKN TOPS 50-70 VSBYS 3-5HZ. ROA-TRI TIL
    01Z CIGS AOB 8 TOPS 40 MTN RDGS OBSCD VSBYS
    BLO 2BR...AFT 01Z BCMG 45 SCT-BKN TOPS AOB
    70 VSBYS 3-5HZ...VLYS RMNG CIGS BLO 8 VSBYS
    BLO 2BR
```

 Have you figured out what AOB stands for? "At or below."

Without a doubt, the TWEB is one of the pilot's best friends. Here is a ready-for-use route format with an excellent forecast of expected conditions along your route. Combine the TWEB with a good weather briefing (remember—the TWEB does not give you forecast conditions for icing and turbulence), and you are now weather-wise.

---

http://www.awc-kc.noaa.gov/awc/awc-tweb.html (AWC's TWEB messages by route)

http://www.nws.noaa.gov/oso/oso1/oso12/d30/map/fulltwebmap.pdf (TWEB route map)

But TWEBs do involve a bit of interpretation. Suppose our estimated time of departure is 0045Z with 2+50 en route to Roanoke, VA and 1+35 from Roanoke to Bristol, TN, or 4+25 en route with an arrival time at TRI of 05:10Z. The next thing to do is check the current weather (0000Z) along the route and compare these conditions with the forecast conditions for 0000Z, and for later times. In short, is this route forecast still a valid forecast? Since the contraction CIG is not used in the route forecast from 0100Z to our projected landing time at 05:10Z, we can do one of the following: either treat the cloud heights as MSL, look at a sectional and get some elevations along the route; or check on PIREPs in this area. Or, be a pessimist and assume that when they say SCT-BKN, that it will be a broken layer, and a broken layer constitutes a ceiling!

Do you need an alternate? ("Well the TWEB is good but let's check the TAF for TRI and…what about valleys? Hmm…") According to the TWEB, the low-lying areas should have marginal weather conditions. Where are airports generally located? In the valleys. Do you have valleys across your route? Yes, this region is an area of strongly folded mountains and narrow SSW–NNE valleys.

```
DCA SYNS 191809 WK CD FRNT MVG FAIRLY RPDLY
   SEWRDS FM PA INTO VA AND NE CSTL STATES
   THIS EVNG. HI PRES MOVG SEWRD FM CANADA
   ERLY MORNING WITH CLRG CONDS.
```

Sometimes forecast cloud conditions can be a bit tricky — for example, a forecast condition of SCT-BKN020 appears quite clear, but consider that this forecast reads a cloud layer that may range from 3/8 to 7/8 coverage. So which condition do you choose in your preflight decision-making? The forecaster should always clarify such forecasts with the use of spatial or temporal qualifiers:

```
SCT 020 BCMG BKN020 OVR SRN SLPS OF MTNS.
```

If such qualifying terms (*see* Figure 7-1) are not used in the forecast, then do opt for the pessimistic, and assume the worst will be occurring over the route. This also applies to the use of variable visibility, always assume the worst forecast conditions. If the TWEB route is based entirely on the use of ASOS AUTO reports, the forecaster may use the contraction CLR BLO 120 if he or she is reasonably sure that the observations are representative of the route.

Figure 7-1. *Descriptive forecast terms used in TWEBs*

Conditional Terms Used in TWEB Messages		
Term	**Coded As**	**Implies**
Isolated	ISOLD (single cells)	Circumnavigation possible
Widely Scattered or local	WDLY SCT LCL	< 25% of route affected
Scattered or areas of	SCT, AREA	25 – 54% of route/area is affected
Numerous or widespread	NMRS, WDSPRD	≥ 54% of route/area is affected

But more often than not, you will find that the TWEB SYNOPSIS contains more *route-specific* information than the FA synopsis, which presents a little information about a rather large geographical area.

Normally the use of CIGS and AGL is limited to cloud layers within 4,000 feet of the surface. The forecast tops of cloud layers is given only for those layers which have their bases below 12,000 feet, and only the top of the highest layer is given.

Winds are only forecast when sustained winds of 25 knots or greater is expected to occur. The area forecast only forecasts winds greater than 20 knots — why the difference? I don't know. But if there is no wind forecast do you assume that there is little or no wind? It's best to check the TAFs as well as current weather conditions. (*See* Figure 7-2 on the next page.)

Enroute Flight Advisory Service (EFAS)

This unique service was expressly designed by the FAA to provide enroute aircraft traffic with weather advisories important for the safety of air traffic. In addition to this service to pilots, EFAS is also the prime collection and distribution point for pilot reports (PIREPs).

The EFAS services are provided by trained specialists at selected AFSS's who control multiple Remote Communications Outlets (RCOs) covering a large region. This service is usually available throughout the U.S. and Puerto Rico from 6:00 AM to 10:00 PM. If the EFAS outlet is in a time zone different from the zone where the flight watch control is located, the availability of EFAS service may be either plus or minus one hour from the normal operating hours. EFAS has a communication capability for aircraft traffic operating from 5,000 feet AGL to 17,500 feet MSL on a common frequency of 122.0 MHz. Discrete frequencies are available for communications from 18,000 to 45,000 feet MSL in each ARTCC area.

Flight Watch can usually be contacted by using the ARTCC facility ID that is serving your area and location. This should be followed by your aircraft ID and the name of the nearest VOR to your location — the latter information is necessary so the specialist can select the best transmitter/receiver outlet for communication coverage of your flight. Also, the A/FD has a chart showing the location of the AFSS's and their outlets.

EFAS should not be used for the following: filing or closing of flight plans, position reports, obtaining complete preflight weather briefings, or trying to get random weather reports and forecasts. Timely destination and alternate TAFs can be provided upon request. If a pilot does request services not normally issued by the EFAS, the pilot will be advised of the correct AFSS/FSS frequency to obtain the information.

Communication with EFAS specialists is a two-way street and pilots are urged to give timely pilot reports of both bad and good weather along the route — especially if weather condition(s) occurred that were not forecast.

See Chapter 9 for ARTCC boundary map, Page 64.

Remember: EFAS is referred to as "Flight Watch" during radio communications.

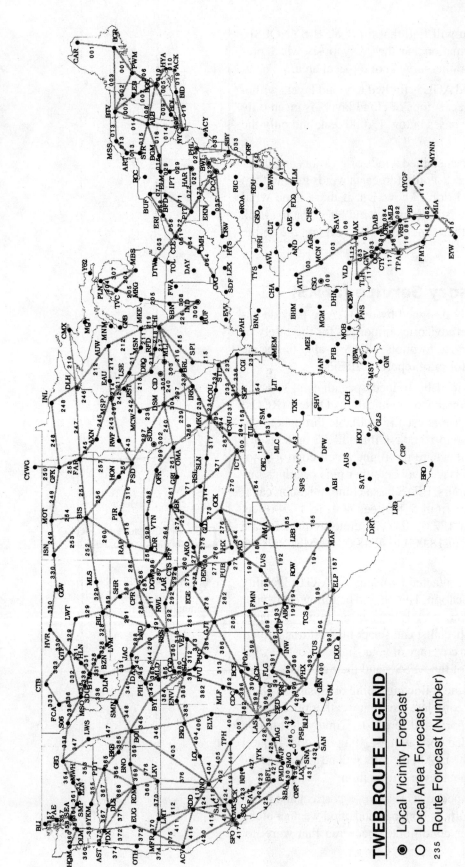

TWEB ROUTE LEGEND

● Local Vicinity Forecast

○ Local Area Forecast

2 3 5 Route Forecast (Number)

Figure 7-2. *TWEB route map*

Aviation Weather Services *Explained*

Practicing TWEBs

1. Using the TWEB synopsis from AC 00-45E Page 4-33, translate the coded information into plain English:

   ```
   CYS SYNS 101402 STG UPSLP WNDS OVR WY TIL 01Z WITH WDSPRD IFR CONDS
       IN LGT SN AND BLOWING SN. CONDS WL IPV FM N TO S ACRS WY AFT 01Z
       WITH DCRG CLDS.
   ```

2. TWEBs are valid for what period of time?

3. How many nautical miles wide is the TWEB enroute corridor?

4. You are planning a flight along this route with a takeoff time of 1630Z with 1:30 time en route to FMY (Fort Myers, FL) and 1:20 time en route to TPA (Tampa Bay, FL). Total flight time is 2:50. What will be the forecast for your route and this time frame?

   ```
   116 TWEB 061402 MIA-FMY-TPA. ALL HGTS MSL XCP CIGS. MIA-FMY CLR 5BR
       TIL 20Z...AFT 21Z BCMG 30-40 BKN OCNL OVC. VSBYS 5-SHRA TS VCNTY.
       FMY-TPA 30 SCT-BKN 5BR TIL 19Z...AFT 21Z 40 BKN TRSA VCNTY.
   ```

Chapter 8: *Winds and Temperatures Aloft Forecast (FD)*

The FD Schedule

Radiosonde observations are routinely taken at 0000Z and 1200Z all over the earth, and this provides meteorologists (and pilots) with a fairly reliable picture of what is going on in the atmosphere. From these upper air observations the NWS prepares the forecast winds and temperatures aloft (FD) in message and plotted chart formats.

The forecast winds are prepared for three use-periods, and these messages are then transmitted at the appropriate time. For example, the 0000Z balloon-run data will be analyzed and forecasts prepared with the first use-period available to the pilots by about 0230Z (FD1). Looking ahead in this scenario, a pilot planning a flight the next morning at 1500Z will be using forecast winds and temperatures prepared from the 0000Z data of the day before (FD3). In other words, the "new" 1200Z data is not normally available to the pilot by 1500Z.

I can hear some pilot saying, "Okay, if I can't get the forecast winds, can I get the actual observed winds and temperatures by 1500Z?" Yes, you can, but you might also raise the stress level of an FAA briefer. Ask the briefer for the current winds aloft chart for 1200Z. Winds aloft charts are prepared for several levels; these are described in AC 00-45E Section 10.

Another thing you should remember is that winds can change, especially over higher terrain where air may be compressed as it flows over mountain ranges or high hills. "2425-04" is a wind/temperature group at 12,000 feet, but don't assume that's what you should get if the forecast winds are accurate. No—that direction can vary as much as 35 degrees with wind speeds between 5 to 30 knots. Adding to our confusion is the fact that the wind speeds can vary by as much as 20 knots before the forecast winds are amended. So what is a pilot to do?

Obviously you have to use the wind information you receive. But if it is in error, then give Flight Watch a PIREP with your best calculation as to the actual winds and temps at your altitude.

AC 00-45E Reading Assignment
Section 4
Pages 4-35 through 4-37; and
Section 10
Pages 10-1 through 10-8

 The Aviation Digital Data Service (ADDS) webpage (*see* address below) has colorful, easy-to-read charts for winds aloft information.

http://www.awc-kc.noaa.gov/awc/awc-fd.html (AWC's Winds and Temp's Aloft page)

http://adds.awc-kc.noaa.gov/projects/adds/winds/index.php3 (ADDS Winds/Progs page)

http://www.rap.ucar.edu/weather/upper/ (National Center for Atmospheric Research)

POH: Pilot's operating handbook

ICAO: International Civil Aviation Organization

Route Planning

Let's assume you have plotted your cross-country route, calculated time en route, fuel burn, etc.; let's say the average temperature at altitude, from the forecast winds/temps, is +1.0°C. Now look in your POH and find the chart that gives the standard ICAO temperature lapse rate. Let's say the value you find for your altitude is -04°C—the forecast air temperature is five degrees warmer than standard. How will this affect your climb performance?

Plan a flight from Dallas, TX (DAL) to Garden City, KS (GCK) via Oklahoma City, OK (OKC). Locate the route on the chart illustration (*see* Figure 8-1). The average winds/temps from DAL to OKC are an easy calculation, average 220 degrees at 33 knots and +2.5°C temperature. But how about from OKC to GCK? Where does the wind direction change? The wind direction changes somewhere east of GAG, and the location of the trough line of low pressure is probably located close to CSM (Clinton-Sherman, OK).

Now obtain the forecast winds/temps for GAG (Gage, OK) to GCK. Notice the drawn lines which are oriented parallel to wind direction. These are called streamlines, and they indicate the pattern of air over the western United States.

Suppose your route was from SAT to ABI to AMA. With the streamlines you could use a protractor and obtain wind direction to a ten-degree accuracy. Again, notice how the winds change direction, in a clockwise direction. If you had the surface analysis chart for this day and time, you would find a frontal low over TUL (OK) with a cold frontal system extending towards the southwest and east of ABI. The trough shown on our wind pattern is nothing more than the position of the surface frontal system at 12,000 feet.

The points of this route just happen to coincide with forecast wind locations (*see* the Winds and Temperatures Aloft Network map on AC 00-45E Page 4-36). But what would you do if you had a route from Durango, CO (DRO) to Wendover, UT (ENV)? These points are in SW Colorado and NW Utah but there are no forecast winds given *directly for* this route, so you will have to interpolate using the GJT, BCE and SLC forecast winds.

The sidebar illustration shows a plot of the forecast winds for SLC, GJT, and BCE and their relationship to the flight line from DRO to ENV:

Winds leg 1 (DRO–route midpoint). Average wind most likely 260 degrees at 30 knots, temp about -6°C, which is an average of the BCE and GJT winds/temps (250+270/2 for the wind direction; average all three temps and speeds to get 30 kts/-6°C).

Winds leg 2 (midpoint–ENV). Average wind is about 290–300 degrees at 30 knots and -6°C, an average of the SLC and BCE winds/temps.

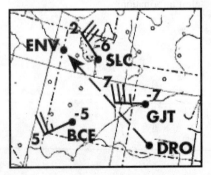

Interpolate the winds in between the points of the route.

Continue to Practice Session.

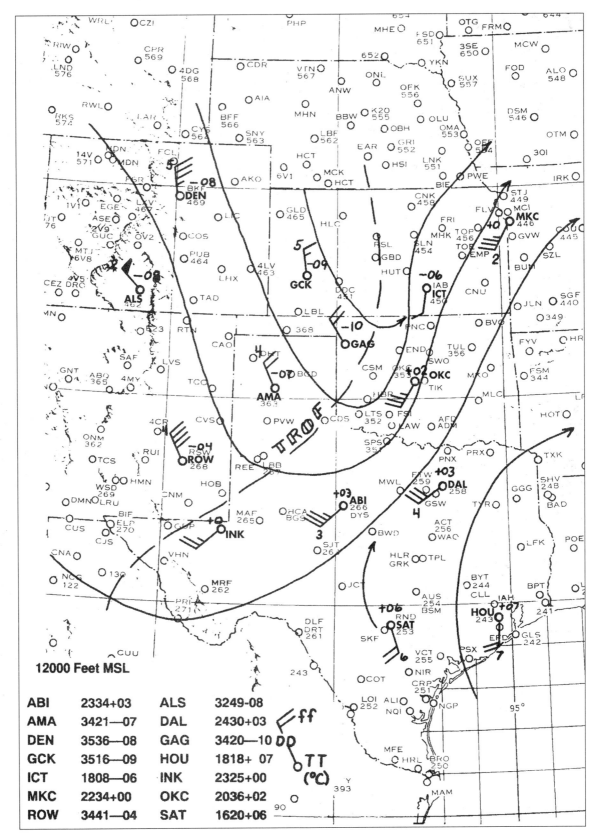

12000 Feet MSL

ABI	2334+03	ALS	3249-08
AMA	3421—07	DAL	2430+03
DEN	3536—08	GAG	3420—10
GCK	3516—09	HOU	1818+ 07
ICT	1808—06	INK	2325+00
MKC	2234+00	OKC	2036+02
ROW	3441—04	SAT	1620+06

Figure 8-1. *Winds and temperatures aloft chart*

Practice FDs

1. Take a look at the winds aloft example below for Kansas City, Missouri (KMKC) and Albuquerque, New Mexico (KABQ) at 9,000 feet. Quite a change in winds for anyone flying from ABQ to MKC! How would you calculate an average wind speed and direction across this route?

```
DATA BASED ON 010000Z

VALID 010600Z FOR USE 0500-0900Z. TEMPS NEG ABV 24000
```

FT	3000	6000	9000	12000	18000	24000	30000	34000	39000
MKC	2426	2726-09	2826-14	2930-21	2744-32	2751-41	275550	276050	731960
ABQ			1912+05	1914+07	1917-06	1820-17	172132	171942	192054

What would be the average temperature (across the route)?

What could be a plausible explanation for the rather drastic temperature drop across the route?

2. A wind is coded at the 34,000-foot level as 802551. What is the wind direction, wind speed and temperature?

3. An airfield has a field elevation of 5,000 feet MSL. If this is a forecast winds location, the first level of forecast winds would be the:

   a. 6,000-foot level

   b. 9,000-foot level

   c. 11,000-foot level

4. The radiosonde determines that the winds at 12,000 feet MSL are less than 5 knots. How would winds at this level be coded for the FD message?

5. A forecast winds aloft location has an elevation of 7,000 feet MSL. Would the first forecast winds aloft group also include a temperature value?

6. Winds aloft at 6,000 feet and 9,000 feet are 2014+12 and 2624+06. What is the wind direction, speed and temperature for the 8,000-foot level?

Chapter 9: *Center Weather Service Unit (CWSU)*

CWA and MIS

AC 00-45E Reading Assignment
Section 4
Pages 4-38 through 4-39

The messages covered in AC 00-45E were not originally intended for use by the general aviation community. But they still are a valuable source of information to the general pilot because they are "short" forecasts with a valid time that ranges from two hours (Center Weather Advisory, CWA) to about ten hours (Meteorological Impact Statement, MIS).

Since these are unscheduled, how do you know if either a CWA or MIS is in effect? There are two places you can check for their occurrence: in PIREPs and SIGMETs. .

An aircraft reports MDT-SVR CAT at FL300. The PIREP issued was an Urgent PIREP or, UUA. The ARTCC, since it can react faster than the Aviation Weather Center at Kansas City, issues a UCWA message (a SIGMET will be issued a bit later). The PIREP might read something like this when issued by Flight Watch:

MDT-SVR CAT: Moderate to severe clear air turbulence.

```
FL300 /TP 737 /SK CLR /TB MDT-SVR CAT ZAB
```

Notice the ZAB at the end of the UA; this is an alert to aircraft that either an MIS or a CWA message has been issued at AB (Albuquerque Center) concerning this CAT. Later, the SIGMET message will also end with ZAB to make pilots aware of the issuance of these messages.

If you're the pilot of a C-172 flying at 7,000 feet MSL, would the UUA affect you? There are times when SVR CAT is reported in the eastern part of the KZAB and KZDV ARTCCs, that conditions might also be favorable for MDT TURBC occurring in the lower altitudes with strong gusty surface winds. So do not assume anything; call Flight Watch and check it out if this is your flight area.

See chart on next page for ARTCC boundaries.

Continued

---

http://www.awc-kc.noaa.gov/awc/cwsu-corner.html (CWSU Corner at Aviation Weather Center)

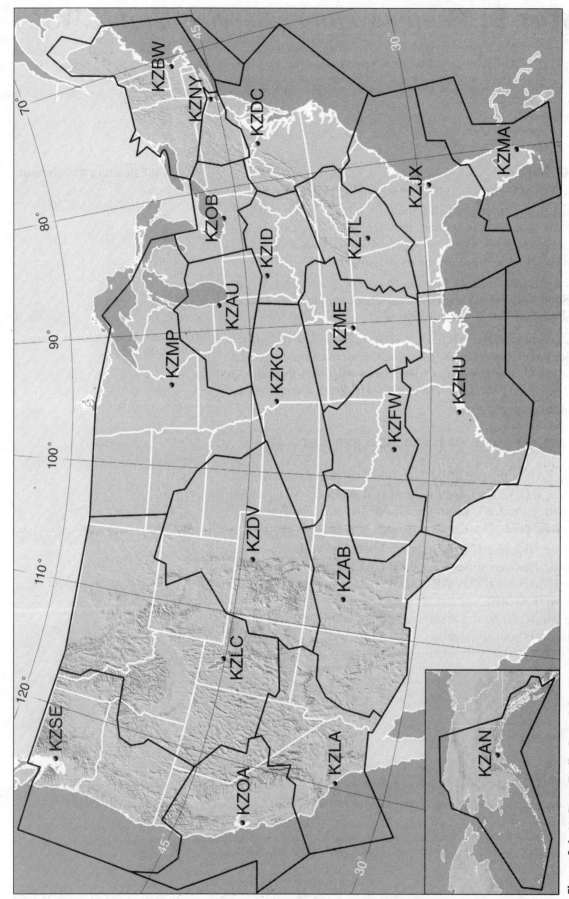

Figure 9-1. *Air Route Traffic Control Center (ARTCC) boundaries*

Aviation Weather Services *Explained*

Example: Nowcast

```
WCUS21 KZBW 281220
ZBW1 CWA 01 281210-281400
FROM 50NE PVD TO 160SSE PVD TO 75SSW PVD TO
   60NE PVD
AREA OF HVY SHWRS/TRW MOVG NE 40 KTS AND WL
   AFFECT SE MA AND
      CAPE COD NXT 1-2 HRS. SEE CONVECTIVE
   SIGMETs...
```

This "nowcast" was issued by the Boston Center (KZBW) and is pretty self-explanatory. A nowcast is a short-term forecast—30 minutes to 2 hours—and CWAs are sometimes referred to as nowcasts.

Example: MIS

```
ZKC MIS 02 061800Z-070100Z
...FOR ATC PLANNING
TERMINAL...STL...SCT OCNL BKN 015-020 BKN
   OCNL OVC CHC LVL 3-4
TSTMS WDLY SCT AND MOVG E 20 KTS. 22Z MVFR
   CONDS WITH BKN-OVC
CIGS 008-015 CHC VSBYS 3-4 FOG/HAZE. SFC WNDS
   250-280 10-15 KTS
SHFTG 280-310 AFTR 22Z.
```

Don't let the second line of the MIS discourage you; you can still request MIS's or CWAs from Flight Watch or your briefer. *See* Figure 9-1 for the locations of the air route traffic control centers (ARTCCs) and their areas of responsibility, so you'll know which one(s) apply to your route. There is an interactive map you can click on and get instant messages at the "CWSU Corner" on the Aviation Weather Center website.

Continue to next page for Practice Session.

"Nowcasting" is a buzzword in aviation weather; NCAR (National Center for Atmospheric Research) in Boulder, CO, and units of the NOAA and NWS prepare both experimental and operational weather nowcasts.

The website address for this is shown at the bottom of Page 63.

Practice CWSU Messages

1. Which is more precise in its forecasting of phenomena such as SVR TURBC or MDT-SVR CLR ICG?
   a. SIGMET
   b. CWA

   Why?

2. Interpret the last two lines of the nowcast from Page 65:

   ```
   AREA OF HVY SHWRS/TRW MOVG NE 40 KTS AND WL AFFECT SE MA AND
   CAPE COD NXT 1-2 HRS. SEE CONVECTIVE SIGMETs...
   ```

3. Now interpret the MIS message (the last four lines):

   ```
   TERMINAL...STL...SCT OCNL BKN 015-020 BKN OCNL OVC CHC LVL 3-4
   TSTMS WDLY SCT AND MOVG E 20 KTS. 22Z MVFR CONDS WITH BKN-OVC
   CIGS 008-015 CHC VSBYS 3-4 FOG/HAZE. SFC WNDS 250-280 10-15 KTS
   SHFTG 280-310 AFTR 22Z.
   ```

4. What are three of the criteria used for issuing an MIS?

5. Can a CWA message be issued as an urgent message? If so, why would this be necessary?

Chapter 10: *Convective Outlook (AC)*
Including CCFPs and other
Severe Weather Advisories

Working Together

The items covered in these sections of AC 00-45E work together in that the convective outlook chart is nothing more than a graphic version of the 24-hour convective outlook (AC) message. The convective outlook chart is sometimes called the "severe weather outlook chart" (but this title is being replaced with "convective outlook"). This chart/message combination gives the pilot an excellent preplanning look at where general convective activity is anticipated for the next 24 hours, and a 48-hour forecast for where severe thunderstorms may develop in the future.

On the next page is an example of an AC message (an excerpt from a Storm Prediction Center message), and its associated convective outlook chart. Read through the message with help from the contractions listed in AC 00-45E Section 14.

CAPE (J/kg)

You can find all of the contractions used in ACs in the list at the back of AC 00-45E, except for one acronym that needs some further explanation:

> SURFACE BASED CAPE VALUES SHOULD BE AT OR
>   ABOVE 2000 3/KG THIS AFTERNOON. BOUNDARIES
>   FROM OVERNIGHT CONVECTION AS WELL AS SEA
>   BREEZE CIRCULATIONS SHOULD BE SUFFICIENT TO
>   INITIATE SCATTERED TO NUMEROUS
>   THUNDERSTORMS ACROSS THE AREA...

CAPE stands for Convectively Available Potential Energy. The Storm Prediction Center (SPC) at Norman, Oklahoma routinely uses this stability indicator in its forecasts. Without using rocket scientist language, CAPE is either a mathematical or graphical expression of the atmosphere's stability or instability, as expressed in joules per kilogram (J/kg). A joule is the amount of work done by a force of one Newton, over a distance of one meter.

AC 00-45E Reading Assignment
Section 4
Pages 4-40 through 4-44; and
Section 12
Pages 12-1 through 12-2

The contraction list starts on AC 00-45E Page 14-6.

See also AC 00-45E Page 4-42, in the paragraph of the AC message that begins, COOL FRONT CONTS...

convection: *In meteorology* — atmospheric motion that is mainly vertical; the vertical transport and mixing of atmospheric properties.

http://www.awc-kc.noaa.gov/awc/aviation_weather_center.html, *then*
http://www.spc.noaa.gov/products/outlook/day1otlk.html
(AWC link to Storm Prediction Center "Day 1 Outlook" page)
http://www.nhc.noaa.gov/ (National Hurricane Center)

```
STORM PREDICTION
CENTER...NWS/NCEP...NORMAN
OK
DAY 2 CONVECTIVE OUTLOOK...REF
AWIPS GRAPHIC PGWI47 KWBC.

VALID 281200Z - 291200Z

THERE IS A SLGT RISK OF SVR TSTMS
TO THE RIGHT OF A LINE FROM 10
ENE FSM 35 NE PRX 25 SSW PRX
45 E JCT 20 NE P07 15 SSE MAF
40 ESE CVS 25 SW EHA 45 N LAA
40 SW MCK 40 S HSI 35 W FNB 10
SSW STJ 25 ESE OJC 50 NW SGF
20 SSE UMN 10 ENE FSM.

GEN TSTMS ARE FCST TO THE RIGHT
OF A LINE FROM 70 NNW CLM 15
SSW OLM 45 SE EUG 20 S MHS 45
NNW SAC 10 W SFO.
```

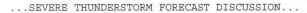

Issued 27/1819Z Valid 281200Z - 291200Z
SPC Day Convective Outlook

```
GEN TSTMS ARE FCST TO THE RIGHT
OF A LINE FROM 15 SW DUG 35 NNW SVC 50 SW GNT 55 WSW GUP 35 S PGA 40 E U24 45 WNW BPI 10 S WRL 50
NE 4BQ 55 SSW FAR 35 N MKT 40 N ALO 15 SW BRL 55 NNW POF 15 NE LIT SHV 15 ESE LFK 45 NNE HOU 30
WSW GLS.


...SEVERE THUNDERSTORM FORECAST DISCUSSION...

...SYNOPSIS...
AN ACTIVE DAY 2 ANTICIPATED AS HIGH AMPLITUDE AND ENERGETIC FLOW REGIME CONTINUES OVER
THE CONUS. DEEP CYCLONE CENTERED NEAR 50N 138W WILL PROVIDE SUFFICIENT DOWNSTREAM FORCING
TO QUICKLY DISLODGE VIGOROUS UPPER TROUGH CURRENTLY MOVING OVER NRN BAJA. THE PACIFIC SYSTEM
WILL PRODUCE IMPRESSIVE 180 M/12-H HEIGHT FALLS ALONG THE COAST OF THE PACIFIC NORTHWEST
WHILE THE BAJA SHORT WAVE EJECTS NEWD ACROSS NEW MEXICO AND INTO THE CENTRAL PLAINS BY
EARLY SUNDAY.

IN THE EAST...MERGING OF STRONG NORTHERN AND SOUTHERN STREAM TROUGHS OFF THE NORTHEASTERN
SEABOARD WILL RESULT IN SIGNIFICANT SURFACE CYCLOGENESIS SOUTH OF NOVA SCOTIA.

...SOUTHERN AND CENTRAL PLAINS...
PERSISTENT SLY FLOW PATTERN OVER THE SOUTHERN AND CENTRAL PLAINS HAS PRODUCED A BROAD PLUME
OF RICH LOWER TROPOSPHERIC MOISTURE  FROM TX NWD THROUGH KS. WIDESPREAD STRONG TO SEVERE
THUNDERSTORMS ARE LIKELY AS THE POTENTIAL INSTABILITY OF THIS AIRMASS COMBINES WITH INTENSE
KINEMATICS ASSOCIATED WITH RAPIDLY MOVING MID LEVEL SHORT WAVE TROUGH.

SEVERAL AVN AND ETA MODEL RUNS HAVE BEEN IN VERY GOOD AGREEMENT AND CONSISTENT WITH TIMING
AND PLACEMENT OF LARGE SCALE FEATURES ASSOCIATED WITH EJECTING SWRN U.S. SHORT WAVE. ISOLATED
SEVERE STORMS ARE POSSIBLE AT THE BEGINNING OF THE PERIOD WITHIN LARGE PRECIPITATION SHIELD
EXPECTED FROM ERN NM NEWD INTO SWRN KS. ALTHOUGH CAPE VALUES ACROSS THIS AREA WILL BE
LIMITED BY EXTENSIVE CLOUD AND PRECIPITATION COVERAGE...STRONGER UPDRAFTS WILL OCCUR WITHIN
AN ENVIRONMENT FAVORABLE FOR STORM ROTATION WHERE SFC-6KM SHEAR EXCEEDS 30 KT. LATEST ETA
SUGGESTS THAT A FEW NW-SE BANDS OF STORMS ARE LIKELY ALONG THE LEADING EDGE OF WARM AIR
ADVECTION ASSOCIATED WITH STRENGTHENING LOW LEVEL JET INVOF E TX PANHANDLE/SWRN OK NORTH
TO KS. THIS LOOKS REASONABLE GIVEN PRESENCE OF STRONG FORCING WITHIN UNCAPPED/MOIST AIRMASS.
DISCREET CELLULAR ACTIVITY WITHIN THESE BANDS MAY POSE A THREAT OF ISOLATED TORNADOES GIVEN
RATHER LOW LCL. LARGE MERIDIONAL COMPONENT OF THE MID AND UPPER LEVEL FLOW SUGGESTS THAT
A N-S SQUALL LINE WILL DEVELOP AHEAD OF THE UPPER TROUGH...ACROSS TX PANHANDLE...BY AFTERNOON.
STRONG INFLOW AND ENHANCED LOW LEVEL SHEAR NEAR WHERE THIS N-S LINE INTERSECTS PREEXISTING
CONVECTIVE BANDS ASSOCIATED WITH WARM AIR ADVECTION MAY ALSO BE AREAS WHERE BRIEF TORNADO/LARGE
HAIL THREAT IS MAXIMIZED.

STRONG MID LEVEL DRY PUNCH SHOULD DEVELOP ACROSS WEST TX SWRN KS BY LATE AFTERNOON/EARLY
EVENING. THIS SHOULD ENHANCE DOWNWARD MOMENTUM TRANSPORT AND POSSIBILITY OF DAMAGING WINDS
ALONG A RATHER EXTENSIVE SQUALL LINE FROM SRN TX...ACROSS MUCH OF OK AND KS THROUGH SUNDAY
MORNING. A FEW SEVERE STORMS...POSSIBLY SUPERCELLS WITH LARGE HAIL...MAY DEVELOP ACROSS
THE HIGH PLAINS OF EXTREME ERN CO/WRN KS LATE ON SATURDAY AS DRY SLOT AND ASSOCIATED
FORCING/COLD AIR WITH UPPER SHORT WAVE OVERRUNS RESIDUAL BOUNDARY LAYER MOISTURE.

..CARBIN.. 10/27/00

NOTE: THE NEXT DAY 2 OUTLOOK IS SCHEDULED FOR 0800Z
```

Figure 10-1. *Textual and charted Convective Outlook for 281200Z–291200Z*

Convective Outlook Chart

The primary use of the convective Day 1, Day 2 chart (*see* Figure 10-1) is to give you a glimpse into the near future for where severe and non-severe thunderstorm activity is expected to occur. AC 00-45E Page 12-2 has a table for determining the levels of risk that are being forecast for convective activity.

Collaborative Convective Forecast Product (CCFP)

This is a new product (therefore not covered in the AC 00-45E), that is an extended forecast for thunderstorms with a lead time of 2, 4 or 6 hours presented in graphical format and updated as necessary. Collaboratively produced by the NWS, the FAA and numerous airline "Met" departments, the CCFP starts with the Aviation Weather Center (AWC) in Kansas City where meteorologists produce an initial forecast for convective activity. The final product evolves after an online collaboration with commercial airlines, the NWS Center Weather Service Units (CWSUs), and the FAA experts at the National Air Traffic Control System Command Center in Herndon, VA.

The product is available to the FAA briefer, and can also be obtained from the Aviation Weather Center website. Figure 10-2 on the next page shows one of the pages you'll see when you go there: a CCFP map for the entire U.S. with an explanatory menu at left. Here in one complete picture is a chart showing where thunderstorm activity is occurring, thunderstorm intensity and growth, area coverage and movement. Most of the major carriers are now using this forecast for air traffic management planning—and so can you (if you have access to the web)!

Other Watches and Advisories of Convective Activity

Hurricane Advisories (WH)

Hurricanes are not the largest storms on the planet but they certainly can cause widespread devastation, so in order to alert the aviation community of a threat near a coastline, the National Hurricane Center first issues the WH. Once the hurricane poses a threat within 24 hours of coastal areas, the NHC will issue a Hurricane Warning.

Pilots might be interested in checking out the Hurricane Hunters site at: http://www.hurricanehunters.com. With the development of high sustained-flight drones, the days of the Hurricane Hunters are probably numbered. Those men and women of the USAF have certainly done a magnificent job, as have the P-3 Orions of NOAA.

Severe Weather Watch Bulletins (WW), Alert Messages (AWW)

Along with the WHs, these messages are meant for public agencies such as the local police and Red Cross, and are therefore always in plain language with no contractions or acronyms, and given in standard time. Nevertheless, no weather message can be completely understood unless you are able to envision its contents in the context of the Big Picture—much of which will be covered in the next several chapters.

Severe thunderstorm criteria:

1. Winds equal to or greater than 50 kts at the surface
2. Hail equal to or greater than 3/4 inches in diameter at the surface
3. Tornadoes

The CCFP page is under AWC's "Publications" link, or go to
www.awc-kc.noaa.gov/ccfp/ccfp.html

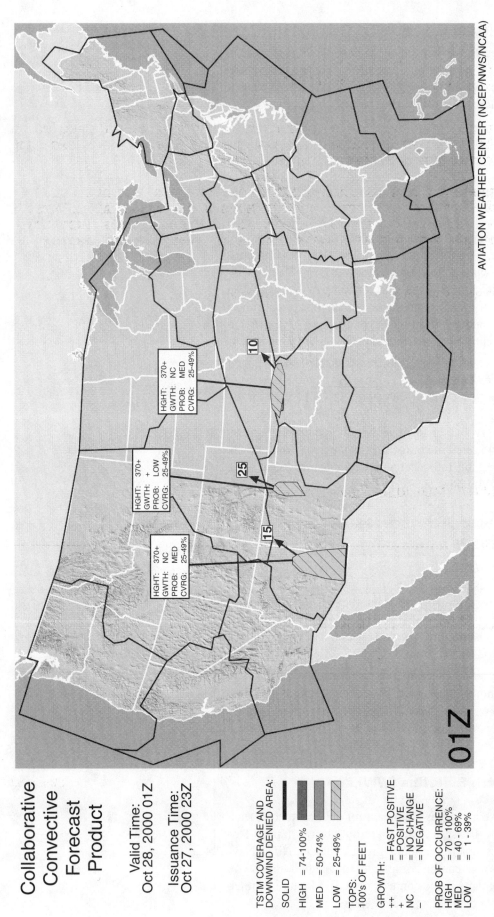

Figure 10-2. *Aviation Weather Center "CCFP" example (solid lines show ARTCC boundaries)*

Collaborative
Convective
Forecast
Product

Valid Time:
Oct 28, 2000 01Z

Issuance Time:
Oct 27, 2000 23Z

TSTM COVERAGE AND
DOWNWIND DENIED AREA:

SOLID

HIGH = 74-100%

MED = 50-74%

LOW = 25-49%

TOPS:
100's OF FEET

GROWTH:
++ = FAST POSITIVE
+ = POSITIVE
NC = NO CHANGE
– = NEGATIVE

PROB OF OCCURRENCE:
HIGH = 70 - 100%
MED = 40 - 69%
LOW = 1 - 39%

HGHT: 370+
GWTH: NC
PROB: MED
CVRG: 25-49%

HGHT: 370+
GWTH: +
PROB: LOW
CVRG: 25-49%

HGHT: 370+
GWTH: NC
PROB: MED
CVRG: 25-49%

10

25

15

01Z

AVIATION WEATHER CENTER (NCEP/NWS/NCAA)

Aviation Weather Services *Explained*

AC Practice

```
KMKC AC 291200
CONVECTIVE OUTLOOK...REF AFOS NMCGPH940
VALID 291200-301200Z

THERE IS A SLGT - MDT RISK OF SVR TSTMS THIS EVNG AND ERLY MRNG TO
   THE RIGHT OF A LN WHICH XTNDS FROM ILM TRI ATL LFK GLD SLN PNC LIT
   MEM 60E BWG CRW BUF ART MWN MHT HVN.

STG CD FNT CURRENTLY ALG LN FROM ERI ZZV BWG MEM 60N TXK DFW. STG
   UPR LVL LOW CNTRD AT 12Z OVER LK ERIE MOVG SLOLY NEWRD AT 10 KTS.
   STG JET STRM WL PROVIDE STG DVRG PTRN ALFT. NARROW ZN OF INSTBLTY
   RANGES FM MINUS 7 TO MINUS 5 WITH GOOD MSTR AVBL ALG AND AHD OF
   FRNTL ZONE.
```

1. Translate the last paragraph of this convective outlook message above:

2. What is meant by SLGT – MDT RISK in the AC above?

3. What constitutes severe thunderstorm criteria?

Continued

4. Table 12-1 of AC 00-45E mentions the term "derecho." What does this word mean?

5. Regarding the two-panel severe weather (convective) outlook chart below, how does the right-hand panel differ from the left-hand panel?

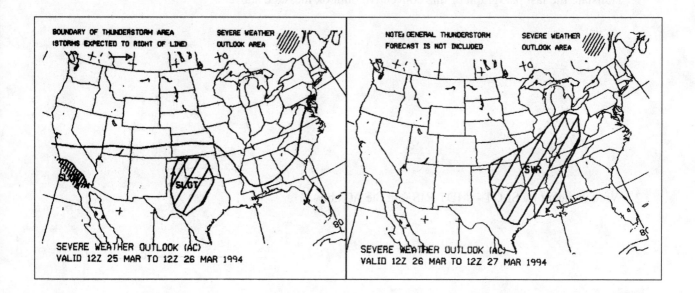

Aviation Weather Services *Explained*

Chapter 11: *Radar Summary Chart and Severe Weather Watch*

Source Information

Radar images and other pertinent weather information can be found for the U.S. and selected other countries at the websites listed below. To update and further interpret the map on AC 00-45E Page 7-6 (the "WSR-88 Radar Network"), an Appendix is included at the back of this book that contains a list of all the current WSR-88 radar installations. Also, Figure 11-1 displays station IDs that correspond to the radar installations shown on AC 00-45E Page 7-6.

AC 00-45E Reading Assignment
Section 7
Pages 7-1 through 7-6

See also radar image information listed in Chapter 3 (Pages 23–24); and *see* Appendix B.

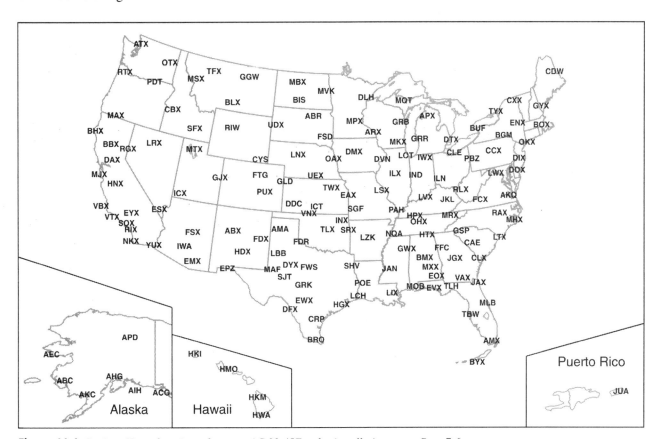

Figure 11-1. *Stations IDs at locations shown on AC 00-45E radar installations map, Page 7-6*

http://www.awc-kc.noaa.gov/awc/aviation_weather_center.html (AWC Official Forecast Products page)

http://weather.noaa.gov/fax/nwsfax.shtml (NWS fax charts)

http://twister.sbs.ohio-state.edu/
   or, http://aps1.sbs.ohio-state.edu/ — *either one works* (Ohio State University weather pages)

http://www.intellicast.com/LocalWeather/World/UnitedStates/Radar/ (Radar loop images)

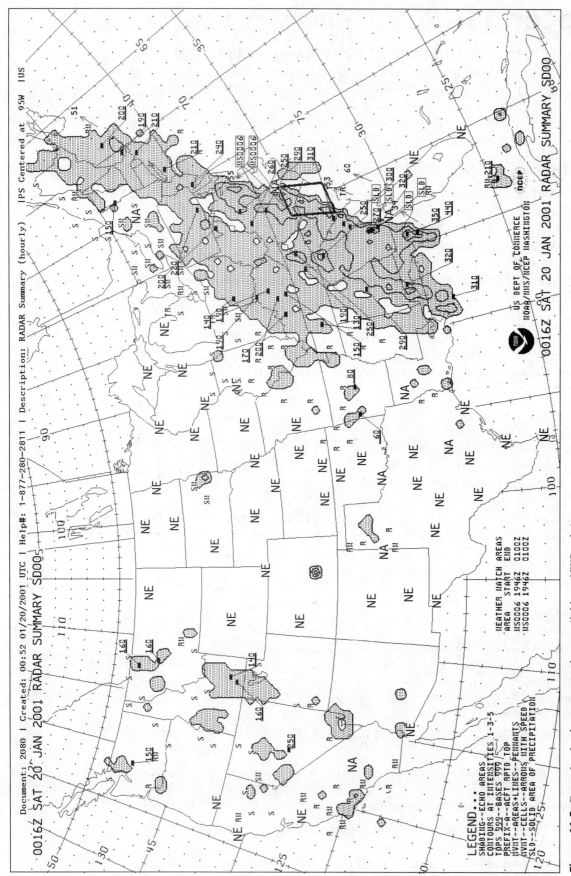

Figure 11-2. *Example of radar summary chart available on NWS website*

The Chart

The basic radar summary chart can be found in different colorized formats at several websites, but I still prefer the old-fashioned black-and-white version—they're easier to read and to print out (*see* the example in Figure 11-2). These can be found at either the NWS Fax Charts page (shown in the list at the bottom Page 73), or at the AWC "Official Forecast Products" page where they list all their links for a "standard briefing."

The radar summary chart has undergone some revisions in the past few years, and AC 00-45E makes statements that represent changes from the way the old charts displayed radar information:

1. No line or area movements are shown on the chart.

2. Precipitation indicated is always reaching the ground.*

3. Precipitation intensity trend is no longer coded.

It would appear that by doing away with intensity trends, and line or area movement, the FAA is hammering home the point of using the radar summary chart *only* as a planning tool.

One point about the chart not addressed in AC 00-45E is that a lot of pilots associate an area of echoes with IMC. This correlation will be true in some cases, but not always! Always fine-tune your weather search by checking on the current weather within a region.

Radar Echo Intensity

It's common knowledge that most radar products on the internet, television, and weather briefing are color-coded. AC 00-45E Page 7-2 has a table showing the charted intensities of precipitation for the radar summary charts, and this can be related somewhat to turbulence. Even though they are based on a different scale (dBZ), the colored areas on weather radar charts should correspond somewhat to these areas on the radar summary chart, with the greens or blues generally on the lighter side, and the intense oranges and reds indicate the more severe, extreme weather situations.

Echo Reflectivity

Stratiform clouds usually produce drizzle, light rain or snow, and there is usually just one contour line surrounding the area of precipitation. As a rule, stratified clouds are turbulence-free. If stratified cloudiness/precipitation is occurring over the mountainous west, you had best refer to the convective rate of rainfall in AC 00-45E Table 7-2, and look for those areas on the radar summary chart. If an area of precipitation is contoured, you should *never* fly through an area showing more then one radar contour line.

Snow will never show more than the one contour line and the new radar summary chart doesn't show intensity trends on the chart. But the individual ROB reports can give you that vital information.

The radar summary chart in Figure 11-2 is also more up-to-date than the one in AC 00-45E, and more legible since chart-transmitting technology at the NWS has improved on the internet. Examine the features in Figure 11-2, and compare it to the excerpt of the AC 00-45E's chart in Figure 11-3 (on the next page).

*This might be true in the humid southeast or east, but in the arid west or southwest? There it would probably indicate a lot of virga.

dBZ: Unit of radar reflectivity, the function of the amount of radar beam energy backscattered by a target and detected as an echo.

ROB reports: Radar observation reports. *See both* AC 00-45E Section 3, and Chapter 3 in this book (Page 23).

Interpreting the Radar Summary Chart

This chart may be for planning purposes only, but you can get a lot of information from it, when you compare it to the other charts (surface analysis, weather depiction, and constant pressure). For example, the discussion on "Echo Movement" in the AC 00-45E refers to the convective activity in Texas as moving southwestward at 8 knots, and to the precipitation in the New England area as moving towards the east-northeast at 25 knots. But what about the rest of the precipitation area(s) on the chart, particularly in the southeast where severe weather is occurring? In this case, you might want to consult the other charts and take your interpretation a bit further, to get the best idea about what's happening here.

The movement of precipitation is largely directed by the mean wind direction and 2/3 of the average speed of the winds between the 700 mb and 500 mb levels. Some thunderstorms, particularly in the southern and central plains states, also appear to move to the right of the average 700 to 500 mb wind direction.

The rule appears to be true for the activity over the New Jersey area and the NE U.S. in the AC 00-45E's chart on Page 7-5. If you compare the constant pressure charts in AC 00-45E to this, the 700 and 500 mb-level charts indicate that the weather will be generally moving towards the east-northeast. The severe weather watch areas on the radar summary chart extend from Florida, Georgia into western South Carolina; following this on the 700 mb and 500 mb constant pressure charts, you can verify that they indicate the severe weather is likely to move towards the north-northeast at about 25–30 knots.

Suppose you did not have access to constant pressure charts; how do you determine the possible direction of the weather? When in doubt as to possible movement of radar echoes on the radar summary chart, check the individual ROBs for the station(s) along your route. These messages give the direction and speed of movement of the echoes. Forecast winds aloft can also help. If you use forecast winds aloft, make sure you gather enough data from different stations/locations to give you an overall idea of the wind pattern and strength in your flight area(s).

Severe Weather Watch (WS, WW)

The radar summary chart is the only place you will find the current "Severe Weather Watch" areas, where they are displayed as a heavy dashed rectangle(s). Remember that the rectangle encloses an area where the severe thunderstorms and/or tornadoes are expected to form, and the weather usually clears back towards the western side of the watch area.

A closer examination of the AC 00-45E chart (Page 7-5) indicates there are three Severe Weather Watch areas: WS004, WS005 and WS006 over the southeastern U.S. WS005 (valid from 0003Z to 0600Z) is the easternmost rectangular area bound by heavy dashes located over extreme NW and W South Carolina and NE and E Georgia. The small rectangular box (WS005) printed over southern North Carolina has a fine thin line pointing and connected to the larger rectangular area in question.

The identifier rectangular box for WS006 is printed over southeastern Georgia and adjacent coastal waters. The severe weather area itself is

---

Constant pressure charts for 700 and 500 mb, for the same day in January 1998 as the AC 00-45E's radar summary chart (Page 7-5), can be found on AC 00-45E Pages 8-9 and 8-10.

The NSSL (National Severe Storms Laboratory in Norman, OK) is developing a new dual-polarization weather radar with radar energy beams that have both a horizontal (which is conventional Doppler radar) and vertical orientation. The new radar will give a faster scan as well as a better representation of the vertical aspects of the storm being scanned.

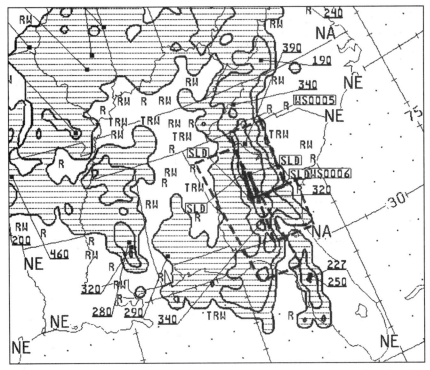

Figure 11-3. *Closeup excerpt of the WS area on AC 00-45E chart (AC 00-45E Page 7-5).*

a continuation of the severe weather area of WS005 and covers SE Georgia and the eastern panhandle of Florida.

Where is the heavy dashed-line rectangle for WS004? *See* Figure 11-3: no ID rectangle such as those for WS005 and WS006 appear on the chart for this WS. It would appear that somebody goofed and forgot to put a small fine line box on the chart telling you where WS004 is. Surprise! They can omit such an identifying feature if by so doing so, important data or information in the same area that might be covered-up will be more visible.

As stated before, weather moves through time and space, and for the U.S., weather moves roughly from west to east. WS004 was the first watch issued and is about to be canceled (valid time 2033Z–0300Z) and is superseded by the other two Severe Weather Watches because the severe weather has moved east and north.

Continue to next page for Practice Session.

The AC 00-45E chart excerpt above reveals a jumbled area of "WS" and "SLD" boxes. The legend in the AC 00-45E Page 7-5 chart doesn't explain SLD, but these are "solid" areas of precipitation. They're combined with the WS boxes on this chart, but the intention of the SLD boxes is to pinpoint the areas of heaviest radar reflectivity (with heavy black lines or dots within the shaded areas of the chart).

Mostly Radar Summary Chart Interpretation Practice

Your practice for using this chapter's chart must include the consultation of other charts: For these questions, use the AC 00-45E charts that are for 0000Z on January 8, 1998. The surface analysis (Page 5-3), weather depiction (Page 6-5), and radar (Page 7-5) charts are for 0000Z, 0100Z and 0235Z respectively, on January 8. (But only flights after 0330Z or 0400Z will have the luxury of having relatively current constant pressure charts—Pages 8-9, 8-10—to examine. Before this time, the constant pressure charts are about 12 hours old, and the forecast winds aloft are also old since they are based on the 1200Z ROB data.)

1. The maximum reported tops of activity on the radar chart in the AC 00-45E is
   _____. This height is
   a. MSL
   b. AGL

2. The maximum tops are located in what state and are most likely moving in which direction?

3. The surface chart indicates two low pressure cells over central Montana. In which direction do you think they will move?

4. The use of NE on the radar chart refers to "No Echoes" which implies that the weather is
   a. VFR
   b. IFR
   c. You can't tell

5. There is snow occurring over southern Idaho along the Snake River plain. Obviously something is causing the snow…determine what it is using the AC 00-45E charts. (Actually, the culprit is given clearly on the surface analysis chart!)

6. Examine the surface analysis chart, radar summary chart, and composite moisture/stability charts in the AC 00-45E. The convective activity across the western Carolinas and western Virginia is probably caused by what?

7. What are the average tops of the precipitation over Illinois on the radar summary chart and what kind of precip is occurring?

   Which direction is the precip most likely moving towards?

Chapter 12: *Surface Analysis Chart*

Looking at the Big Picture

The surface analysis chart, along with the radar summary chart (Chapter 11) and the weather depiction chart (Chapter 13), gives the pilot a look at the *big picture*. Every three hours, hourly surface weather reports are plotted graphically and analyzed to show where the surface pressure systems are located as well as the current position of frontal systems and troughs of low pressure. The "companion" weather depiction chart indicates where the areas of marginal VFR and IFR weather are located at the time of the chart (an hour later than the surface analysis).

On the next pages are examples of the surface analysis and weather depiction charts for 1500Z, March 25, 1994. By the time the data has been checked for errors, machine plotted and analyzed, 2 to 3 hours have passed, so *always* make sure you are looking at the most current chart and related weather information.

Looking at Figure 12-1: From a low-pressure cell (pressure 1,008) over northern California, there is a weak and weakening diffuse occluded frontal system (618]) extending east and southeast to a low cell (1,007 mb) over southern Nevada. Also, there is a weak cold front (little or no change) just east of the Colorado River area of California/Arizona (420]).

In the New England area there is a moderate cold front with waves (457]) and this system extends southwestward into the Carolinas, northern GLFMEX and into the Brownsville, TX area. The frontal system is weak and quasi-stationary ([010) along the Rio Grande and into central New Mexico. High pressure dominates much of the eastern half of the United States with excellent VFR weather (*see* Figure 12-2), and a trough of low pressure is dominant from eastern Colorado northward into the western Dakotas.

If you have access to earlier charts you can also get a fairly good idea of how the frontal and pressure systems have been moving. However, the best way to determine frontal/pressure system movement is to use the 12- and 24-hour weather prognostic charts, described in AC 00-45E Section 11, and Chapter 16 of this book.

AC 00-45E Reading Assignment
Section 5
Pages 5-1 through 5-10

Just *how* the surface chart's graphics are plotted from METARs, and what this chart's "station models" *mean*, are partially explained in the AC 00-45E's series of Figures 5-3 through 5-7. However, *see* Appendix A, Pages 147–152 ("Surface Chart Symbology Explained") for further clarification of the AC 00-45E's tables and diagrams in this section.

A bracket ([or]) before or after the code number for the front points to the weather front the code is referring to.

618]   [010

Clouds	
⌒	Cumulus (Cu)
⊠	Thunderstorms (Cb)
⦫	Altostratus (As)

Weather	
⚡	Thunderstorm/rain
∴	Rain, moderate
∿	Freezing rain

---

http://www.nws.noaa.gov

http://weather.noaa.gov/fax/nwsfax.shtml (NWS "Difax" charts*)

http://www.hpc.ncep.noaa.gov/html/sfc2.html (Hydrometeorological Prediction Center)

*See Appendix E, Page 186 for more information about this webpage.

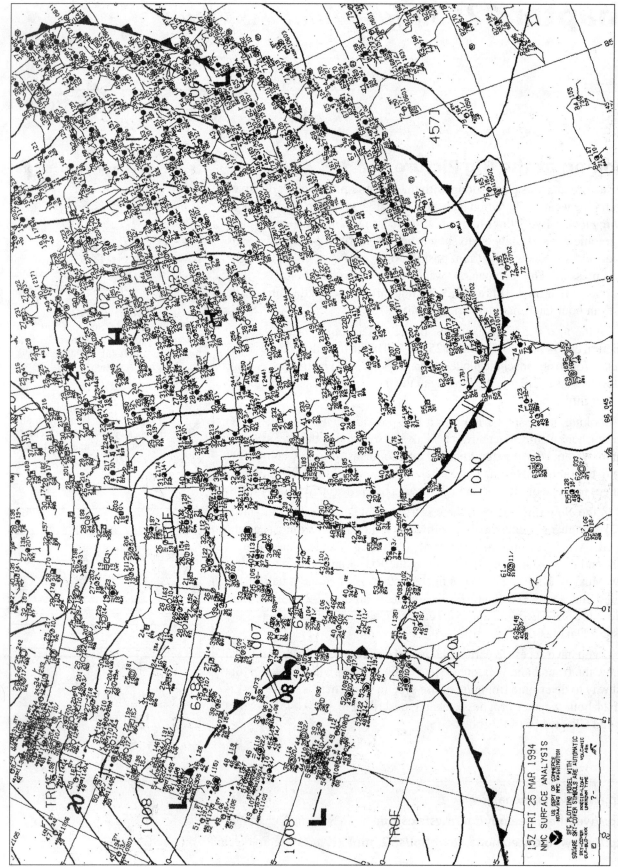

Figure 12-1. *Surface analysis for March 25, 1994*

Aviation Weather Services *Explained*

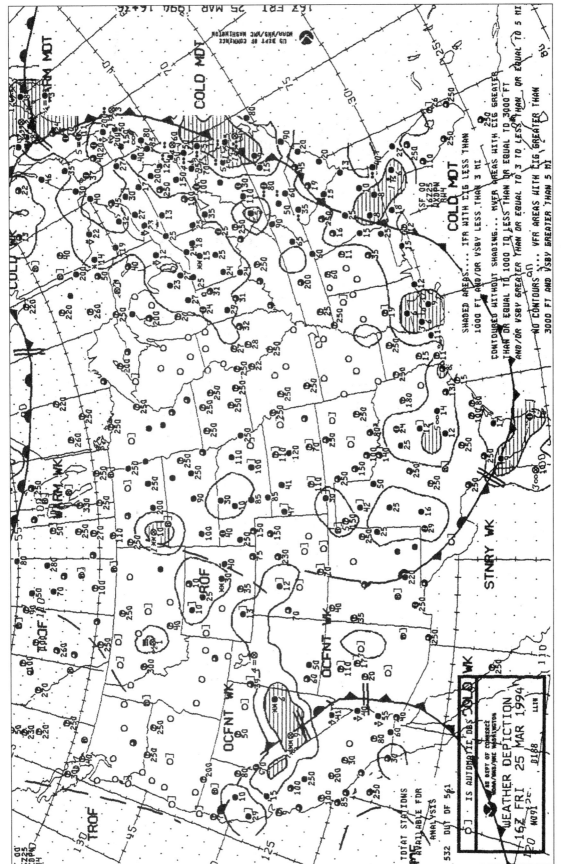

Figure 12-2. *Weather depiction for the same day*

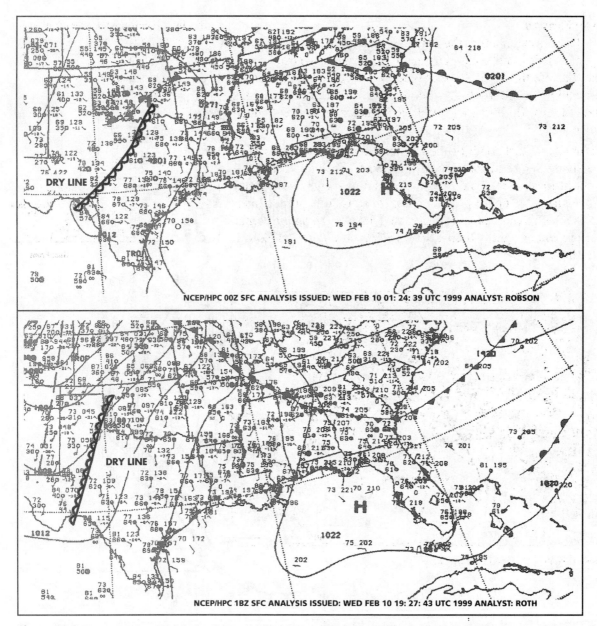

Figure 12-3. *Two examples of a "dryline"— notice the movement of the dryline over the time interval.*

On Other Fronts

Figure 12-3 shows examples of the "dryline" that the AC 00-45E alludes to on Page 5-2. This is a line that separates dry hot air (west) from cooler more humid air (to the east). Weather-types in the central United States might also call this a "Marfa Front" but it really isn't a front. Under the right conditions, the dryline is a good place for heavy to severe thunderstorms to erupt.

In Figure 12-4, just south of the low that sits on the Gulf coast of Louisiana, there is an "outflow boundary" shown by a curved dashed line bulging out in front of the cold front. (This is also mentioned on Page 5-2.) This is where two or more thunderstorm gust fronts happen to intersect; an area where rapid violent lifting of air occurs (*see* diagram of gust front development at right). Often a SVR TSTM, or a mesocyclone will rapidly develop.

dryline: A moisture boundary that separates warm moist air from hot dry air in west central or western Texas; a zone of instability where severe thunderstorms may occur. Also called the Marfa or dewpoint front.

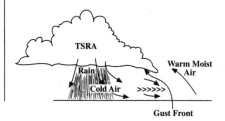

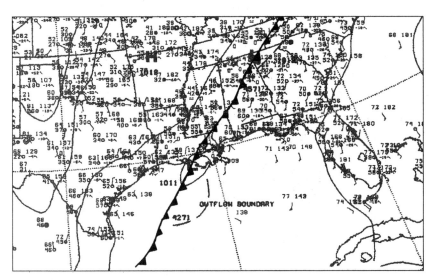

Figure 12-4. *Example of an outflow boundary*

Practice Surface Analysis

1. Use the chart on AC 00-45E Page 5-3: Examine the area on the chart immediately north and south of the cold front running east-west through Montana. Extend a mental 300 NM line (5 degrees of latitude) both north and south of the frontal zone into Canada and Wyoming. What range of temperatures and winds do you find north and south of the cold front?

   North of front

   South of front

   What type of front is lying across central Montana? How strong is it?

2. Using the same chart, carefully study what weather is occurring over the state of Missouri and answer the following questions:

   The temperatures range from _____ to _____ from north to south over the state.

   The sea level pressure ranges from _____ mb to _____ mb from north to south over the state.

   The average wind direction and speed over the state is from _____ at _____ knots.

   The pressure is rising or falling over the state?

3. Using the surface analysis chart in Figure 12-5 (at right), determine the mean wind direction and speed, temperature and dew point over the Texas/Louisiana region.

4. Using AC 00-45E Table 5-1 (Page 5-6), determine the type and characteristics of the frontal system that bisects eastern Mississippi on the surface analysis chart in Figure 12-5.

5. What is the pressure doing behind the front that bisects Mississippi?
   a. Little or no change
   b. Rising
   c. Falling

6. Using the AC 00-45E figures on Pages 5-5 through 5-8, decipher the plotted weather data for the data plot in the center of the Texas panhandle.

7. In which direction would you expect the frontal system over Mississippi and the Gulf of Mexico to move?
   a. North
   b. East
   c. West
   d. South

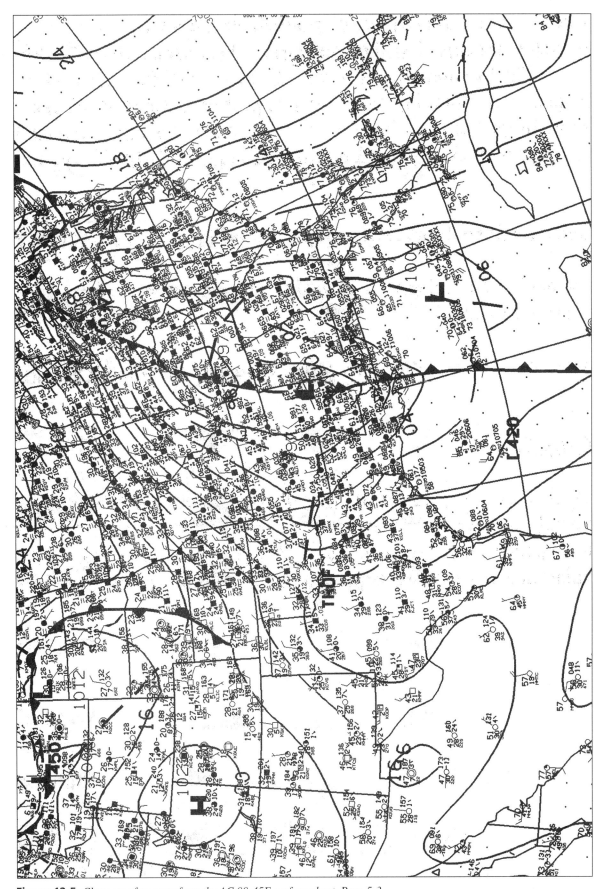

Figure 12-5. *Close-up of an area from the AC 00-45E surface chart, Page 5-3*

Chapter 13: *Weather Depiction Chart*

Use All Resources for the Big Picture
Compare to Surface Chart

If you compare AC 00-45E Figures 5-1 and 6-3, you can see the depicted fronts are the same ones, even though the weather depiction chart is one hour later than the surface chart. Normally there would be a notation at the bottom part of the weather depiction chart about the frontal positions being an hour old.

Remember the "four W" questions: What is it? Where is it? Why is it? and When is it? Use this kind of inquiry while examining the weather depiction chart on AC 00-45E Page 6-5.

What is Being Depicted?

What is causing the widespread LIFR and IFR conditions to the north and west of the frontal system shown on these two charts? It certainly appears that the weather immediately north of the front from Illinois, through Ohio and New York, and into New England—could be typical warm frontal weather since there is a strong pronounced southerly flow of warm moist air. This is coming northward off the Gulf of Mexico and overrunning the cooler air north of the front.

If you also compare the radar summary chart (AC 00-45E Page 7-5), you'll see that much of the area north of the front has continuous light rain (*see* Page 5-9). However, some of the stations at or near the frontal zone are experiencing continuous *moderate* rain, which appears to be associated with the smaller, second closed-contour over southeast Ohio northeastward into Pennsylvania. Now think for a moment, what kind of terrain do we find in this area? That's right—the western area of the Appalachian Mountains (hills, that is!).

In the lower left-hand area of this chart, southwest of San Diego, there is a legend that tells you how many stations were available for the analysis. If every station is reporting their observations there will be a total of 1,363 data plots on the chart; in reality, this number is seldom realized. For example, the chart on Page 6-5 tells us that only 1,133 weather observations are reporting at the time of the chart. That means that some of those circles (which can denote clear skies or clouds above 12,000 feet)

AC 00-45E Reading Assignment
Section 6
Pages 6-1 through 6-5

 You should always try to determine:
- *WHERE* is the weather occurring?
- *WHAT* type of weather?
- *WHY* is this weather occurring?
- *WHEN* will the weather be affecting my flight region?

LIFR: Low IFR conditions

overrunning: This occurs when warm moist air is either forced aloft by colder denser air (cold front) or, when retreating cold air is overtaken by warm moist air (warm front).

More about the data plots:

Cross-reference the plotted station symbol examples in AC 00-45E Figure 6-2 with the weather symbols in the previous section on Page 5-9. The AC 00-45E doesn't say so, but Figure 5-6 consists of the World Meteorological Organization's official symbology for all weather phenomena. (*See also* Appendix A for a more complete description of the weather symbols on these charts.)

---

http://www.nws.noaa.gov

http://weather.noaa.gov/fax/nwsfax.shtml (NWS "Difax" charts)

AC 00-45E Figure 6-3 shows some weather symbols not listed in Figure 6-2, and it takes cross-referencing with Figure 5-6 to interpret them:

3 = ● Examine the data plots in central
14 and northern California—these double-lines are fog, but not of the total-sky-obscuring type shown in Figure 6-2.

3 ⧍● In two areas of New England and
3 the upstate New York border this triangular symbol is indicating ice pellets or sleet.

on the chart might have some significant cloud layers and/or restricted visibility. How can you tell which is which? If the surface analysis chart shows a pretty strong high cell over a region, that usually implies pretty good weather—but there can be exceptions to this!

And When is it Being Depicted?

Examine the composite moisture-stability chart (Pages 9-11 through 9-15) and look at the stability over this eastern third of the country where there are three severe weather watches in effect (radar chart). It doesn't look very unstable over the area. Now look at the bottom left corner of the moisture-stability chart and note the date/time legend—it's 1200Z (that's only 2:35 hours earlier then the radar summary chart!) In fact, the composite moisture stability chart is for 1200Z, the radar summary, surface analysis, and weather depiction charts are for 0235Z, 0000Z and 0100Z. *Always check the date and time for all weather information before using it.*

Knowing that the composite moisture chart can be fairly old or fairly new (depending upon flight time), you can see why the Lifted Index values are so out of whack with the reality of the situation—i.e., severe weather developing! Atmospheric stability is not static—it can change through time.

Why is it Occurring?

Now let's examine the weather occurring *behind* the front in part of Texas, Oklahoma, Arkansas and Missouri. Hey, isn't weather supposed to be clearing out behind a cold front? Sometimes yes, sometimes no. In this case, the radar chart does indicate rain-shower activity in convectively unstable air over Texas and Oklahoma moving, as we already know, towards the southwest. Look at the constant pressure charts on AC 00-45E Pages 8-8 through 8-10. Using a colored pencil and Figure 13-1 (which is an excerpt of this area from those charts), carefully mark the location of the cold front (blue) onto the 850, 700 and 500 mb chart excerpts.

Note that the surface position of the frontal system does not, will not, match up with the trough over this area on the upper air charts. Fronts slope with height back over the colder air behind the frontal systems.

Now take a hi-lighter pen, and again on Figure 13-1, shade-in the area(s) on the 850, 700 and 500 mb charts where the temperature/dewpoint is a five-degree spread or less. What we are doing is trying to pinpoint the area(s) of high moisture content.

Where is it Occurring?

Should you hilight areas over this *entire* chart? No of course not, just over the eastern two-thirds of the country because it is pretty obvious there is a large area of deep moisture both east of the frontal system as well as north and northwest. Believe it or not, all of this moisture is from the Gulf of Mexico and advected, moved northward, ahead of the frontal system in Mississippi–Tennessee–Kentucky, and then upward over the colder air north of the frontal system. The air then wraps or curves counterclockwise into Indiana, Illinois, Missouri, Arkansas and Louisiana.

Continue to Practice Session.

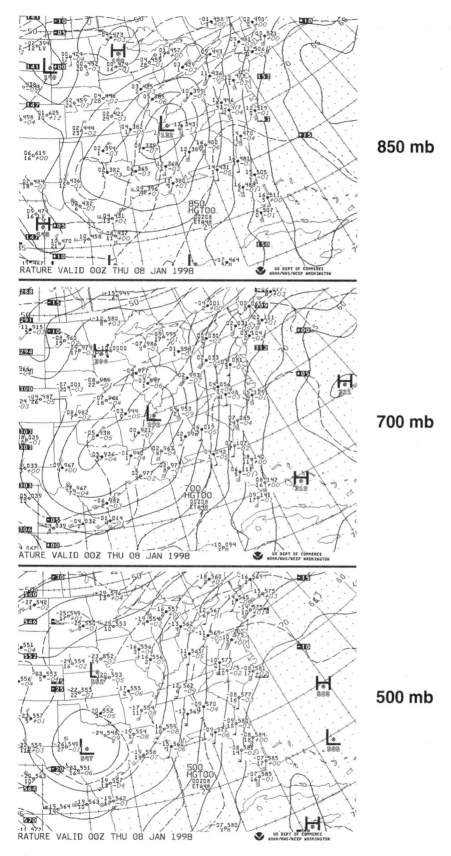

850 mb

700 mb

500 mb

Figure 13-1. *AC 00-45E chart excerpts (from Pages 8-8 through 8-11).*

Practice Weather Depiction

1. If the total sky coverage is less than 5/8ths, what does the cloud height located below the data plot indicate?

2. How is a partially obscured sky condition plotted on the data plot?

3. How is a thin overcast layer indicated on the chart?

4. Identify the flight conditions (IFR, MVFR, LIFR, and VFR) for each of the data plots shown below:

   a. 3 ═○ _____   d. 3/4 ═⊗ _____
        6   7

   b.   ◑ _____   e. 6 ∞● _____
       30   200

   c. 1 ✱✱⊗ _____   f. 4 •• ● _____
         12   40

For the rest of the questions, use the weather depiction chart on AC 00-45E Page 6-5.

5. Notice the thin dashed line starting over eastern TN and stretching southward into GA and the Florida panhandle. What does this line indicate?

6. Examine the weather occurring over central and northern Georgia (a magnifying glass might prove helpful)…What is happening here?

7. Maine is really having some weird weather—but what kind?

8. Towards which direction would you suspect the weather over Georgia and the Carolinas to be moving?
   a. S
   b. N
   c. W
   d. E

Chapter 14: *Composite Moisture Stability Chart*

One of the most important things to remember about the composite moisture stability chart (AC 00-45E Page 9-11) is that it is *observed data taken from the radiosonde balloon runs at 0000Z and 1200Z.* Therefore your weather briefing may include information from this chart which is old, very old! For example, you receive a briefing at 1400Z, but this chart would be from the 0000Z chart of the 14th, since the new 1200Z data chart hasn't been received yet by the FSS. In this chapter we'll review some of the panels in this chart and how they should be used with other charts from different times of the day.

AC 00-45E Reading Assignment
Section 9
Pages 9-1 through 9-15

Lifted and K Index Panel

AC 00-45E clearly explains the whys and whens of the "lifted index and K index" panel, one of the four panels on this chart. But let's take a look at three other charts in AC 00-45E: the weather depiction chart (Page 6-5), the radar summary chart (Page 7-1), and the composite moisture stability chart (Page 9-11). These charts, compared with each other, give a good example of why you must be careful in using "old" information.

LI/K or LI/KI: Both refer to lifted index and K index.

LI: Indicator of stable/unstable air
K: Indicator of moist/dry air

The LI/K index panel of the moisture-stability chart indicates the air is slightly stable — and then slightly unstable in a region from Pennsylvania/Kentucky southward to the Gulf coast and Florida (Figure 14-1). Yet the radar chart, which is over 14 hours later then the stability chart, shows strong (level 5 — *intense*) thunderstorms from northern Florida through Georgia and the Carolinas. Obviously the instability (LI) has shown a remarkable change, and the question you should be asking is, *why?*

As the AC 00-45E points out on Page 9-2, the LI can change (become more negative — unstable) through increasing surface temperatures and/or dew points, as well as through other factors such as a trough of low pressure located to the west of a suspect severe weather area (*see* Chapter 11 of this book). It could also be a combination of one or more of the factors listed below. There is an old saw about weather that states: "If you want to make air unstable, just lift it!" Significant upward vertical motion can often occur:

1. Along frontal zones

2. Over the windward slopes of hills or mountains

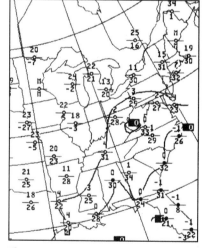

Figure 14-1. *LI/K values for Wednesday, January 7, 1998 at 1200Z.*

http://weather.noaa.gov/fax/nwsfax.shtml

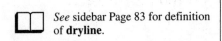

See sidebar Page 83 for definition of **dryline**.

3. With mass convergence of air around a low-pressure system

4. Heating (convection)

5. Along a dryline

6. Along thunderstorm outflow boundaries (particularly converging gust fronts)

7. A strong jet stream aloft over an area of weak instability

8. An upper-level trough of low pressure located west of an area of weak instability.

Potential for Thunderstorms?

Any one or several of these factors may combine to change an area of weak instability (or weak stability) into an unstable environment for thunderstorm activity.

Take a look at AC 00-45E Table 9-1, "Thunderstorm Potential"—these two tables should be used with caution. For example, a station might have an LI value of -7, quite unstable. But the KI might be 15, which is a very low probability of thunderstorms! This type of LI/KI data is seen frequently in the summertime over hot desert regions. The thunderstorm probability inferred by the right-hand side of this table is for air mass thunderstorms, not severe frontal or squall-line thunderstorms. If the LI is -3 or -4 and the K index is in the 25–35 range, there is a very good chance of convective activity—but they may not be severe or tornadic thunderstorms.

Average Relative Humidity Panel

This panel can give the pilot a pretty good indication of the moisture distribution in the vertical (850 mb to 500 mb). But compare again: you can also get some good ideas of the "current" vertical moisture distribution by examining the partial METAR reports plotted on the weather depiction chart. The one on AC 00-45E Page 6-5 indicates widespread low overcasts and somewhat restricted visibilities from Louisiana Mississippi and northward through the eastern Great Plains, then eastwards into the Great Lakes states. Steady precipitation, like that observed on this chart over Missouri and Illinois, needs a fairly deep layer of cloudiness to produce precipitation.

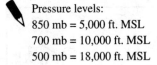

Pressure levels:
850 mb = 5,000 ft. MSL
700 mb = 10,000 ft. MSL
500 mb = 18,000 ft. MSL

But north of Missouri and into northern Illinois, there is no rain— only low stratus clouds with good visibility. The implication here is that the cloud tops are fairly low and the amount of water vapor in the vertical (amount between 5,000' and 18,000') is fairly low. Now look at the panel on Page 9-15*—it indicates a rapid drop of relative humidity from 76% in central Illinois to 43% and lower in northwest Illinois, northwestward into Iowa and the Dakotas.

*This panel is the same as the lower right-hand panel on Page 9-11.

Yes, the panels of the composite moisture stability chart are 12 hours old, but this panel shows the humidity parameter was fairly low, and remained that way as evidenced by the later weather depiction and the radar summary chart coverage of this area.

Note something else occurring at Grand Forks (KGFK), North Dakota, where the average relative humidity probably approached or exceeded

50%: yes, it is snowing but the radar chart tells us "NE"—no echoes. Snow can be an elusive radar target because it absorbs radar energy rather than reflecting the energy back to the radar receiver. Suffice to say that what you see is not always what you get!

Freezing Level Panel

AC 00-45E uses the data plot of North Platte, Nebraska as a good example of multiple freezing levels. But examine the number of multiple freezing levels around North Platte: with below-freezing surface temperatures all over the northern Plains states, there is also a layer of above-freezing air aloft, its base averaging about 4,000' MSL and the tops of the layer at about 5,400' MSL. Compare this with the vertical temperature profile in the sidebar. This diagram for North Platte, Nebraska exhibits a classic profile that could create icing hazards for aircraft operating below 4,400' MSL. An aircraft operating below 4,400 feet is flying through below-freezing air. Water droplets falling from an above-freezing layer of air down through the colder air will cool, and either freeze or become supercooled. These supercooled droplets will freeze on impact with any surface—especially aircraft.

But in this case there is no icing occurring and none was forecast. Why? The weather depiction and surface analysis charts show skies are clear over this part of Nebraska, which is west of the stationary frontal system running north-south through eastern North and South Dakota and Nebraska. You might also notice the number of *square* sky cover symbols on the surface analysis chart, and the number of symbols used on the weather depiction chart. Both of these symbols indicate an automated weather station which may or may not be augmented.

Continue to next page for Practice Session.

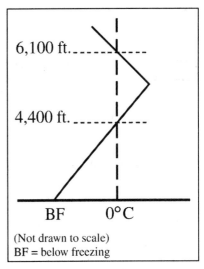

Vertical temperature profile

Hints:
AC 00-45E Page 5-2, in the first paragraph—

☐ square station symbol = observation by automated system

AC 00-45E Page 6-1 under "Plotted Data"—

] right bracket = weather information obtained by automated system

Practice Reading Panels

1. On the stability panel, the analysis of data is based on
   a. LI
   b. KI
   c. LI and KI

2. A large positive KI value is most representative of what type of thunderstorm activity in what season?
   a. Frontal, in the summer
   b. Air mass, in the winter
   c. Frontal, in the winter
   d. Air mass, in the summer

3. The information shown on the panels of the chart is
   a. forecast information.
   b. observed information.

4. Radiosonde runs (observations) are taken
   a. hourly.
   b. every three hours.
   c. every six hours.
   d. every 12 hours.

5. Heights on the freezing level chart are given in feet
   a. MSL.
   b. AGL.

6. A radiosonde reports three freezing levels. Which level is used in the analysis of the freezing level panel?
   a. Highest level
   b. Middle level
   c. Lowest level

7. Shown below are several data plots from the Lifted Index/K Index panel.

    a. -2/36

    b. 12/10

    c. -4/06

    d. 0/24

    Which one of the plots indicates the most unstable air at the time of the run? _____

    Which one indicates the most stable air? _____

    Which one indicates the greatest probability of air mass TSTMS? _____

    Which data plot shows the driest air mass? _____

8. The Lifted Index is calculated by assuming that air will be lifted to the _____ mb level.

    a. 300

    b. 500

    c. 700

9. Which reporting station might have a higher precipitable water vapor content? All other factors are held constant.

    a. Station at 500 meters

    b. Station at 2,000 meters

    c. Not enough information given

Chapter 15: *Constant Pressure Charts*
and the Four-Dimensional Weather Picture

3D vs. 4D?

AC 00-45E makes a strong point about being able to see weather information in both the horizontal and vertical dimensions, calling this the "three-dimensional aspect." You should actually think this one a bit further, and imagine weather as a four-dimensional picture:

1. East-West changes
2. North-South changes
3. Vertical changes
4. Changes through time

All four aspects should be part of a good weather briefing. Constant pressure charts help this picture become clearer, because they are a device for a better understanding of how the atmosphere behaves at different heights and pressure levels. The earth's atmosphere is a tremendous, deep river of air that flows continually over the Earth's surfaces. It may form eddies and waves both in the horizontal and vertical, and it is the prime mover in the creation of weather over the planet.

These charts are really horizontal "slices" or layers taken from the twice-daily balloon runs—the "vertical profile" of the atmosphere. Each chart ("slice") contains plots of temperature, temperature/dew point (humidity), wind direction and speed, height of the layer, and changes in height of that particular pressure. In other words, on each chart the pressure is the same, but the heights will vary.

Let's examine the 850 mb chart on Page 8-8. The height of 850 mb is approximately 5,000 feet MSL, which means that this chart is of limited use in the higher terrain of the western United States. Locate the data plot at this height for Jacksonville, Florida (JAX). Now, let's assume that we took off from Jacksonville, climbed to an altitude of 4,770 feet (4,900 meters) and then flew northward to Churchill, in northern Manitoba (lat. 59°N, long. 94°W), and maintained our constant altitude with no change in our altimeter setting. *See* the sidebar figure at right, and Figure 15-1.

Obviously, there has been a drastic change in temperature as well as a change in the height of 850 mb. Now the question is this: Did we main-

AC 00-45E Reading Assignment
Section 8
Pages 8-1 through 8-12

 Understanding these charts and pressure levels is key to understanding weather; therefore you should supplement this section with studies in some of the "Suggested Reading" on Page 197 of this book.

"balloon runs"—radiosonde weather balloons. *See* Chapter 3, Page 28, and Appendix B.

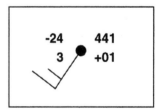

Churchill data plot

---

http://weather.noaa.gov/fax/nwsfax.shtml

http://www.met.tamu.edu/weather/mp/models1.html (Forecast Products from Texas A & M)

http://weather.uwyo.edu/upperair/uamap.html (University Wyoming Dept. of Atmospheric Science)

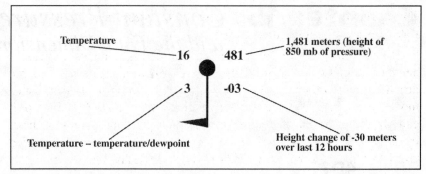

Figure 15-1. *Jacksonville data plot*

tain a constant altitude? No, we actually lost height: From 1,481 meters at KJAX to 1,399 meters at KCVG (Covington, KY); but we then gained height from there to Churchill with its 850 mb height of 1,441 meters. This should not come as much of a surprise; pressure surfaces are lower in colder air, higher in warmer air. So we flew a constant pressure slope rather than a constant altitude; thus the old rule, "High to low, look out below."

Flow Patterns and Frontal Systems

The flow of air over the U.S. on the constant pressure charts (Pages 8-8 through 8-12) indicates a meridional pattern—a strong looping pattern with troughs of lower height (pressure) and ridges of higher height (pressure). There is a strong ridge of high pressure over the eastern Pacific and the adjacent western U.S.; low pressure over the central U.S.; and a high-pressure ridge over the western Atlantic and the northeastern U.S. The meridional pattern is easily recognizable on these charts. You can see that the low-pressure center on the surface chart slopes back to the west from the surface, upwards to the 500 mb chart. From this height upward, the low cell appears to be vertical.

Another flow pattern often observed (usually in spring or fall) is called a "zonal flow," which is an airflow that moves west to east roughly parallel to latitude lines. The height contours of the constant pressure charts are also oriented west to east. A zonal flow pattern is not conducive to the development of strong mid-latitude wave cyclones, with their accompanying frontal systems.

Turn back to AC 00-45E Page 5-3, the surface analysis chart. Note how the surface position of the low-pressure system in Tennessee slopes back to the west—up to the 500 mb level. Then the low center is approximately vertical up to the 250 mb level, especially from the 700 mb upwards to the 250 mb chart. This is a good example of a deep cold core low, so-called because the temperatures around the central area of the low-pressure cell (trough) are lower then the surrounding areas at the same latitude.

For example: On the 700 mb chart, going from Arizona to the low-pressure area over Texas, then eastwards into the southeastern U.S., the temperatures are -03, -08, -09, -05, and in Shreveport, Louisiana, a -01°C.

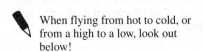

When flying from hot to cold, or from a high to a low, look out below!

meridional pattern: An airflow that exhibits a looping pattern. Figure 15-2 on the next page is a good example of this.

zonal flow: An airflow pattern that is essentially west–east. Some zonal flow can be see on the constant pressure charts on AC 00-45E Pages 8-9 through 8-11 over southern Canada from Lake Superior to Maine.

This is true for all the charts; the *troughs* of low pressure and/or low-pressure cells are areas of colder temperatures.

Deep cold core lows are associated with mid-latitude wave cyclones and their frontal systems. Sometimes there will be an upper-level low, but no surface low-pressure system with fronts. As the upper-level disturbance moves, it can help to create strong surface pressure falls (PRESFR), or it can certainly weaken an existing surface high-pressure system. In many instances the end result will be an area of precipitation and unsettled weather; clues as to why may show on the surface analysis chart.

There are shallow pressure systems, and these are generally created by strong surface heating and cooling: thermal low- and high-pressure systems. A thermal low is a warm core low, a heat low that might form over the southwestern desert in the summer season, and this weakens with height. A thermal high is a cold core high; a cold high pressure system created over the higher latitudes of Canada and Siberia in the winter (there is a perennial thermal high over Antarctica). These also weaken with height, as opposed to the deep systems that intensify with height.

The surface analysis chart on Page 5-3 does indicate one shallow cold-core high which persists up through the 850 mb level over northwest Canada. A weak warm-core low is in Mexico at 25 degrees north latitude and persists up to the 850 mb level. Obviously these lows are strongest and somewhat deeper in the summer months.

Let me give you a simplified rule regarding the upper-air patterns and the occurrence of "weather": *Inclement weather is associated with an upper-level trough of low pressure and is found east of the trough line.*

This can easily be seen on your surface chart and weather depiction charts when you examine the 850–500 mb charts and note the position of the trough in relation to the MVFR/IFR weather on the weather depiction chart. Good weather is associated with the ridge line and eastward to the trough line.

One interesting way to track these troughs and ridges is to pick a mid latitude height contour on the 700 or 500 mb chart, for example the contour of 300 (3,000 meters). Mark its location on a blank map of the U.S. (a copy of the flight advisory chart will do). Then the next day, 24 hours later, locate the same height contour and sketch it on the same chart with

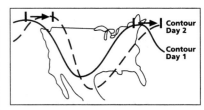

Tracking method

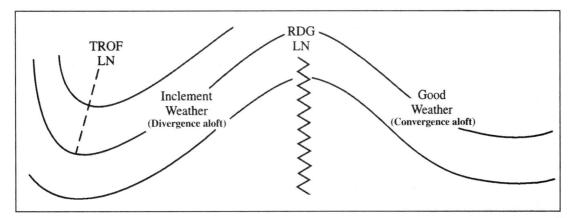

Figure 15-2. *The constant pressure chart, simplified: TROF of low pressure, RDG of high pressure.*

the other contour height. There should be a striking difference in the pattern of the 3,000-meter contour over time, which graphically illustrates that the Earth's atmosphere is like a vast river of air.

But suppose you are getting a weather briefing and the briefer (or computer) indicates a trough of low pressure west of your route. The weather briefing does not indicate any significant cloud layers and/or precipitation east of the trough where you would normally expect such weather. Conclusion? It could very well be that there isn't significant moisture in this region. Check the upper-air charts and/or the composite moisture stability chart panels for moisture availability before jumping to any conclusions.

The 850 mb Chart

The contour height pattern illustrates the location of ridges and troughs of high and low pressure. The isotherm pattern shows where the thermal ridges (warm air) and troughs (cold air) are located. Let's examine the 850 mb chart again (Page 8-8) and note that the isotherms (drawn as dashed lines for every 5°C) do not run parallel to the contours. Instead, the isotherms cross the contours at some angle. A pattern like this is called a "baroclinic atmosphere" and gives rise to cold and warm air advection.

Weak surface fronts and warm frontal systems are often difficult to locate on the surface analysis charts. Why? Terrain effects and even the time of day can "mask" the actual position of these systems.

Locate the frontal systems on the 850 mb chart: The cold front through Louisiana and northward lies to the east and south of pretty good "thermal packing"; that is, the isotherms are close together. This packing is more obvious north of the frontal system over the Great Lake states and eastward into New England.

The stationary frontal system running east west through Washington and Montana (stationary because the winds are parallel to the front) shows strong thermal packing north of the frontal system. Remember that the constant pressure charts and the latest surface chart may not be for the same time.

Cold and Warm Air Advection

Examine the frontal low over western Tennessee, the isobar pattern around the low, and its frontal system: East of the low over the southeastern U.S., the southerly winds are crossing the isotherms (+15 degrees, for example) from south to north—this is warm air advection. This is also occurring for some distance north of the trough-front—another example of "overrunning."

Look closely at both the 850 and 700 mb charts and you'll find cold air advection occurring over northeast Mexico and southwest Texas. This means cooler air is moving southwards in warmer areas and "packing" (albeit loosely) behind the weak cold front. I say weak, because a strong active cold front would have very strong, tightly packed isotherms aligned west or north west of the surface frontal position.

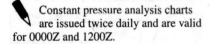

Contour pattern for heights shown by solid lines:

Isotherm pattern for temperature variations shown by bold, dashed lines:

Constant pressure analysis charts are issued twice daily and are valid for 0000Z and 1200Z.

Below 500 mb, cold air advection is typically observed west of the trough line and east of the ridge line. Warm air advection is typically observed east of the trough line and west of the ridge line. It would appear that warm air advection is somehow linked to "bad" weather and cold air advection is associated with "good" weather. Time for another simplified rule: Good weather is associated with sinking air (compressed/warming with pressure rising at the surface). Bad weather is associated with rising/cooling/condensing air. Does this make sense to you? So, cold air advection is associated with sinking air; warm air advection is associated with inclement weather, as long as there is sufficient moisture present.

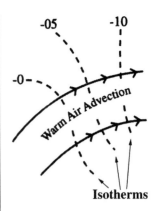

On the western half of the 850 mb chart: Remember that 850 mb is approximately 5,000 feet which means this part of the 850 mb chart is now a *surface* chart for most of the mountainous west!

There is a surface, stationary frontal system extending from southern British Columbia to central Montana, then oriented south to north through eastern South Dakota/central Nebraska. Notice the **L** over the southeast corner of Montana with a trough extended down the western edge of South Dakota and Nebraska. This is the 850 mb position of the surface front in east central South Dakota and Nebraska. In other words, fronts slope back to the west or northwest over the colder air. You can also see that there is some cold air advection in eastern Wyoming and warm air advection occurring over the northeast corner of Montana into Canada; plus there is good moisture (temp/dew point), and the weather depiction chart indicates snow and snow shower activity north of the frontal zone.

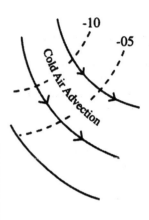

But why do we call this a stationary front? Simply because it isn't going anywhere very fast! Notice that the front is parallel to the contours on the 850 mb chart across much of its length which means the winds aloft are parallel to the front. Compare this low and front with the one in Louisiana where the winds in front of the system are blowing northward; west of the front, the winds are actually blowing towards the front.

Water Vapor Content

How about moisture at these levels? Remember that we have a temperature-minus-dewpoint value plotted right below the temperature. When this temp/dewpoint value is equal to or less than 5°C, the station circle is darkened in. Thus it is relatively easy to locate areas of high moisture content, and when you correlate this with areas of warm air advection, the chances are you will find cloudy, and perhaps, wet weather.

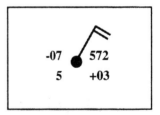

Moisture content—high

Height Changes (HC)

The height change can be compared to the changes of pressure with time by a barometer. The height change is the change of height of the pressure level (850 mb, for example) within a 12-hour period. This value is not plotted when the wind is either missing or light and variable. Positive height changes (higher height values on current chart) imply cold air advection and pressure rising at the surface.

The 700 mb Chart

All of the aforementioned uses of the 850 mb chart can be applied to the 700 mb chart (Page 8-9). This is a good chart to look at if you are flying in the western half of the U.S., because 10,000 feet is approximately the crest level for most of the western mountain ranges.

Another use of this chart is for calculating the steering winds of thunderstorms and rain showers (convective activity). Unfortunately, the NWS chose not to tell us the movement and speed of areas or lines of activity, so we have no idea as to where the thunderstorm activity over the SE U.S. is moving or at what speed. But we can use the 700 and 500 mb charts to give us a pretty good idea as to the movement of TSRA activity. The average wind direction at 700 and 500 mb levels is from the S-SW at an average speed of 50 knots. Using 50% of that speed (25 knots) we can declare with some confidence that this activity is moving to the NNE at about 25–30 knots. (Unfortunately we cannot verify it with any of the related material in the AC 00-45E since the messages (WST, AC, or AWWs) do not correlate with the charts in the book.)

One word of caution on using this rule ("50% of the average…") over the central plains: storms often move to the right of the average 700–500 mb level winds.

On the surface chart (Page 5-3), notice the quasi-stationary front that extends from Ohio to southern New York State. On the 700 mb chart, the data plot for Detroit, MI has evidence for the frontal system at that level. An examination of the wind field from the surface to 700 mb indicates that the wind is blowing from warmer regions to colder ones. This is called warm air advection, but it is also called overrunning (as mentioned previously — refer back to the sidebars on Pages 87 and 100). This is typical of warm fronts and some quasi-stationary frontal systems. Notice where the IFR weather is occurring with respect to this front on the weather depiction chart (AC 00-45E Page 6-5): north of the frontal system is where the warm air is lifting over colder air and creating one huge mess of lousy flying weather.

The 500 mb Chart

The 500 mb chart (Page 8-10) contains the level in the atmosphere where one half of the atmosphere by weight will be found below this level and one-half above it.

First compare the 850 mb chart with the 700 and 500 mb charts. The 850 mb chart, being relatively near the Earth's surface, closely resembles the surface chart; the 700 and 500 are somewhat cleaner in their patterns. Note that there is still a ridge of high pressure over the eastern Pacific Ocean, northwestward into southwest Alaska; a trough of low pressure intruding into the northwestern U.S.; a cold-core low over Texas (the upper position of the surface low over western Tennessee); and a ridge of high pressure over the western Atlantic into the New England states. This pattern is obviously "cleaner" than the 850 mb chart which is at 5,000 feet MSL and at the surface in the higher terrain areas of the western U.S.

A careful look at the 850, 700 and 500 mb will also show that the eastern trough of low pressure at each successive higher level is further to the west; the trough of low pressure tilts westward with increasing height. Remember what a trough is — the location of the front aloft.

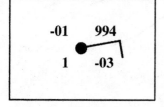

Detroit, MI data plot

From the 500 mb chart upwards short waves are not to be found; the pattern ridge-trough-ridge-trough is repeated around the globe with a wavelength of 40 to 50 degrees of longitude and a wave amplitude 30 to 40 degrees of latitude. These are called the Rossby Long Waves, and they increase in intensity above the 500 mb level.

Cold and warm air advection above the 500 mb level is the exact opposite of what I described for the 850 and 700 mb charts. Cold air advection will tend to make the upper atmosphere more unstable; warm air advection will stabilize the upper atmosphere. By examining the temperature-minus-dewpoint values of 5° or less, you can locate the areas of high vapor content. By comparing what you find at 850–500 mb levels, you can get a good idea of the horizontal and vertical distribution of the water vapor in relation to the troughs and ridges.

300 and 250 mb Charts

The 300 mb and subsequent higher constant-pressure charts (Pages 8-11, 8-12), are called the jet stream charts. The two main jet streams, the polar front jet (PFJ) and the subtropical jet (STJ) are much in evidence. The wind field is analyzed at this and the higher level charts for every 20 knots starting with 10 knots. The jet stream looping over the top of the Pacific Ridge, and then south around and northeast of the low-pressure system over Texas is the polar front jet stream (PFJ).

The other jet stream running west to east near 25 to 30 degrees north latitude is the subtropical jet stream (STJ). These two jets appear to merge at 32 degrees north latitude and 115 degrees west longitude, but in reality the two jets overlap; the PFJ is below the higher STJ. This merging area is also known for lots of turbulence.

The area of maximum winds in a jet is called a jet streak. A careful look at both the 300 and 250 mb charts will show smaller areas of the strong winds: 110 and 130 knots. These actually migrate downstream like a small craft would drift downstream in a river if it were in the middle of the river, as opposed to being near the banks of the river.

The jet streams on the 300 and 250 mb charts loop north of the severe weather area over the SE U.S. Jet streams can really aid and abet severe weather but in this case the jet stream is too far north. So…what is aiding severe weather over the SE U.S.? It isn't very obvious on the AC 00-45E's upper-air charts but the contours are diverging, or spreading apart (*see* Figure 15-3). Divergence aloft (500 mb and upwards) can aid in the development of severe weather.

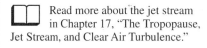

Isotach gradients identify these wind fields on 300 and 250 charts and are shown graphically by short, fine dashed lines:

- -

Read more about the jet stream in Chapter 17, "The Tropopause, Jet Stream, and Clear Air Turbulence."

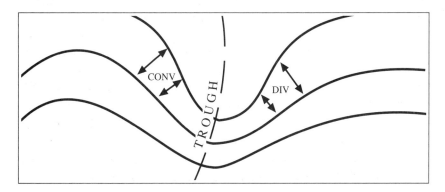

Figure 15-3. *Convergence and divergence*

Constant Pressure Practice

Use AC 00-45E tables and charts on Pages 8-6 through 8-12 to answer the following questions.

1. Contours are drawn for every _____ meters on the 850 and 700 mb charts and _____ on the 500 mb chart.

2. Is the temperature-minus-dewpoint plotted on the 300–250 mb level charts? _____

   When might this value be omitted from these higher-level charts?

3. Isotachs of wind speed are only included on what level charts and for what increment of speeds?

4. A _____ (zonal, meridional) flow pattern of air across the U.S. is conducive to good weather.

5. Which of the two jet streams is found at a lower latitude and which one is found at a higher height?

   a. PFJ, STJ

   b. PFJ, PFJ

   c. STJ, STJ

   d. STJ, PFJ

Chapter 16: *Significant Weather Progs*

Future Perspective

The 12/24- and 36/48-hour significant weather prognostic charts are overview charts that I call the "Readers' Digest" version of the weather services. They condense into graphical format all the information found in other messages and charts such as the TAFs, FAs, WAs, WS's, and a future surface analysis and weather depiction chart. In short, you get a lot of information on two charts.

Before you decide to take a short cut and omit checking out the TAFs and FAs, etc., let's put this chart in perspective with the rest of your weather briefing. You should first look at current conditions, then examine the forecast conditions, and these prognostic charts then can help put all of the above information into a "future perspective" view.

As we've seen before, the surface analysis chart (AC 00-45E Page 5-3) is based on the 0000Z data, January 8, 1998. The weather depiction chart (Page 6-5) is based on 0100Z data, with frontal positions for 0000Z. By comparing the "latest" surface analysis and weather depiction charts with the future positions, as shown in the 12- and 24-hour low-level significant weather prog charts (Page 11-11), pilots can easily get a pretty good idea of how things are expected to change over time.

A good exercise for pilots (and weather enthusiasts) is to make a quick sketch of the current frontal and pressure systems shown on The Weather Channel as well as where they forecast these fronts and systems to be by the next day. Then check the same channel in the next day's report to see just how accurate yesterday's forecasts were. Same thing can be done by surfing the net for these same weather charts and forecasts, and now of course the NWS has excellent charts, graphics, and images available at no cost (*see* websites mentioned at the beginning of each chapter). This is good practice in looking for the possibilities of where the weather is moving.

AC 00-45E Reading Assignment
Section 11
Pages 11-1 through 11-14

 The AWC webpages below have particularly clear examples of the "SIG WX" charts, in full color.

http://www.awc-kc.noaa.gov/awc/lolvl.html (Low Level SIGWX Charts)
http://www.awc-kc.noaa.gov/awc/hilvl.html (High Level SIGWX Charts)

36- and 48-Hour Low-Level Significant Weather Prog Chart

There are some differences between the 12/24 hour prog and the 36/48 hour progs, such as the fact that areas of MVFR and IFR which are depicted on the 12/24 hour progs, are not depicted on the 36/48 hour progs—only precipitation is shown. Also, the 36/48-hour prog chart doesn't give you forecast values for freezing levels or turbulence.

Also different of course, is the included prognostic discussion. Since these 36- and 48-hour forecasts are an extended look into the future, I like this feature which gives me an insight into the forecaster's thinking. However, this discussion was written primarily for the field forecasters and the chances are good that the average FAA flight weather briefer does not use this part of the chart when briefing a pilot or discussing what the NWS is forecasting for the next 24 to 48 hours. Even so, with some patience and questions (always ask questions!) you will be surprised at how much you can grasp about the fascinating, and sometimes frustrating, subject of meteorology!

High-Level Significant Weather Prog Chart

AC 00-45E does a pretty good job of describing the high altitude (above 24,000 feet MSL) significant weather prog charts. But there are several prognostic charts available from the NWS that the AC 00-45E doesn't mention—if you need to have additional information for above flight level 24,000 feet, consult the Aviation Weather Center (AWC) webpage shown at the bottom of Page 105 (the High Level SIGWX Charts). Here they give you a table of linked charts that is pretty complete for current as well as forecast charts for different times and geographic locations. These charts are the color version of the NWS "facsimile" charts; there is even a link to a page that explains the symbols.

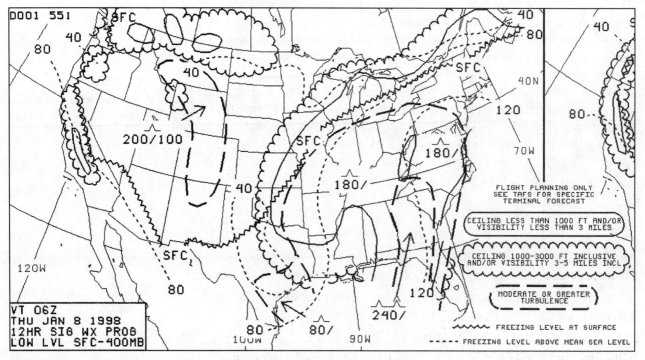

Figure 16-1. *Excerpt of AC 00-45E chart on Page 11-11, top left—06Z "surface" prog.*

Practice Progs

Low-Level Prog Chart

Using Figures 16-1 and 16-2, (excerpts of the chart in the AC 00-45E), plot an imaginary route from KSTL (St. Louis, MO to KBNA (Nashville, TN) to KATL (Atlanta, GA)...the Inflight Advisory Plotting Chart (Page 49 in this book) is also helpful for finding these locations on the prog chart. This route applies to the questions below:

1. Using the VT (valid time) 06Z panel, determine the freezing level across the route. How does it change?

2. For KSTL, how does the freezing level change from the 06Z panel to the 18Z panel?

   Examine the VT 18Z panel—is icing a possibility for the KSTL area?

3. Is any turbulence forecast for the route from KSTL to KBNA? You are flying a King Air at an altitude of 16,500 feet MSL. What severity is forecast?

Continued

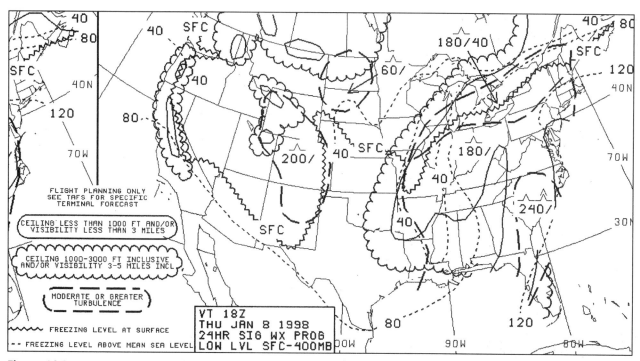

Figure 16-2. *Excerpt of AC 00-45E chart on Page 11-11, top right—18Z "surface" prog.*

4. Same as question #3, but now for the route segment from KBNA to KATL:

5. From KSTL – KBNA – KATL...What conditions are forecast on the route for 0600Z — MVFR? IFR?

Now look at the chart on AC 00-45E, and examine the bottom part of the chart, for this same route for questions 6 and 7.

6. For frontal systems over the route, what type of front, intensity and character is expected (use 0600Z panel)?

7. What type of precipitation is expected across the route, continuous...intermittent? Explain where you would expect to encounter the precipitation and if it changes, approximately where would you expect to find that change.

36- and 48-Hour Significant Weather Prog

For questions 8 through 10, refer to AC 00-45E Page 11-12, the 36/48-hour prog chart:

8. You are expecting to return to KSTL later with an arrival time of 0200Z on the 9th of January. Study the 36/48-hour chart, and write down what conditions you would expect to find upon arrival at KSTL.

9. What kind of frontal system is extending through Montana into southern Alberta (type, intensity and character)?

10. What type of precipitation and coverage is expected to occur over Pennsylvania on the 0000Z panel? The 1200Z panel?

High-Level Prog

For questions 11–16, use the high-level prog chart in Figure 16-3 on the next page. Locate the jet stream that extends from the Pacific over southern California, then east-northeast into Ohio.

11. Interpret the changes forecast for the wind speeds along this jet and give an approximate location where wind speeds are forecast to change. What are the strongest winds forecast and at what flight level?

12. What turbulence, if any, is anticipated along the jet stream and where is it forecast to occur?

13. What are the highest and lowest tropopause heights indicated on the prog, and where do these values occur?

14. As a general rule we find that the highest tropopause heights are located at the _____ latitudes and the lowest tropopause heights at the _____ latitudes.

15. In which direction is the frontal system over southern Arizona into Baja, Mexico forecast to move and at what speed?

16. What significant weather is forecast for the cold front moving through South Carolina and just offshore of North Carolina?

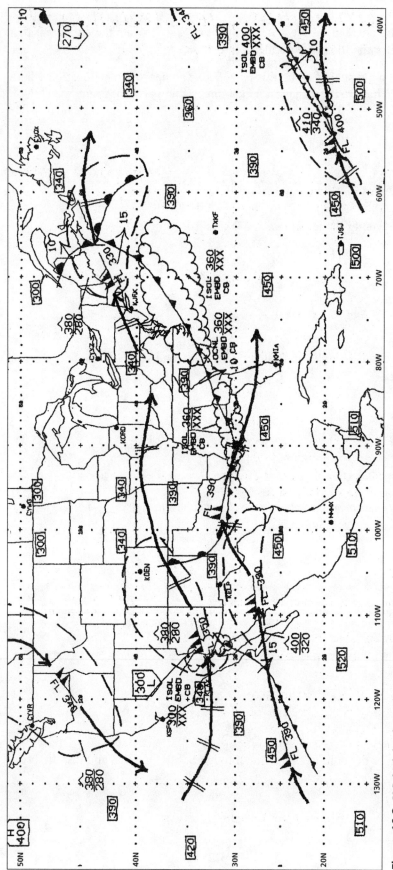

Figure 16-3. *U.S. high-level significant weather prog. showing jet streams and tropopause heights.*

Chapter 17: *The Tropopause, Jet Stream, and Clear Air Turbulence*

High Altitude Factors

The tropopause is the boundary between the troposphere and the stratosphere, very close to where we find the subtropical and polar front jet streams where there are areas of strong horizontal temperature contrast. Sometimes the tropopause can be visibly located at the top of a cirrostratus or cirrocumulus layer of clouds.

A tropopause chart can still be found on the NWS website, but the two-panel chart they present is so small as to render it worthless for pilots. Far better for your use is the High-Level Significant Weather Prognostic chart (Chapter 16), which depicts tropopause heights as well as forecast positions of the jet stream, and forecasted values and heights of clear air turbulence, or CAT.

In the previous *Aviation Weather Services* book, the 00-45D, there was a section covering the tropopause data chart (which has since pretty much disappeared from the NWS weather chart services). Now, the revised AC 00-45E retains some discussion of the effects of the tropopause, at least as far as the likely occurrence of turbulence at different flight levels. For more discussion of high altitude weather and its possible effects on flight, read the FAA's handbook, *Aviation Weather* (AC 00-6A), Pages 135 through 143.

Jet Streams

Figure 17-1 illustrates an average summer vertical profile of the jet streams along with the mean surface pressure pattern. The jet streams are created by the influence of a strong thermal gradient in the horizontal, with colder air to the north and warmer air to the south. This thermal gradient is reversed above 38,000 to 42,000 feet (the subtropical jet, or STJ), where we find cold air to the south and warmer air in the lower stratosphere the north of the jet stream.

We are concerned with two jet streams over North America and Central America: the polar front jet (PFJ) and the subtropical jet. The PFJ shows a strong seasonal latitudinal change in location and speed—usually being much stronger in the winter (when the thermal contrast between

AC 00-45E Reading Assignment
Section 14
Pages 14-1, 14-2

Review AC 00-45E Pages 11-6, 11-7, and 11-13, 11-14 about the high-level sig wx chart.

See the website below, and Pages 172–173 in Appendix C, for some interesting examples of jet stream winds analysis superimposed on IR satellite images.

http://squall.sfsu.edu/crws/jetstream.html
(California Regional Weather Server at San Francisco State University)

the high and low latitudes is stronger), as well as being located at a lower latitude. In 1979, the PFJ was actually located as far south as south central Mexico.

The STJ's location doesn't really show as much movement from season to season as does its northern cousin. But this jet is very persistent in terms of speed.

What is even more remarkable about these turbulent rivers of air is that they change altitude as well as latitude. The average PFJ stream has a vertical extent of 20,000 to 25,000 feet with winds equal to 70 knots or greater. Caution! In the winter over the mountainous west, a strong jet over this region can mean 70 knot winds or stronger at or near mountain ranges, spawning *severe* turbulence. Usually the strongest winds (the jet maxima, or jet streak) lie between 25,000 to 35,000 feet. The 300-mb constant pressure chart is also excellent for finding these jets (*see* Chapter 15).

AC 00-45E Page 8-11 shows this 300-mb chart.

Jet Streams and CAT

Much of the following information comes from the FAA Advisory Circular 00-30B, *Atmospheric Turbulence Avoidance.* "Clear air turbulence" (CAT) is defined by the National Committee for CAT, as well as by the FAA's *Aeronautical Information Manual (AIM),* as "turbulence encountered outside of convective activity." This definition can then easily be used to cover turbulence due to terrain effects (mountain waves), low-level inversions, and thermal effects. In practice, pilots consider turbulence at and above flight level 24,000 feet to signify CAT; other forms of turbulence are then identified, i.e., LO LVL WND SHR, MTN WV TURBC.

Moderate CAT can usually be found along the northern side of the PFJ in a narrow, elongated band that may stretch along the jet axis for a considerable distance. Surprisingly enough, this zone can be turbulence-free more often than it is turbulence-laden. This zone is also called the "upper front" and is the upper-level position of the surface polar front.

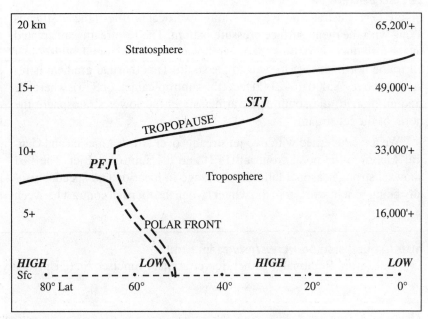

Figure 17-1. *Average location of jet streams, tropopause (in cross-section)*

Aviation Weather Services *Explained*

MDT OR GTR CAT can be found in the vicinity of the jet streak. In the diagram in Figure 17-2, the best chance for turbulence is in the downwind part of the jet streak. This is particularly true if there is a high rate of wind speed decrease eastward from the center of the jet streak. Figure 17-2 shows a strong west to east jet stream—but most jets, along with the upper-air pattern of height contours, show a meridional pattern. If the jet stream is looping around a sharp trough where there is a strong change in wind direction (horizontal shear), MDT OR GTR turbulence can be anticipated. This is illustrated in Figure 17-3.

Another favored area for a high probability of CAT is northeast of a developing surface low-pressure area. These storm systems are always located east of a trough of low pressure—the orientation of the isobars on the surface chart can give you a good indication as to the direction of movement of the low-pressure cell. The surface pressure falls at weather stations located northeast of the low-pressure cell are clues to possible areas of CAT (*see* Figure 17-4 on the next page).

MDT OR GTR CAT: Moderate or greater CAT

The jet streak is the area of strongest winds within the jet stream. (The jet streak is also referred to as the jet maxima.)

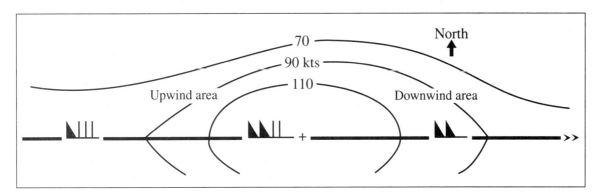

Figure 17-2. *Wind flag symbols show differences in wind speed in cross-section of a jet streak.*

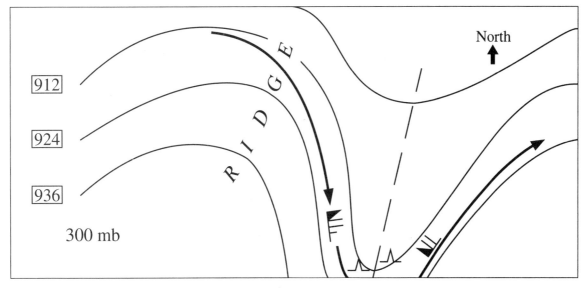

Figure 17-3. *Jet stream looping around a trough in a strong north-south (meridional) pattern.*

CAT can also be generated at the near-confluence of the PFJ and the STJ. Bear in mind that the PFJ is always found at a lower height than the STJ. Therefore on a chart, if they do appear to merge, in reality a vertical cross-section through the two jets would show them stacked up, one on top of the other, separated by a vertical zone of lighter winds (Figure 17-5). What is causing the turbulence here is the shearing of wind either in the horizontal and/or the vertical. The table below gives the threshold values of shear for moderate or greater CAT.

In order for CAT to be generated the winds in the jet stream must equal and/or exceed 110 knots. This is the threshold from which we measure vertical and horizontal wind shear. One easy way to determine horizontal shear is to examine the jet stream charts (300, 250 and 200 mb): wind speed lines (isotachs) are drawn for every 20 knots, and if they are spaced closer together than 150 nautical miles (2.5° latitude), there is a good possibility that moderate CAT will occur. This turbulent area is usually on the polar, low-pressure side of the jet stream.

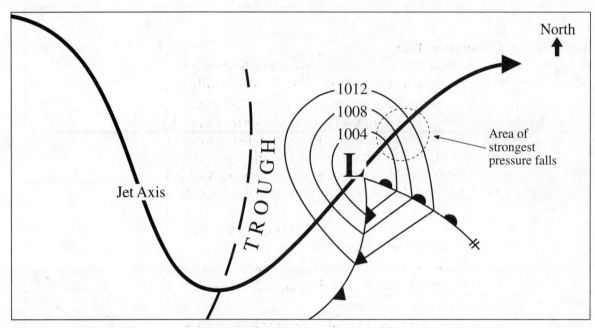

Figure 17-4. *Surface chart clues to pinpointing areas of CAT*

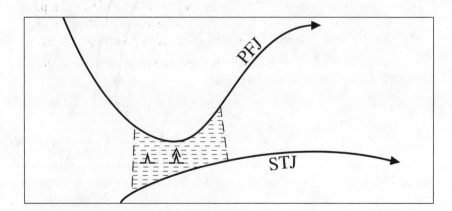

Figure 17-5. *Wind shear areas (horizontal and vertical)*

Aviation Weather Services *Explained*

Vertical shear cannot be easily obtained from the jet stream charts but it might be worthwhile to check out the change in wind speed, in the vertical, over a suspect area by using the forecast winds aloft. CAT is not easy to forecast! This is mainly because it is erratic in time and space (vertically and horizontally). A common dimension of turbulence associated with the jet stream is: an area 100 to 300 miles in length, elongated in the direction of the wind, 50 to 100 miles in length, and with a vertical extent of some 5,000 feet. These may persist for half an hour, or as long as one day.

This is a good use for the upper-air data provided at many meteorology websites such as the University of Wyoming, etc. (*see* web addresses in Appendix E, Page 186).

Horizontal Shear kts/150 nm	Vertical Shear kt/1,000 ft	Turbulence Intensity
20 - 40	5 - 6	MDT
> 40	≥ 6	SVR

Table 17-1. *Critical horizontal and vertical shears for significant CAT*

Turbulence Avoidance Tips

Nevertheless, there are several rules that can help the pilot tell where turbulence is most likely to occur. These tips come from the AC 00-30B:

- A point to remember is that the strength of jet stream CAT can be acerbated where a strong jet stream crosses mountainous terrain; especially where terrain height drops off abruptly downwind of the jet stream. The strongest jet stream winds, and related turbulence, have been observed over eastern China, and the western Pacific where the polar front jet emerges out from over the mountainous mass of continental Asia.

- Curving jet streams will be more likely to have turbulent edges, especially when they are curving around a deep trough.

- If you do encounter CAT with a direct headwind or tailwind, consider a change in altitude rather then a change in heading…Why? Because the turbulent areas are long and shallow.

- CAT with a crosswind? You should be out of the turbulence quickly, because CAT areas are narrow.

- CAT due to penetration across a tropopause boundary (the "upper front")—watch the OAT. The coldest temperature will be upon penetration of the tropopause. The worse turbulence will be in the temperature-change zone on the stratosphere side of the tropopause.

OAT: Outside air temperature

- When crossing a jet stream: if the temperature increases, *climb*. If the temperature starts to drop, *descend*.

Jet Stream Clouds

Cirrus-form clouds (Cirrostratus, cirrocumulus) may be associated with the jet. Often the satellite imagery will show "transverse" rolls of cirrus type clouds, which with the right wavelength and amplitude prove to be quite turbulent. A transverse roll is made up of waves of turbulent air oriented perpendicular to the jet stream and exhibiting strong vertical shear. These seem to occur most frequently when the strongest winds of the jet stream are greater then 110 knots.

Two clues for locating the jet stream from satellite imagery:

1. If there is strong-to-severe thunderstorm activity, the tops of these storms can easily punch through the tropopause and the anvils are then stretched out along the zone of maximum winds.

2. The subtropical jet stream usually has an extensive deck of cirrostratus lying along the south (low-latitude) side of its strongest winds.

Jet Stream Chart Examination

"Jet stream charts" can be found on AC 00-45E Pages 8-11 and 8-12 (the 300 and 250-mb constant pressure charts). Unfortunately they did not include a 200-mb chart, but we can glean quite a bit from these two charts.

First, examine the low-pressure cell over west central Texas, which is in evidence on all of the upper-air charts. From 500 mb upward, the low is vertical, as are all the other features on these charts. Over the eastern Pacific, we find a rather strong ridge of high pressure (heights) with the ridge line along the 145° West longitude line over Alaska to 125° West longitude (where winds change from being southwesterly to northwesterly).

A large trough of low pressure emanates from the low-pressure cell at 65° North and 98° West and extends southward into Idaho, Wyoming and then southward into western Kansas and Texas. The eastern one-third of the U.S. is dominated by southwesterly winds; the western limb of another large ridge of high-pressure (heights).

We are primarily concerned with the 300 and 250 mb charts, and it appears that we have one continuous jet stream looping over the top of the western ridge, then plunging down the western coast of the U.S. and into Arizona and Mexico. At the 300-mb level, the band of strongest winds (110 knots) of the jet is located in northwestern Mexico. This band, the jet streak, continues to the southeast before it curves eastward around the bottom of the trough of low pressure (heights), then northeastward over the Gulf of Mexico.

Look carefully at the 300-mb chart and notice that the jet stream's maximum winds increase once again to 110, then 130 knots with a small area of 150-knot winds over Nova Scotia. Another interesting feature of this jet stream is the movement of the jet streak through the slower-moving air around it and ahead of it. Thus, the jet has two types of horizontal motion:

• the movement of the ridges and troughs themselves (west to east) which is relatively slow, and

• the movement of the faster-moving areas of fast-moving air.

These complex motions can cause turbulence as well as enhance pressure rises and falls at the Earth's surface!

Why does the jet stream's winds seem to weaken and then strengthen? The main factor at work here is the horizontal temperature contrast across the front from north to south. Look at the temperatures over Canada north of the jet stream where the 130 knot winds are found: east of Hudson Bay we see temps ranging from -51°C to -56°C. South of the jet streak we find -41°C and -44°C, a difference of 10 to 12 degrees. This horizontal temperature contrast is the main mechanism behind most wind systems: the greater the contrast, the stronger the winds. (Further complicating factors are high terrain and the strength of the associated surface frontal system(s).) A quick look at the jet lying along the western coast of the U.S. will show a 5–6 degree temperature difference across the jet stream.

The greater the temperature contrast across a frontal area (horizontally), the stronger the winds.

The 250-mb chart (34,000' MSL) exhibits the same pattern as its lower relative but appears to be much stronger with a much longer slender area of 110+ knots from Seattle, WA. The wind field over the top of the eastern ridge is also stronger with a much larger area of 130–150 knot winds. Yet the temperature gradient doesn't appear to be as strong as the gradient at the 300-mb level. Why the weaker thermal gradient?

One reason is the fact that if we were to fly across the jet at 34,000 feet, we would notice a temperature drop as we cross the "upper front" which is nothing more then the upper air location of the frontal surface feature. Furthermore, we would now be in the stratosphere over Canada where the temperature increases upwards from the tropopause. Some of the stronger temperature gradient is nullified by this stratospheric temperature inversion.

As mentioned earlier, CAT can also occur many other places besides the jet stream. It is beyond the scope of this book to cover every aspect of MDT OR GTR TURBC. But I certainly encourage you to learn as much as you can about this fascinating and potentially dangerous subject. Several sources of further information are listed in *Suggested Reading* on Page 197.

One final note about encountering high-altitude CAT and the jet stream: Give a timely, accurate PIREP, and monitor the traffic for other PIREPs.

Chapter 18: *North American Weather Services*
North of 48° Latitude

The AC 00-45E does not devote much space or information to our largest state, Alaska, and the Alaskan Aviation Weather Unit (AAWU). And since it is an FAA publication it would not discuss the excellent weather facilities/messages prepared and disseminated by NavCanada. Therefore this chapter will discuss in some detail these two regions and their suite of data and forecasts, because these services are beneficial for pilots who fly in and near these areas.

Alaskan Aviation Weather Unit (AAWU)

This forecast office offers a fantastic array of data and some excellent and unique graphical forecast charts, along with the usual collection and distribution of TAFs, METARs, FAs, PIREPs, etc. On the AAWU website, a clickable map divided by region gives instant access to weather data and forecasts. You can also click through to the NWS Doppler radar webpage from here.

Hourly Weather Depiction Chart

This special chart is prepared at 10 minutes past the hour. Individual station plots, color coded for IFR (red), MVFR (blue) and VFR (black), look very similar to the station data plot found on AC 00-45E Page 5-5 (*see* Figure 18-1). These plots include temperature/dew point, wind direction and force, visibility, ceiling, weather, and station four-letter ID. The wind direction and force is conventionally displayed as shown on AC 00-45E Page 5-5. The station circle is darkened in to describe total sky cover (*see* AC 00-45E Page 5-7).

AC 00-45E Reading Assignment
Section 1
Page 1-3

There's also a link on the NWS Alaska Regional Headquarters website* that introduces Alaska's Public Broadcasting System (PBS) television show, "Alaska Weather," another good weather information source for the entire state.
*http://www.alaska.net/~nwsar/

See a full-color example of this chart in Appendix C, Page 174.

Alaska
http://www.alaska.net/~aawu/ (Alaska Aviation Weather Unit)

http://www-das.uwyo.edu/surface/sfclist.html (University of Wyoming Dept. of Atmospheric Sciences)

http://www.alaska.net/~aawu/aktaf.html (AAWU's Alaskan TAFs)

Canada
http://www.cmc.ec.gc.ca/cmc/gfa/index.html (Graphical Area Forecast)

http://canfltbrf.ec.gc.ca/navcan/flight/indexe.htm *or*
http://canfltbrf.ec.gc.ca/navcan/flight/weather3/index_3E.htm
    (NavCanada aviation weather and flight planning website)

http://www.weatheroffice.com/ (Environment Canada's weather website)

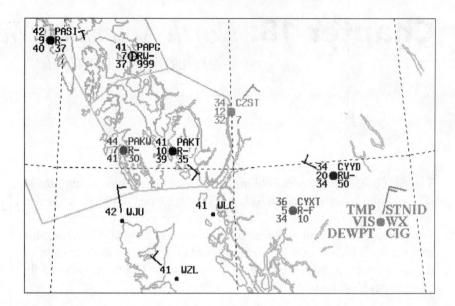

Figure 18-1. *Example of a station data plot*

 See full-color Appendix C, Page 175.

See examples on Page 129, in Figure 18-4 (at the end of this chapter):
• upper-air chart, top of figure
• surface analysis chart, bottom of figure

"Upper-air chart" is another name for the constant pressure chart.

Graphical Area Forecast

This chart is based on the current textual FA, and is the U.S. version of the new Canadian "graphical area forecast." Figure 18-2 (at right) is an example of the four-panel version, and full-color versions of two of these have been included in the color appendix at the back of the book.

These forecast panels closely resemble two of the panels of the 12- and 24-Hour Significant Weather Prog charts with two notable exceptions:

• The Alaskan products are issued in color and include icing forecasts, which are *not* part of the 12- and 24-Hour Sig Wx progs used in the lower 48.

• These charts are not amended, so the pilot must also check the *latest text FA* to see if there have been any changes.

Constant Pressure Charts

Another somewhat unusual product is the set of upper-air charts available from AAWU. These charts are analyzed with contours of height just like the charts in the lower forty-eight. But there are no temperatures or moisture content values on the chart—only wind barbs showing the strength of the wind field at that level. *See* the example in Figure 18-4 on Page 129—this is a forecast winds upper-air chart for the 6,000-foot level.

Surface Analysis

AAWU also offers the Alaskan surface analysis chart which is slightly different then the ones most of us are accustomed to. Take a look at the excerpted example of this chart on Page 129, just underneath the upper-air chart example: Alaska's version of the surface chart includes the four-letter station IDs. These two chart examples are from the same day, so you can see that the upper-air chart's forecast winds are an upper-air-flow pattern that resembles the surface pressure isobar pattern. Remember that aloft, winds tend to parallel any height contours (*see* any constant pressure chart in AC 00-45E or this book); whereas the near surface levels

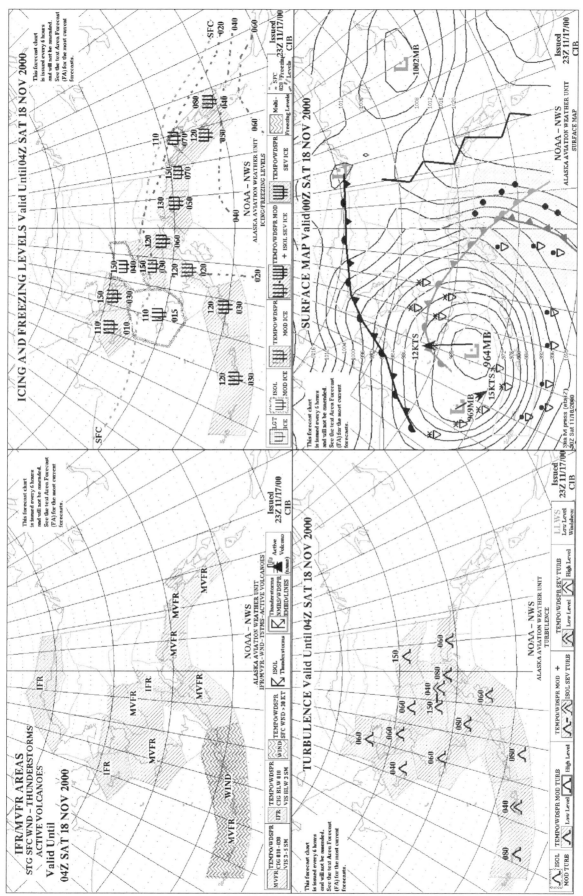

Figure 18-2. *Four-panel graphical area forecast charts from AAWU website*

(3,000', 5,000') winds will tend to flow parallel to the isobars on the surface chart. Therefore, examining the surface chart can give you a pretty good idea of the winds aloft (usually somewhat stronger), over your area of interest.

Alaskan METARs and TAFs

Besides the clickable map at the AAWU home page, you can also get hourly METARs and TAFs for Alaska from the University of Wyoming's website (*see* address at bottom of Page 119). Here, you can obtain decoded METARs or the standard METAR format. Also, the AAWU website links to other internet places for METARs.

Alaskan TAFs are grouped by forecast regions: Anchorage (PANC), Fairbanks (PAFA), and Juneau (PAJN). These are easily obtained from the AAWU TAF webpage (address at the bottom of Page 119). A complete list of Alaskan METAR/TAF stations is given in Appendix B on Page 159.

Volcanic Ash Advisory Centers (VAAC)

This service at Anchorage is one of nine such offices in the world. You can get information that has been collected from the other eight offices on volcanic ash (assuming a volcano is active). AC 00-45E Page 13-2 has a sample of one of the VAAC's messages from the Anchorage office.

Canadian Weather Services

On April 20, 2000, the NavCanada website introduced the world's first graphical area forecast (GFA), their charted version of the textual weather forecasts.

There are four main forecast centers (Kelowna, Edmonton, Toronto, and Gander) that prepare regional GFA products to be sent to Montreal, where the regional GFAs are integrated into a comprehensive Canada GFA. What our friends to the north have essentially done, is do away with their previous low-level significant weather prognostic chart (SFC–24,000') as well as create a new and easy-to-use, comprehensive forecast product for the pilot. This new product incorporates AIRMETs and SIGMETs into the graphical forecast. Each GFA consists of a suite of six charts: two charts for the start of the forecast period, two charts for the 6 hours following, and two charts for 12 hours total.

To follow along in this description of a GFA, go to the color chart on Page 176 in Appendix C. This chart depicts clouds and weather; others depict icing, turbulence, and freezing levels. The last forecast chart will also include an IFR outlook for an additional 12-hour block of time. GFAs are issued every 6 hours at 30 minutes prior to the start of the forecast period, and amendments will be issued as required.

At first glance this new product seems complex with different colors and types of lines all over the chart. But if you focus on one color or line pattern at a time, interpreting the chart is much easier. The heavy dark line is the boundary of the GFA superimposed on the lighter lines that show the provinces in that forecast area. Cloud cover is delineated by scal-

Also, on AC 00-45E Page 4-16 there is a map showing the location of Alaska observation stations that have a TAF.

See this page of their website for details about the graphical area forecast—

http://canfltbrf.ec.gc.ca/navcan/ flight/gfa/gfa.htm

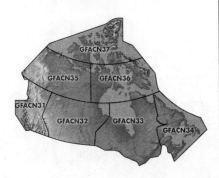

loped lines; cloud type and amount are shown along with bases and tops (as in Figure 18-3). There is a link under "Supporting Information" that goes to a page with an explanation of all this chart's symbols and coding.

Another helpful feature: isobars are drawn for every 4 mb, making it easy to determine the approximate wind direction over an area. Winds are included if they are expected to be over 20 knots; on the color chart example at the top, gusts to 30 are forecast ("G30" next to the wind flag).

These GFA charts show you every bit of weather information that you would need! (The question is, when will the U.S. weather services get in step with Canada?)

Figure 18-3. *GFA symbols for cloud type, amount, bases and tops.*

Canadian METARs and TAFs

The best website for finding these reports fast is the NavCanada one — go to the address shown at the bottom of Page 119 and use the menu at the left-hand side of your screen. Under "Reports and Forecasts" and then METARs/TAFs, you can select the province or region you want, then either type-in the four-letter ID of the airport(s) you want, or just check the box(es) in the airport list that comes up for that region (up to six at a time). For help finding the airport ID you need a TAF for, see the list of Canadian station IDs in the tables at the end of this chapter.

These tables start on Page 124.

One nice thing about the Canadian METARs is that they identify cloud types — *all* cloud types:

```
CYXX 182300Z 21005KT 253M FEW050 BKN120
   OVC250 19/08 A3017 RMK CU1AC5CA2 HZ SLP 218
```

CU1: Cumulus clouds cover 1/8 of the sky

AC5: Altocumulus clouds cover 5/8 of the sky; total sky cover is 6/8

CA2: Cirrus covers 2/8 of sky; total sky cover is 8/8 OVC

The Canadian TAF is just like the U.S. version; however, take a look at this one from an automated station, Mackenzie (CYZY):

```
TAF CYZY 181935Z 182008 22010KT P6SM SCT050
   SCT100 RMK FCST BASED ON AUTO OBS NXT FCST
   BY 02Z
```

What is the 6-digit group "182008" for? *"Is this the valid date/time?"* Yes, this forecast is valid from 2000Z on the 18th to 0800Z on 19th. The previous group gives the date/actual time of issuance.

See Chapter 19, Page 131, for a list of international TAF terminology and forecast groups that differ from NWS usage.

Canadian Forecast Winds

Some of the stations in the tables on the following pages have "(W)" after the name: this indicates that forecast winds and temperatures (FDs) are available at these locations. A significant number of the FDs issued by NavCanada are for points designated by latitude and longitude, while others are for specific geographic locations (i.e., AWOS sites). Those points iden-

The easiest way to get FDs from the NavCanada website is to use their "Route Forecast" section (*see* the menu at left when you're on their main webpage for flight planning). Choose a route in your area of flight, then choose low or high-level FDs among the forecast links provided for the route.

tified by latitude and longitude in FD messages use the three-letter IDs that start with "W." Below is an example of an FD message:

```
FDCN01
FCST BASED ON 191200 DATA VALID 191800 FOR
  USE 17-21
          3000    6000      9000      12000      18000
  VBI   1615    1914+08   2507+04   3010+00   3117-13
WCK 74N 135W
          0908    0606-08   9900-11   9900-16   3106-27
```

Note: Canadian winds and temperatures aloft forecasts are identical to ours, and the winds at and above 24,000 feet MSL are prepared by the U.S. National Weather Service.

Canadian Radiosonde

If you are into interpreting the upper-air data on a Skew-T Log P format, you can easily access the individual radiosonde sites in the U.S., Canada, Mexico, and Central America from the University of Wyoming website:

http://www-das.uwo.edu/upperair/sounding

If you wish to learn more about radiosondes and Skew-T's, visit the tutorial at the Unisys website:

http://weather.unisys.com/upper_ait/skew/index.html or,

http://www.nemas.net/edu/

Flying in Canada

There are some differences between the lower 48 and our northern friends when it comes to flight:

1. There are user fees up north!

2. There are no TWEB routes or TWEB messages.

3. No WSTs, CWAs or MIS's.

4. Canada does not use "low IFR" as we do in our FAs.

5. Free access to AWBS and AWIS briefing services are available at 1-800-INFO-FSS (NavCanada).

Canadian Weather Stations and Radar Units

Much of Canada is sparsely populated and therefore automatic weather stations are widely used. Table 18-1 is not intended to furnish the names and locations of every weather station in Canada, but rather, those weather observation sites that also prepare TAFs for their location. Also, a list of the radar units across the country is given in Table 18-2. *See* the "Environment Canada" website (weatheroffice.com) for looped and composite radar images, updated frequently.

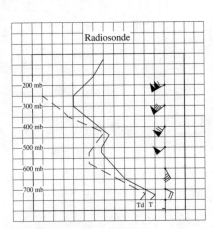

Rough example of a Skew-T chart.

Table 18-1. *Canadian weather observation sites that also prepare TAFs (continued through the next two pages).*

BRITISH COLUMBIA (B.C.)
Southwestern Canada

Name	ID	Lat./Long. N W	Name	ID	Lat./Long. N W
ABBOTSFORD	CYXX	49°00/122°00	PORT HARDY (W)	CYZT	50°41/127°22
CAMPBELL R.	CYBL	49°57/125°16	PRINCE GEORGE (W)	CYXS	53°53/122°41
CASTLEGAR	CYCG	49°19/117°40	PRINCE RUPERT	CYPR	54°18/130°26
COMOX	CYQQ	49°40/125°00	QUESNEL	CYQZ	53°02/122°31
CRANBROOK (W)	CYXC	39°27/115°47	SANDSPIT (W)	CYZP	53°15/131°49
FT. NELSON (W)	CYYE	58°50/122°35	SMITHERS (W)	CYYD	54°49/127°11
FT. ST JOHN (W)	CYXJ	56°14/120°44	TERRACE	CYXT	54°28/128°35
KAMLOOPS (W)	CYKA	50°42/120°127	TOFINO AIRPORT	CYAZ	49°05/125°46
KELOWNA	CYLW	49°58/119°23	VANCOUVER INT'L (W)	CYVR	49°11/123°10
MACKENZIE	CYZY	55°18/123°08	VICTORIA	CYYJ	48°39/123°26
NANAIMO	CYCD	49°03/123°52	WILLIAMS LAKE	CYWL	52°11/122°03

Western Canada
This area includes the following provinces/territories: Yukon Territory (YT), Northwest Territory (NWT), Nunavut (NUN), and Alberta (Alb).

Name	ID	Lat./Long. N W	Name	ID	Lat./Long. N W
ARVIAT Nun	CYEK	61°06/094°04	KUGLUKTUK (W) NUN	CYCO	67°49/115°08
BAKER LK.(W) NWT	CYBK	64°18/096°05	LETHBRIDGE Alb	CYQL	49°38/112°48
BROUGHTON IS. Nun	CYVM	67°33/064°02	LLOYDMINSTER (W) Alb	CYLL	53°19/110°04
BURWASH (W) YT	CYDB	61°22/139°02	LUPIN NUN	CYWO	65°46/111°15
CALGARY (W) Alb	CYYC	51°07/114°01	MAYO (W) YT	CYMA	63°37/135°52
CAMBRIDGE (W) NWT	CYCB	69°08/105°04	MEDICINE HAT Alb	CYXH	50°01/110°43
CAPE DORSET (W) NWT	CYTE	64°13/076°32	NANISIVIK NUN	CYSR	72°59/084°38
CLYDE NWT	CYCY	70°29/068°31	NORMAL WELLS (W) NWT	CYVQ	65°17/126°48
COLD LK.(W) Alb	CYOD	52°25/110°17	OLD CROW (W) YT	CYOC	67°34/139°49
CORAL HARBOR (W) NWT	CYZS	64°12/083°22	PAULATUK NWT	CYPC	69°21/124°02
DAWSON YT	CYDA	64°03/139°08	PEACE R. Alb	CYPE	56°14/117°26
EDMONTON (W) Alb	CYEG	53°18/113°35	PELLY BAY NUN	CYBB	68°32/089°49
EDMONTON MUNI Alb	CYXD	53°34/113°31	POND INLET NUN	CYIO	72°42/077°58
" " NAMAO Alb	CYED	53°40/113°28	RANKIN INLET (W) NUN	CYRT	62°49/092°07
FARO YT	CZFA	62°12/133°22	RED DEER Alb	CYQF	52°11/113°54
FT. MCMURRAY (W) Alb	CYMM	56°39/111°13	REPULSE BAY NUN	CYUT	66°32/086°15
FT. SIMPSON (W) NWT	CYFS	61°45/121°14	RESOLUTE (W) NUN	CYRB	74°43/095°59
FT. SMITH (W) NWT	CYSM	60°01/111°57	SACHS HARBOR (W) NWT	CYSY	72°00/125°17
GJOA HAVEN NUN	CYHK	68°38/095°51	SLAVE LK.(W) Alb	CYZH	55°18/114°47
GRAND PRAIRE Alb	CYQU	55°11/118°53	SPENCE BAY (W) NUN	CYYH	69°53/093°35
HALL BEACH (W) NWT	CYUX	68°47/081°15	TESTLIN YT	CYZW	60°10/132°44
HAY R. NWT	CYHY	60°50/115°47	TUKTOYAKTUK NWT	CYUB	69°27/133°01
HIGH LEVEL (W) Alb	CYOJ	58°37/117°10	WATSON LK.(W) YT	CYQH	60°07/128°49
HOLMAN AIRPORT NUN	CYHI	70°46/117°48	WHITEHORSE (W) YT	CYXY	60°43/135°04
INUVIK (W) NWT	CYEV	68°18/133°29	YELLOWKNIFE (W) NWT	CYZF	62°28/114°27
IQALUIT (W) NUN	CYFB	64°45/068°33			

Central Canada
Provinces of Saskatchewan (Sas) and Manitoba (Man)

Name	ID	Lat./Long.	Name	ID	Lat./Long.
BRANDON (W) Sas	CYBR	49°55/099°57	PORTAGE SOUTHPORT (W) Man	CYPG	49°54/098°16
CHURCHILL (W) Sas	CYYQ	58°44/094°04	PRINCE ALBERT Sas	CYPA	53°13/105°41
DAUPHIN Man	CYDN	51°06/100°03	REGINA (W) Sas	CYQR	52°26/104°40
GILLAM Man	CYGX	56°21/094°42	SASKATOON(W) Sas	CYXE	52°10/106°41
ISLAND LK.	CYIV	53°47/094°25	STONY RAPIDS Sas	CYSF	59°15/105°50
LA RONGE (W) Sas	CYVC	55°09/105°16	SWIFT CURRENT Sas	CYYN	50°17/107°41
LYNN LK (W) Man	CYYL	56°51/101°05	THE PAS (W) Man	CYQD	53°58/101°06
MOOSE JAW Sas	CYMJ	50°20/105°33	THOMPSON Man	CYTH	55°48/097°51
N. BATTLEFORD Sas	CYQW	52°46/108°15	WINNIPEG (W) Man	CYWG	49°54/097°14
NORWAY HOUSE Man	CYNE	54°00/097°50	YORKTON Sas	CYQV	51°13/102°28

Eastern Canada

This section will include Ontario, Quebec and the Atlantic ("Maritime") provinces.

Ontario

Name	ID	Lat./Long. N W	Name	ID	Lat./Long.
ARMSTRONG (W)	CYYW	50°18/089°02	PICKLE LK.	CYPL	51°27/090°12
BIG TROUT LK. (W)	CYTL	53°50/089°52	RED LK. (W)	CYRL	51°04/093°48
CHAPLEAU	CYLD	47°49/083°21	SARNIA	CYZR	43°00/082°19
DRYDEN	CYHD	49°50/092°45	SAULT STE MARIE (W)	CYAM	46°29/084°30
EARLTON	CYXR	47°42/079°51	SIOUX LOOKOUT	CYXL	50°07/091°54
ELLIOT LK.	CYEL	46°21/083°34	ST. CATHERINES	CYSN	43°12/079°10
GORE BAY	CYZE	45°53/082°34	SUDBURY	CYSB	46°37/080°48
HAMILTON	CYHM	43°10/079°56	TERRACE	CYTJ	48°49/086°06
KAPUSKASING (W)	CYYU	49°25/092°28	THUNDER BAY (W)	CYQT	48°22/089°19
KENORA	CYQK	49°47/094°22	TIMMINS	CYTS	48°34/081°22
KINGSTON	CYGK	44°13/076°36	TORONTO BUTTONVILLE	CYKZ	43°52/079°22
LONDON	CYXU	43°02/081°09	TORONTO ISLAND	CYTZ	43°38/079°24
MOOSONEE (W)	CYMO	51°16/080°39	TORONTO PEARSON(W)	CYYZ	43°40/079°38
MUSKOKA	CYQA	44°58/079°18	TRENTON	CYTR	44°07/077°32
NORTH BAY (W)	CYYB	46°21/079°26	WATERLOO WELLINGTON	CYKF	43°28/080°23
OTTOWA	CYOW	45°19/075°40	WAWA	CYXZ	47°58/084°47
PETAWAWA	CYWA	45°57/077°19	WIARTON (W)	CYVV	44°45/081°06
PETERBOROUGH	CYPQ	44°140/078°22	WINDSOR (W)	CYQG	42°16/082°58

Table 18-1. *Canadian weather observation sites that also prepare TAFs (Eastern Canada, continued).*

Quebec

Name	ID	Lat./Long. N W	Name	ID	Lat./Long. N W
BAGOTVILLE	CYBG	48°20/071°00	MONTREAL (W) DORVAL	CYUL	45°28/073°45
BAIE-COMEAU	CYBC	49°08/068°12	MONTREAL MIRABEL	CYMX	45°41/074°02
BLANC-SABLON	CYBX	51°27/057°11	NATASHOUAN (W)	CYNA	50°11/061°49
CHIBOUGAMAU (W)	CYMT	49°46/074°32	PUVIRNITUO	CYPX	60°03/077°17
GASPE (W)	CYGP	48°50/064°29	QUAQTAQ	CHYA	61°03/069°38
GATINEAU	CYND	45°45/075°50	QUEBEC (W)	CYQB	46°48/071°23
HAVRE ST PIERRE (W)	CYGV	50°17/063°37	ROBERVAL	CYRJ	48°32/072°15
ILES LA MADELEINE (W)	CYGR	47°30/062°45	ROUYN	CYUY	48°22/079°03
INUKJUAK (W)	CYPH	58°16/078°05	SCHEFFERVILLE (W)	CYKL	54°48/066°48
IVUJIVIK	CYIK	62°17/077°52	SEPT-ILES (W)	CYZV	50°12/066°23
KUUJJUAQ (W)	CYVP	58°06/068°25	SHERBROOKE (W)	CYSC	45°24/071°53
LA GRANDE IV (W)	CYAH	53°45/073°40	ST-HUBERT	CYHU	45°31/073°25
LA GRANDE RIVIERE	CYGL	55°55/077°30	VAL D'0R (W)	CYVO	48°04/077°47
MONT JOL (W)	CYYY	48°36/068°13	VALCARTIER (W)	CYOY	46°56/071°28
			WASKAHGANISH	CYKQ	51°29/078°45

Atlantic (Maritime) Provinces

New Bruinswick (NB), Nova Scotia (NS), Prince Edward Island (PEI) and Newfoundland (NFL).

Name	ID	Lat./Long. N W	Name	ID	Lat./Long. N W
BATHHURST NB	CZBF	47°38/65°45	NAIN NFL	CYDP	56°33/061°41
CARTWRIGHT NB	CYCA	53°36/057°00	ROWAN GORILLA	CWXO	43°53/060°33
CHARLO NB	CYCL	47°59/066°20	SABLE ISLAND NS	CYSA	43°56/060°01
CHARLOTTETOWN PEI	CYYG	46°17/068°08	SAINT JOHN NB	CYSJ	43°20/65°53
CHURCHILL FALLS NFL	CZUM	53°33/064°06	SHEARWATER NS	CYAW	44°38/060°30
DEER LAKE NFL	CYDF	49°13/057°24	ST. ANTHONY NFL	CYAY	47°37/056°05
FREDERICTON (W) NB	CYFC	45°52/066°32	ST. JOHN'S NFL	CYYT	47°37/052°44
GAGETOWN NB	CYCX	45°50/066°26	ST. LEONARD NB	CYSL	47°09/067°50
GANDER (W) NFL	CYQX	48°57/054°34	ST. PIERRE IS.	LFVP	46°46/56°10
GOOSE BAY (W) NFL	CYYR	53°19/060°25	STEPHENVILLE NB	CYJT	48°33/058°35
GREENWOOD NS	CYZX	44°59/064°55	SYDNEY NS	CYQY	46°09/060°11
HALIFAX (W) NS	CYHZ	44°53/063°30	WABUSH LK.(W) NFL	CYWK	52°56/066°52
MARY'S HARBOUR NFL	CYMH	52°18/055°51	YARMOUTH (W)	CYQI	43°50/066°06
MIRAMICHI NB	CYCH	47°00/065°27			
MONCTON	CYQM	46°07/064°41			

Continued

Canadian Weather Radar Units

Provinces: British Columbia (BC), Alberta (ALB), Saskatchewan (SASK), Manitoba (MAN), Ontario (ONT), Quebec (QUE), Newfoundland (NFL), New Bruinswick (NB) and Nova Scotia (NS).

Prov.	Site	ID	Prov.	Site	ID
BC	Aldershot	WUJ	ONT	Franklin	WKR
ALB	Carvel	WHK	ONT	King	WKR
ALB	Spirit R.	WWW	ONT	Montreal R.	WGJ
ALB	Vulcan	WUN	ONT	Upsala	WIM
SASK	Jimmy Lake	WYN	QUE	Lac Cas	WMB
SASK	Bethune	XBE	QUE	McGill	WMN
SASK	Broadview	WIK	QUE	Villeroy	WVY
SASK	Radisson	XBA	NB	Mechanic Settlement	WMK
MAN	Vivian	WVJ	NS	Halifax	YHZ
MAN	Woodlands	XWL	NFL	Goose Bay	WVA
ONT	Britt	WBI	NFL	Holyrood	WTP
ONT	Exeter	WSO			

Table 18-2. *Some Canadian weather radar sites*

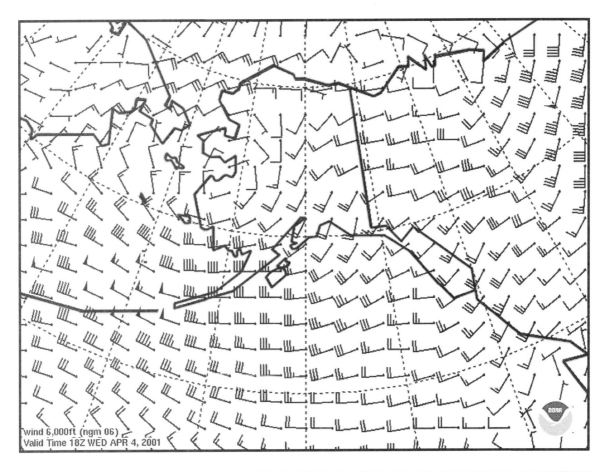

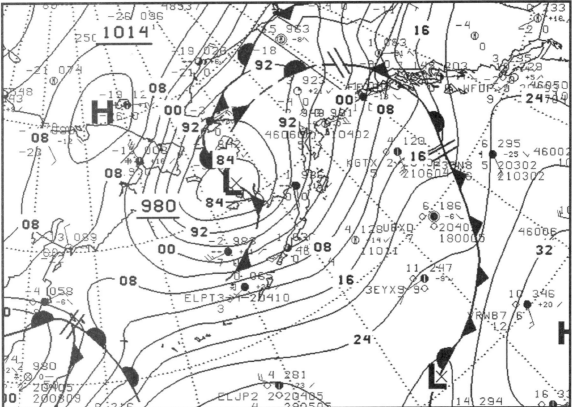

Figure 18-4. *Upper-air and surface analysis charts from AAWU, for 4/4/2001.*

Chapter 19: *Aviation Weather Services of Mexico*

South of the Border

Just about everything that the pilot needs for planning a flight into Mexico or Central America, can be found at the *Landings* website. For those people who do not have access to the internet and the World Wide Web, your local Flight Service briefer can furnish you with all the weather info you will require. But there are other sources beside *Landings* for data such as METARs and TAFs—the best of the lot is the NWS webpage (address at bottom of page).

Weather Radar in Mexico

At www.skywarn-texas.org/doppler.htm, users can click on the individual radar sites to receive reports. But be careful to check the date and time, as these messages may be late. They are supposed to be updated hourly, so check them twice to detect any change in echo pattern, intensity, and movement.

International TAFs, Terminology and Forecast Groups

This section describes some of the terminology and code groups used in international TAFs that are not being used in NWS TAF products. This material has been extracted from the NWS Ops Manual, ("Aviation Terminal Forecasts D-31"), and the *World Meteorological Organization Code Book*.

1. CAVOK (KAV-OH-KAY). Essentially this says that the term can be used when the sky is clear, the visibility is unlimited and there is no forecast for significant weather.
   a. No clouds below 1,500 meters (5,000') AGL, or below the highest minimum sector altitude, whichever is greater, and no thunderstorms are in the area.
   b. Visibility is more than 6 statute miles (10 km).
   c. There is no forecast for significant weather to occur (fog, precipitation).
2. NSC. No significant clouds indicates that no clouds are forecast below 5,000 feet or below the highest minimum sector altitude, whichever is greater, and no cumulonimbus at any height is expected

Continued

NWS webpage: Here you can search by ICAO identifier, state, or country; choose Mexico under *country*, select a city/airport, and then the individual station reports for METARs and TAFs will come up onscreen.

http://www.landings.com (Landings website)

http://www.nws.noaa.gov/oso/siteloc.shtml (Meteorological Station Information Lookup)

NSW: No significant weather

See the example TAF on
AC 00-45E Pages 4-7 and 4-8.

to occur. This would be used where the use of CAVOK or SKC (Sky Clear) would not be applicable.

3. NSW. The international community only uses NSW in the BECMG and/or FM groups, and as in U.S. TAFs, will not use NSW in the initial time period.

4. PROB40 and PROB30. These are to be used for the probability of thunderstorms or other precipitation vents. Used by the WMO and NWS: The WMO places PROB immediately before the TEMPO group (i.e. PROB40 TEMPO 1214); NWS use of PROB40 and PROB30 is different in that they are placed after the TEMPO or BECMG group.

5. Use of BECMG. This transitional phrase is normally for a period from 2–4 hours in WMO use.

6. Cloud Heights. WMO forecast and observed cloud-height and vertical-visibility values are in hundreds of feet for all levels. Cloud heights between 5,000 and 10,000 feet are to the nearest 500 feet. Above 10,000 feet heights are reported or forecast to the nearest thousand feet. (NWS uses hundreds of feet for heights near the surface upwards to and including 5,000 feet.)

7. Visibility. WMO uses meters for reporting visibilities (NWS uses miles). In the U.S., the military, particularly the USAF, follows the WMO practice.

8. Minimum Altimeter/Pressure. The expected minimum altimeter (QNH, inches of mercury) or pressure (hectopascals) until the next forecast change group.

9. Wind Shear. Forecast of non-convective low-level winds up to 2,000 feet AGL, entered after forecast minimum altimeter; gives the height of the wind shear, and wind direction and speed at that height:

WS020/24045KT Low level wind shear at 2,000 feet, wind is 240 degrees at 45 knots.

10. Temperatures (Max/Min). There are times the anticipated maximum and minimum temperatures may be of operational significance. These forecast values are used with the BECMG group as illustrated below:

BECMG 0304 20008KT 9999 BKN080 QNH3001INS T17/23 T07/11

Maximum temperature is 17°C, expected to occur at 2300 UTC. Minimum temperature of 7°C is expected to occur at 1100 UTC.

Mexico and Western Caribbean Weather Stations

See Figure 19-1 for METAR/TAF locations in Mexico and parts of the Caribbean (also includes a couple of stations in Central America).

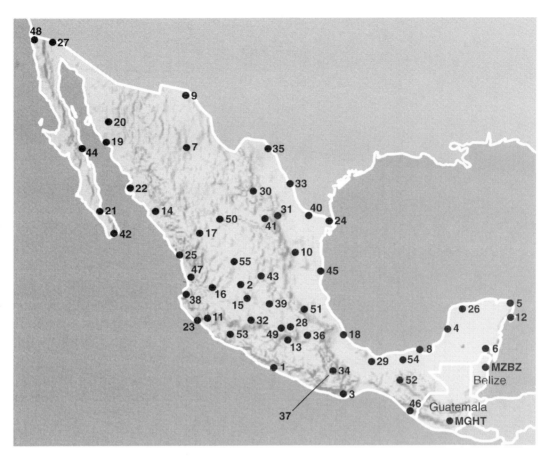

MEXICO METAR & TAF STATIONS

Name	ICAO	Name	ICAO	Name	ICAO
1 Acapulco	MMAA	20 Hermosillo	MMHO	38 Puerto Vallarta	MMPR
2 Aguascalientes	MMAS	21 La Paz	MMLP	39 Queretaro	MMQT
3 Bahias De Huatulco	MMBT	22 Las Mochis Airport	MMLM	40 Reynosa	MMRX
4 Campeche	MMCP	23 Manzanillo	MMZO	41 Saltillo	MMIO
5 Cancun Int'l Airport	MMUN	24 Matamoros	MMMA	42 San Jose Del Cabo**	MMSD
6 Chetumal	MMCM	25 Mazatlan	MMMZ	43 San Luis Potosi	MMSP
7 Chihuahua Int'l Airport	MMCU	26 Merida	MMMD	44 Santa Rosalia	MMCN
8 Ciudad Del Carmen	MMCE	27 Mexicali Int'l Airport	MMML	45 Tampico	MMTM
9 Ciudad Juarez	MMCS	28 Mexico City	MMMX	46 Tapachula	MMTP
10 Ciudad Victoria	MMCV	29 Minatitlan	MMMT	47 Tepic	MMEP
11 Colima	MMIA	30 Monclova	MMMV	48 Tijuana Int'l Airport	MMTJ
12 Cozumel	MMCZ	31 Monterrey	MMMY	49 Toluca/Jose Maria	MMTO
13 Cuernavaca	MMCB	32 Morelia	MMMM	50 Torreon	MMTC
14 Culiacan	MMCL	33 Nuevo Laredo	MMNL	51 Tulancingo	MMTL
15 El Bajio (city of León)	MMLO	34 Oaxaca	MMOX	52 Tuxtla Gutierrez	MMTG
16 Don Miguel	MMGL	35 Piedras Negras	MMPG	53 Uruapan	MMPN
17 Durango Airport	MMDO	36 Puebla, Pue.	MMPB	54 Villahermosa	MMVA
18 Vera Cruz (Gen. Heriberto Jara)	MMVR	37 Puerto Escondido*	MMPS	55 Zacatecas Airport	MMZC
19 Guaymas Int'l Airport	MMGM				

*located in the city of Oaxaca **located in Los Cabos, Baja California

Figure 19-1. *METAR and TAF locations for flying south of the border*

Chapter 20: *Weather Decisions and The Weather Briefing*

Author and aviator Richard L. Taylor once stated that "There are two kinds of VFR pilots: those who *have* flown inadvertently into instrument conditions and those who *probably will*."* After reading the latest Nall report from AOPA, I am inclined to agree. Becoming fluent in weather-flying decision making, then, is essential.

*Richard L. Taylor, *IFR for VFR Pilots* (1997 Aviation Supplies & Academics)

But opening this book and seeing first the section entitled "The Big Picture of Aviation Weather Services," some readers' first reaction might be astonishment: "All this must be checked before a flight?...No way!" Relax Ace! It's true there is a lot of weather information to check, but actually, there's only a few flight scenarios wherein you should have to check every single weather forecast listed.

To Fly or Not to Fly

Chapter 1 discussed a good example of a VFR situation and what weather data a pilot should check before launching a flight with good unrestricted VFR weather. In this concluding chapter, let's take a good look at what is needed for the following flight conditions:

Restricted VFR Ceiling greater then 3,000' but less then 10,000' with visibility between 5–7 miles

Marginal VFR Ceiling 1,000' to 3,000' and/or visibility 3–5 miles

IFR Ceiling less than 1,000'–500' and/or visibility 1–3 miles

This use of the term "restricted VFR" is *not* an official definition, yet it certainly describes VFR conditions that are somewhat "restricted."

What follows is an in-depth look at what weather services are appropriate for scenarios involving restricted VFR, marginal VFR, and IFR. Low IFR (LIFR) is not described simply because this category pretty much puts a damper on the flight, unless the pilot is hauling serum somewhere to halt an epidemic—i.e., in a state of emergency.

As you read through these scenarios, keep in mind that same checklist we've covered in this book, of questions you should always try to answer when dealing with the weather: What is it? Where is it? Why is it? and When is it? If you can't answer them, then find someone who can.

 You should always try to determine:
- *WHERE* is the weather occurring?
- *WHAT* type of weather?
- *WHY* is this weather occurring?
- *WHEN* will the weather be affecting my flight region?

Also be sure to determine *both* what weather information you need to use for planning the flight, as well as that needed to carry the flight to completion. Please understand that a lot of this information would also be used for MVFR and IFR flights as well.

Restricted VFR Flight

You are planning a cross-country flight from Covington, KY (KCVG) to Hot Springs, AR (KHOT) and want to file VFR. According to a check of the METARs for over the flight region, the weather two days (48 hours) before your flight looks pretty good. The present conditions across the proposed flight region are averaging:

```
33010G18 6SM HZ BKN060 BKN250 13/06 A3012 RMK
8/016
```

From the above weather description, you should deduce that the current local-regional situation is stable and not very humid (layer clouds, haze conditions, and a good temp/dewpoint spread). Now let's see what weather products you should use and the sequence in which you would use them.

48-Hour Preview

TWEB routes. A quick examination of the route map on AC 00-45E Page 4-34 tells you there is no TWEB route for your particular flight. But when there is a route on this chart that fits your particular flight, use the TWEB forecast within the 24-hour block of your flight planning.

Current surface analysis chart. Check this chart so you know what the current weather pattern is like over the whole U.S. as well as your region—this allows you to track changes over the next 48 hours. Sketch a map of the current weather, or if you have access to a computer, get a printout of this chart (as well as other info) from The Weather Channel or the National Weather Service websites. No computer access? The Weather Channel gives a look at the surface weather chart every hour as do most TV weather reports. You can also obtain a word-picture from the nearest AFSS.

In this scenario, there is a large area of high pressure dominating the midwestern U.S., with a low-pressure area over the eastern Great Lakes. An eastward-moving cold frontal system extends southward into the east central Atlantic states.

Weather depiction chart. Compiled from METAR reports, this chart gives you a broad-brush, bird's-eye look at the VFR/MVFR and IFR conditions across the U.S. See if you can make an association between the synoptic picture (high- and low-pressure areas, fronts and troughs), and the distribution of MVFR and IFR conditions on the chart.

Constant pressure charts. If you have a pretty good idea of what altitude you will be using for your flight, try to determine the wind pattern at or near your flight level. Let's assume you want to fly about 9,000–10,000 feet MSL: see what the 700 mb constant pressure chart looks like currently.

Why are we bothering to do this when the AFSS briefer will give you the forecast winds aloft? At this stage of flight planning, you need to get that "four-dimensional picture" so you can better understand what is brewing weather-wise *before* you get the briefing.

If you have internet access, go to the NWS website and then click "Weather Maps." These are the NWS "facsimile charts" of which they

---

Note "8/016" in the RMK section: if there is no low cloud layer, "0" will be reported in the code group. But in a "8/6//" code report, for example, a solidus (/) following the low cloud number indicates (for each layer) that the middle and/or high cloud types cannot be determined because of the obscuring layer (6). *See* Appendix A, Page 150.

You can check the latest TWEB routes available on the web, or see the current chart printed on Page 56 of this book.

Hint: Use the Inflight Advisory Plotting Chart (Page 49) for sketching weather maps—make photocopies of this chart for future use.

See Appendix E for internet weather addresses.

synoptic picture: A chart showing the viewer the location and strength of surface pressure systems along with their frontal zones at a given time (a surface analysis chart).

have every size, shape, and description; you're looking for the standard pressure levels—the 850, 700, 500, 300 mb levels, and etc. Get the 700 mb chart, the level appropriate to your flight. (You can even download a plug-in viewer to display and print out the TIFF images.) Also, other web-sites such as "Landings," and the Aviation Weather Center will lead you right back to the facsimile charts since many folks access these NWS products. No computer access? Turn on The Weather Channel and watch their programming for about 30–40 minutes.

Winds aloft forecast. If you cannot find anything about the upper-air flow from The Weather Channel, then call the nearest AFSS and get the latest forecast winds aloft. You won't use them to fly with, but with a verbal description from the briefer and a couple of forecast winds from 10,000 to 18,000 feet MSL, you can easily determine the pattern.

See the Winds Aloft Network chart, AC 00-45E Page 4-36.

Let's say you got the following winds for 9,000 feet for KCVG, KCGI, and KLIT (which is northeast of your Hot Springs, AR destination):

```
KCVG   3412-03
KCGI   3020+01
KLIT   2914+03
```

These winds are backing (320°, 300°, and 290°), changing direction across your route in a counterclockwise manner. There is a ridge probably centered over the east central plains states, and a trough of low pressure (associated with the frontal system) east of Covington and moving eastward.

"Buys Ballot's Law" (*see* Glossary) is a handy rule for determining where low pressure is with respect to your location. *See* Page 143 in this chapter for a diagram showing how to do this, using the winds shown at left for example.

Significant weather prog chart. Now locate the 34-48 hour significant weather prognostic chart to see what is being forecast for the day of flight. Compare this forecast chart with the initial sketch map or print-out that you made. If you don't have access to the internet, The Weather Channel also offers a two- to four-day weather outlook, and the friendly FSS or AFSS is only a telephone call away.

See Section 11, AC 00-45E.

You will notice that the 36-48 hour prognostic chart does not show areas of MVFR/IFR conditions like the weather depiction chart does. Instead it reveals the forecast areas of precipitation (i.e., clouds). Another nice feature of this prog chart is the forecast discussion (as mentioned in an earlier chapter). Reading one can be cause of a minor migraine, but stay with it and use AC 00-45E Section 14's contraction list, and the glossary in this book…and don't be afraid to ask questions!

You now have enough to put together a pretty good picture of what the weather is; the next task is to see what happens over time.

24-Hour Preview

METARs and TAFs. The day before the flight you want to start looking at the current conditions along your route corridor (60 NM wide) to get an idea of what is being reported and what the "weather gurus" are forecasting.

Next, repeat the drill you did the day before and check the surface analysis and weather depiction charts. Since weather patterns do change with time, you should be able to spot any significant movement in fronts, pressure systems and areas of MVFR/IFR weather. Mark the new posi-

Why check in those particular directions? Because weather generally moves from a westerly to easterly direction in the middle latitudes.

Lifted Index, or LI, is a measure of stability.

tions of the fronts, highs and lows onto your original chart; that is, those over your region and to the southwest, west and northwest of that.

Composite moisture stability chart. This chart is nice because it is a picture of the atmosphere's freezing levels, moisture content, and Lifted Index; although it's true that it isn't very "current" if you're looking at the 12Z chart at 1800Z... at least it gives you a general idea. Once again, the best places to obtain a copy of this chart is from the NWS website facsimile charts, or from the AFSS briefer.

If conditions appear to be relatively stable, there is no need to check any of the convective forecasts at this time because AIRMETs and SIGMETs are only valid for 6 hours and 4 hours respectively. You can check on AIRMETs, SIGMETs and convective SIGMETs (if necessary) when you receive your morning flight briefing.

Next, check out the 12/24 hour surface weather prognostic chart and get the weather folks' forecast for the frontal and pressure systems and MVFR/IFR areas.

24-Hour Preview, Evening

Later that same day, you should also check the airport directory for EFAS sites and communication outlets/frequencies as well as those FSS's with HIWAS capabilities. Have you checked to see what type of terrain you are flying over? Have you marked your sectional with possible diversion/ emergency fields and alternate?

abbreviated weather briefing: Requested after receiving a standard weather briefing earlier in the day; includes only elements that may have changed since the standard briefing such as current weather, updated forecasts, NOTAMs.

Call the AFSS/FSS, inform them of your flight plans and obtain an abbreviated weather briefing. Also get the forecast winds and temperatures for your planned altitude over the region and for the route. These forecast winds/temps values should have been calculated from the latest radiosonde (weather-balloon run) data (0000Z). Last, check the latest TAFs for Hot Springs and Little Rock. These forecasts should cover all or most of the time interval of your flight and will give you a good idea of what the forecasters are thinking with respect to your route area.

Flight Time!

Depending upon the weather picture, you may want to have a good quick overview of the weather that you get with a standard weather briefing— the basic format of this is covered in the last section of this chapter.

An example of a standard weather briefing and the weather services used therein is covered at the end of this chapter.

All the weather information you have gathered over the past 48 hours certainly doesn't indicate an IMC flight. The METAR reports for your route the morning of the flight (*see* below) indicates a high deck of clouds (probably cirrostratus) with a broken middle cloud deck at 10,000 feet at KHOT, your destination. Visibility appears to be slightly restricted with haze, which does tell you that the lower atmosphere is pretty stable this morning—but this might change with daytime heating.

```
METAR KCVG 131348Z 30010KT SCT030 BKN300 10SM
   04/M02 A2998 RMK AO2
METAR KEVV 131351Z AUTO 06006KT 4HZ SCT015
   SCT080 BKN300 05/01 A3002 RMK AO2
METAR KHOT 131350Z AUTO 27007KT 6HZ SCT020
   BKN100 300OVC 06/01 A3003 SLP200
```

Your flight time with a 1415Z takeoff calls for a ETE of 2+45 to KEVV where you plan to refuel and get some good airport coffee. Wheels up at 1800Z and a 3+30 ETE flight to KHOT; ETA at KHOT is 132130Z. The TAFs along your route (*see* below) do confirm your earlier weather research and weather briefing—the only "bad" weather is the restricted visibility. Still, it would be wise (and a good habit as well) to recheck your en route and destination weather while you are enjoying that good coffee.

```
TAF KEVV 131140Z 131212 VRB04KT 6SM HZ SCT100
BKN300
BECMG 1821 SCT100 BKN300
TAF KHOT 131140Z 131212 20008KT 5SM HZ SCT030
   BECMG 1922Z 3010 P6SM OVC250
```

If you have a morning flight, the chances are very good that the constant pressure chart alluded to in your standard briefing will be the same one that you looked at last night—because the latest radiosonde data has not yet been analyzed and put online. So once you're at cruise altitude you may want to check with the nearest AFSS to see if the new 1200Z winds/temps are available yet. Always fly with the latest info!

It doesn't appear that there will be anything of importance developing in terms of radar activity with this stable air mass, so your briefing will probably be brief (excuse the pun), with no need to check the convective messages.

The AIM has some excellent advice for VFR pilots: File a VFR flight plan, but practice IFR procedures on your flight by using the NAVAIDs, maintaining a constant altitude, estimating en route position times, and making accurate and frequent position reports to FSS/AFSS's along the route. It's just good practice!

One final question for you before you depart: With hilly terrain over much of your route and most weather stations located in valleys, how much terrain clearance would you have if ceilings of 4,000 to 6,000 feet were being reported? Always be aware of the terrain features.

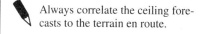 Always correlate the ceiling forecasts to the terrain en route.

Marginal VFR Flight

You are working for a large software firm and based out of Tallahassee, FL. Your boss, a guy named Bill, calls you at 0600 and wants you to fly some needed computer equipment to the company's Atlanta, GA (KATL) and Louisville, KY (KLOU) offices. As usual, calls like these don't give you much time to plan out a mission, so you tell Bill you will be airborne within three to four hours.

Quick-Briefing Charts

In your quick check of the company's computer you find the latest surface weather analysis chart which gives you this broad-scale information: Temperatures, in advance of the trough and its surface frontal system, are already in the high 70s and low 80s, and the entire southeastern U.S. is covered by a very moist and potentially unstable air mass (high dewpoint temperatures, in the low 70s).

The constant pressure chart(s) show a low-level southerly flow over the southeastern part of the states which becomes more southwesterly at the 10,000- to 30,000-foot levels. A trough of low pressure extends from a deep low-pressure cell (centered over northeastern Oklahoma) southward into eastern Texas.

The weather depiction chart indicates a rather large area of MVFR weather from east Texas/Oklahoma, across Louisiana, into Alabama and northward to a weak stationary front lying east-west over the Ohio River Valley. A smaller area of IFR conditions dominates all of western Louisiana northward through the western third of Tennessee, with ceilings of 500–800 feet and 1 to 2 miles in mist. The basic cloud type over the MVFR area is stratocumulus (Sc) and stratus (St) with fog in the IFR area. Several stations in east Texas, Oklahoma, Louisiana and Arkansas are reporting light rainshower activity.

Best Bet

With the potentially unstable situation confronting your flight, it would be wise to check for current AIRMETs, SIGMETs and particularly, the convective SIGMETs. Also a good clue as to future developments is the convective outlook (AC) and the latest moisture/stability chart for 1200Z, if it is available. A quick solution to all this is the Aviation Weather Center (AWC) on the web for an instantly-available look at these products. On this webpage, everything laid out like a standard weather briefing, making this information easy to scan and relatively fast to pick up. This is no substitute for an official weather briefing from the FSS (1-800-WX-BRIEF), but it is a great preview you can use to get an idea of what lies ahead. Below is an example of the AWC "standard briefing" page arrangement, which starts out with "Adverse Conditions":

AIRMETs and SIGMETs. Remember that these are short forecasts and you should check en route for possible changes if any are in effect for your flight period.

Convective SIGMETs (WST). If none are valid for your flight time to your first destination, make a mental or written note to check with EFAS once you are at cruise altitude.

Current AC (convective outlook). As the AC 00-45E states, these messages are prepared and transmitted every hour at H+55 and are valid for 2 hours. Examine the latest AC (as well as the one previous, if available); here again, you are looking for how things are developing and changing. (These and other weather-watches from the SPC are linked a bit further down the AWC briefing page.)

Severe weather watch (WWs) or alert messages (AWWs). Are there any in effect for your route? Probably not. But, with surface heating as the day progresses, convective activity looks like a distinct possibility for the *second leg* of your flight. So, remember to check at Atlanta and with EFAS for any updates on these and other convective forecasts/messages.

VFR Flight Recommendation. "Not recommended." Given the information that you gathered from the computer, the chances are that you will be filing an IFR flight plan.

Stratocumulus is the most common cloud in the world, and a stable cloud…but it can, with heating/lifting, turn into an unstable cloud.

On the web, go to **www.awc-kc.noaa.gov**, and click on the link for "Official Forecast Products."

Another convective outlook product not directly linked to this page is the Collaborative Convective Forecast Product (CCFP)—*see* Chapter 10. This is a new product for the NWS/FAA, and a really neat one. Go to the AWC home page and click on CCFP.

SPC: Storm Prediction Center at Norman, Oklahoma

Obviously a detailed weather check involving one to two days is nice when you have the time. But for short notice flights, the best approach is to use such resources to gather an overview of what's going on, in order to give yourself extra time — so you aren't rushed when you do get the weather briefing and plan the flight.

IFR Flight Conditions

The same drill as outlined for all the previous flight conditions should be followed where practicable — after you have looked in the mirror and asked yourself this question: "Is this flight really that vital or necessary?" Below are some real-life questions about possible IMC and flying weather decisions.

Real World Practice

Consider the following scenarios:

Scenario 1. The sun has just come up and the airport and surrounding area are blanketed with a thick layer of radiation fog, with a visibility of $1\frac{1}{2}$ miles, light variable wind and a high thin overcast of cirrostratus. A few minutes later, the fog layer appears to have thinned a bit and has moved off the approach end of the runway. So — what to do?

    a. Yes, it looks good — let's launch!

    b. No, let's wait until the fog has cleared the area.

    c. Cancel flying and go fishing.

Scenario 2. The following METAR report is fictitious yet contains all the elements of a real-world weather situation. You already know how to read a METAR report, but can you understand and *interpret* these reports?

```
KACT METAR 051152Z 14008G15KT 5SMHZ BKN020
BKN280 30/25 A3004 RMK SLP990 60000 56018
8/203 UA ACFT RPT WND FL 120 240/40 LGT TURBC
```

1. Where is this report from? Check the map on AC 00-45E Page 4-46.

2. Does this report represent a potentially stable or unstable air mass?

    a. Stable.

    b. Unstable.

    c. Cannot tell.

Continued

3. Defend your choice of answer of #2 by giving at least two reasons for your decision.

4. Where is low pressure aloft with respect to this airport?

   a. East

   b. Southwest

   c. Northwest

   d. South

5. Based on the information you have, what conditions would you forecast for this location/area within the next few hours, and why?

6. Given this report and information you have deduced, would you recommend a 4-hour cross-country VFR flight for an inexperienced pilot during this time frame?

7. What direction are the lowest clouds most apt to move from? (North, South, East, West)

Scenario 1

Answer—b. Wait! In this scenario, fog will start to thin but as it is warmed from the surface heating, the fog lifts into a low stratus layer which can put the field under IFR conditions once again. These conditions might persist for a couple of hours with a light wind condition; breaking up sooner with a stronger wind.

Scenario 2

Your answers should go something like this:

1. KACT is Waco, Texas.

2. and 3. Potentially unstable. Lower 2,000 scattered deck is developing cumulus, pressure is falling (characteristic 6: decreasing then decreasing more slowly), 1.8 millibars in 3 hours. Winds are out of the SE with light gust conditions. There is some haze that implies there may be a surface-based inversion, but the air appears to be unstable above 2,000 feet (cumulus clouds). Surface heating will dissipate the inversion, thus the atmosphere could become even more unstable.

3. Using Buys Ballot's rule, low pressure is west of the station. The upper winds (240/40 kts) indicate a trough of low pressure is west of the station and the winds appear to be veering with increasing height—a vital ingredient for severe thunderstorm development. Also, the cloud group (8/203) indicates that the clouds are unstable. Additionally, the PIREP reveals a vital ingredient for strong thunderstorm development—the winds aloft show that the winds have veered in a clockwise direction.

   Note: Did you let the haze fool you into thinking that the air mass was stable? Often the lower few-thousand feet of the atmosphere is stable in an inversion, but if air can be lifted beyond this lower level via convection, terrain, etc., it could very easily turn unstable. This is called "conditional instability" and it is common over the central and east-central U.S. regions.

4. By afternoon, scattered thunderstorm and rain showers are likely to occur with their usual display of winds, turbulence, possible hail, and certainly deadly lightning.

5. No!

6. Probably will move from south to north.

The Standard Weather Briefing

This weather briefing, probably the most frequent one given by FAA briefers, consists of several sections. This is a breakdown of which weather messages or charts are applicable to each section of a briefing.

Adverse Conditions: AIRMETs (WA), SIGMETs (WS), convective SIGMETs (WST). When applicable, severe weather watch bulletins (WW) and/or alert messages (AWW) from SPC, or a hurricane advisory (WH) will be discussed where appropriate.

Synopsis: Surface analysis chart, weather depiction chart, radar summary chart, and constant pressure charts will be discussed.

Current Conditions:

- METARs (ICAO ID), METARs (plain English) and temperature/dewpoint graphics.

- Satellite imagery (visible, water vapor, and infrared).

- The national radar summary chart and radar weather observations (old SDs, now called ROBs).

   Note: If the briefer does not mention the ROBs and convective activity is called for in your flight area, ask for ROBs, since they show much more detail than the radar summary chart.

Enroute Weather: Area forecast(s) (FAs), transcribed weather enroute broadcast (TWEB), and the low- and high-level significant weather prognostic charts are covered.

Continued

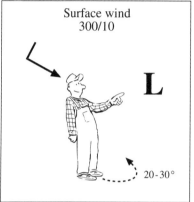

Buys Ballot's Law: At the surface, with your back to the wind, rotate your body to the right about 20–30 degrees and then point left to low pressure. (*See also* Appendix D, Glossary.)

 Call 1-800-WX-BRIEF for a weather briefing.

You should check the TWEB route map before the briefing (AC 00-45E Page 4-34 or Page 56 in this book) to see if one of these routes would be appropriate for your flight. If so, you then have a detailed enroute forecast of anticipated weather conditions.

Destination: Provides terminal airport forecast (TAFs, ICAO ID), regional TAFs, and TAF graphics. But if your destination does not have a TAF prepared for it, you should use the area forecast to determine your destination weather.

Winds/Temperatures Aloft (FDs): Forecast winds, temperatures aloft.

NOTAMs: U.S. NOTAM Office (ICAO ID), NOTAM publications.

Additional Information: From the Center Weather Service Unit (CWSU), includes text messages for meteorological impact statements (MIS) and center weather advisories (CWA). The Aviation Weather Center also has a link to these messages and a chart showing the area of responsibility of the ARTCCs of the U.S.

This ARTCC chart is also found on Page 64 of this book.

Conclusion

Several times during the course of writing this book, I have found myself thinking back over the astonishing rate of aviation growth over the past decades. Equally as fascinating has been the ever-increasing rate of new developments in such industries as radar, satellites, and telemetry, and by no means least, the computer industry.

Hand-in-glove with the computer revolution has been the development in voice and video communications, and most important of all, increased knowledge and awareness of our world and those natural forces which still dictate to a large extent our lives and activities.

Yesterday we had the aviation industry growing rapidly out of its infancy, and the Weather Bureau under the direction of the Department of Agriculture. Today we have the NWS with its fine array of weather products and services available to all customers via the fast and very dependable internet and satellite relay systems. In addition are free and fee-for-service companies such as those at many universities and Weather Service International, who offer their version of the weather services and charts described in this book and the FAA's AC 00-45E.

Therefore it is easy to feel somewhat overwhelmed by the wide selection of weather products and services almost instantly available to the pilot. You can be certain that our future weather services will be changing and evolving, and we have only one constant to contend with: change itself! Sometimes we are not going to approve of or like the changes that will take place. One change slowly taking shape on the horizon is that of privatization of weather services. Some countries (Canada, for example) already charge a fee for aviation and related weather services. Do we want to go that route in this country? Last year a group of private weather companies asked Congress to stop the NWS from issuing weather forecasts. These companies argued that the NWS was unfairly competing with the pay-for-service companies. As I write this, there is now a bill, HR 1553, before a house committee that is examining the suggested "Privatization of the Weather Services."

But whatever the changes that occur over the next few years, it's a sure thing that the pilot will always be in a learning mode—which has been the reason for this book! To help you make sense out of those weather services currently in use. The computer and its handmaiden, the internet and worldwide web, are valuable learning tools to use in conjunction with this book in your quest for better understanding of the weather services, as well as for gaining new knowledge and information about weather in general. Remember that the nature of the internet is change, as well. I should also point out that one way to help keep tabs on changes to this book, as well as other regulatory updates, is to periodically check the Aviation Supplies & Academics (ASA) website (**http://www.asa2fly.com**) for any regulatory or procedural changes that may occur.

Here, then, is a set of tools for you to practice with and learn to become a safer, more weather-wise pilot. And remember that old adage, "use it or lose it"—you can apply that to both body and health but it also applies to your personal inner computer (aka brain).

May you always be learning and always be Weather-Wise!

Appendix A: *Surface Chart Symbology Explained*

The following charts and figures further explain the weather symbols described in AC 00-45E in Section 5 on the surface analysis chart, and Section 6, the weather depiction chart. Figure 6-2 in AC 00-45E interprets the various plots, but does not explain where they get their precipitation amount and type. You must cross-reference Figure 6-2 with Figure 5-6 in Section 5 to find the actual precip expression.

The symbols in Figure 5-6 are displayed in a grid, but the grid itself is not explained. The numbers at the left and top side of the layout of symbols indicate the amount and intensity of the precipitation being depicted by each symbol. The line at "50" indicates light intermittent drizzle, but if you follow it over to fall under column 5 (making it "55"), then you have "continuous thick drizzle" (thick like a heavy damp blanket—the type you could stay outside in for a couple of hours without actually getting soaked). Therefore the further to the right in the chart, the more intense that type of precipitation reported:

,	slight intermittent drizzle
•	slight intermittent rain
*	slight intermittent snow
,,	slight continuous drizzle
••	slight continuous rain
**	slight continuous snow
,',	continuous heavy drizzle
•:•	continuous heavy rain
:	continuous heavy snow
⌁	slight freezing drizzle
⌁	slight freezing rain
⌁	moderate heavy freezing drizzle
⌁	moderate heavy freezing rain

Continued

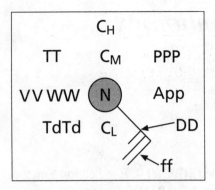

Station Model Explained

The station model is nothing more than a graphical code for the METAR information that comes in from the observation and then gets plotted onto the surface analysis charts. The diagram below shows how the parts of a METAR are arranged about a circle that represents the location of a weather station. While the use of letters to represent values (i.e., TT, App, etc.) are not used in the AC 00-45E Figure 5-3 to explain a station model, these are letter-symbols that have been used for some time by the NWS and FAA to represent places for the numerical values in the codes.

TT	Used to indicate the air temperature in degrees Celsius.
VV	Used to indicate the visibility in statute miles and fractions of miles.
WW	"Present weather"—i.e., the weather symbols added from the grid shown in AC 00-45E Figure 5-6.
TdTd	Used to indicate the dewpoint temperature in Celsius.
C_H, C_M, C_L	These are the types of clouds an observer might report at a station. H is for high clouds, ice clouds located above 20,000 ft. AGL. M is for middle-level clouds between 6,500 ft. AGL and 20,000 ft. AGL. L is for low-level clouds from near the surface to 6,500 ft. AGL. This information is taken from the 00, 03, 06, 09, 12, 15, 18, and 2100Z observations where there are observers who can identify the clouds. The data is reported in the 8/ClCmCh group in the REMARKS of the METAR.
N	This is the total sky cover, as shown in AC 00-45E Figure 6-1, in which the station circle is darkened in to show the total amount of sky cover at the station.
PPP	Sea level pressure (SLP), found in the REMARKS section of the METAR. It is coded as 3 numbers and plotted the same way: 125 is read as 1012.5 mb …995 would be 999.5 mb. Sea level pressure will never exceed 1045.0 mb, or be less than 900.0 mb (a low number like that would be a very strong hurricane!)
App	Pressure tendency and amount of pressure change during the past 3 hours. The amount of change is plotted just to the right of the station circle with the pressure tendency "diagram" at far right. It is plotted as whole numbers: a coded 001 would read as 0.1 mb, a coded 032 would read as 3.2 mb. This information is found in the "5appp" group in the 3-hourly METAR reports— *see also* the following table for an explanation of the pressure tendency "diagram" and coding.
DD	Wind direction, reported for every 10 degrees of direction (360, 350, etc.), and drawn as a shaft that connect to the station circle.
ff	Wind force in knots; a barb is 10 knots and a half-barb is 5 knots. 50 knots is drawn as a triangular flag. A calm wind is indicated by a circle drawn around the station circle (rather than a shaft).

Characteristics of Barometer Tendency			
Primary Requirements	**Pressure is changing by...**	**Tendency coded as (in METAR/TAF)**	**Graphic used on surface chart**
Atmospheric Pressure is now **higher** then 3 hours ago	Increasing, then decreasing	0	
	Increasing, then steady; or increasing, then increasing more slowly	1	
	Increasing steadily or unsteadily	2	
	Decreasing or steady, then increasing; or increasing, then increasing more rapidly	3	
Atmospheric pressure is now **the same** as it was 3 hours ago	Increasing, then decreasing	0	
	Steady	4	
	Decreasing, then increasing	5	
Atmospheric pressure is now **lower** than 3 hours ago	Decreasing then steady; or decreasing, then decreasing more slowly	6	
	Decreasing steadily, or unsteadily	7	
	Steady or increasing, then decreasing; or decreasing, then decreasing more rapidly	8	

Pressure change information is determined every 3 hours (00Z, 03Z, 06Z, etc.) and coded as part of the Remarks section of the METAR. This can be very useful in giving the pilot an idea of how the pressure has been changing over the previous period. Pressure rises usually mean good or improving weather; falling pressure is the usually the opposite. A good example of how this information can be used appears in the top chart on Page 170 in Appendix C.

Cloud type abbreviations used in Cloud Chart

St or Fs	stratus or fractostratus
Ci	cirrus
Cs	cirrostratus
Cc	cirrocumulus
Ac	altocumulus
As	altostratus
Sc	stratocumulus
Ns	nimbostratus
Cu or Fc	cumulus or fractocumulus
Cb	cumulonimbus

Using this chart, an observer would report this coding in the METAR:

For a sky containing stratocumulus for low clouds, slightly obscuring altostratus in the middle cloud levels, and cirrostratus at 30,000 feet, the METAR code would read **8/527** (the format is **8/ClCmCh**, with the "8" expressing the total sky cover, broken into the three layers as shown by the "low-middle-high clouds" expression, in that order). The "5" is for stratocumulus that is not formed by cumulus spreading; the "2" expresses thick altostratus; and the "7" means a veil of cirrostratus covering the entire sky at high altitude.

If the code given in the METAR is **8/7//**, for example, the two solidus characters following the low-cloud code number indicate that the cloud types at the middle and high level cannot be determined by the equipment (due to obscuration). But you can still figure it out:

```
METAR KXYZ 051752Z 06008KT 3SM RA FG OVC012
   RMKS...8/7//
```

For Low Clouds C_L

Number code reported in METAR	Graphic symbol used on Chart	Description of cloud cover type (from W.M.O. Code)
1		**Cu**, fair weather, little vertical development and flattened
2		**Cu**, considerable development, towering with or without other **Cu** or **Sc** bases at same level
3		**Cb** with tops lacking clear-cut outlines, but distinctly not cirroform or anvil-shaped; with or without **Cu**, **Sc**, or **St**
4		**Sc** formed by spreading out of **Cu**; **Cu** often present also
5		**Sc** not formed by spreading out of **Cu**
6		**St** or **Fs** or both, but no **Fs** of bad weather
7		**Fs** and/or **Fc** of bad weather (scud)
8		**Cu** and **Sc** (not formed by spreading out of **Cu**) with bases at different levels
9		**Cb** having a clearly fibrous (cirroform) top, often anvil-shaped, with or without **Cu**, **Sc**, **St**, or scud

Interpretation: Low layer cloud type 7 with no upper layers indicated; however, it is raining which would indicate a cloud layer of some depth— greater than 4,000-5,000 feet. The higher the precipitation intensity, the greater the cloud layer thickness, so you can bet there is obscuration above the low-cloud layer given in the code.

For Middle Clouds C_M

Number code reported in METAR	Graphic symbol used on Chart	Description of cloud cover type (from W.M.O. Code)
1		Thin **As** (most of cloud layer is semitransparent)
2		Thick **As**, greater part sufficiently dense to hide sun or moon, or **Ns**
3		Thin **Ac**, mostly semitransparent; cloud elements not changing much at a single level
4		Thin **Ac** in patches; cloud elements continually changing and/or occurring at more than one level
5		Thin **Ac** in bands or in a layer gradually spreading over sky and usually thickening as a whole
6		**Ac** formed by the spreading out of **Cu**
7		Double-layered **Ac**, or a thick layer of **Ac**, not increasing; or **Ac** with **As** and/or **Ns**
8		**Ac** in the form of **Cu**-shaped tufts or **Ac** with turrets
9		**Ac** of chaotic sky, usually at different levels; patches of dense **Ci** are usually present

Continued

For High Clouds $$C_H$$

Number code reported in METAR	Graphic symbol used on Chart	Description of cloud cover type (from W.M.O. Code)
1		Filaments of **Ci**, or "mares tails" scattered and not increasing
2		Dense **Ci** in patches or twisted sheaves, usually not increasing, sometimes like remains of **Cb**, or towers tufts
3		Dense **Ci**, often anvil-shaped, derived from or associated **Cb**
4		**Ci**, often hook-shaped, gradually spreading over the sky and usually thickening as a whole
5		**Ci** and **Cs**, often in converging bands or **Cs** alone; generally overspreading and growing denser; the continuous layer not reaching 45 altitude
6		**Ci** and **Cs**, often in converging bands or **Cs** alone; generally overspreading and growing denser; the continuous layer exceeding 45 altitude
7		Veil of **Cs** covering the entire sky
8		**Cs** not increasing and not covering the entire sky
9		**Cc** alone or **Cc** with some **Ci** or **Cs**, but the **Cc** being the main cirroform cloud

Appendix B: *Handy Weather Information Tables*

North American Time Zones and GMT

Weather observations are always taken with respect to Greenwich Mean Time (GMT). These observations, as well as all other aviation messages, also use the 24-hour military clock-format. GMT is also known as Universal Time Coordinated (UTC).

In order to convert from GMT/UTC to local time, we must know the time difference between GMT and local time, for both standard time as well as summer daylight savings time. Complicating the calculation is the fact that some states simply do not use daylight savings time—in the case of Indiana, for example, part of the state is daylight savings time, and the rest of the state does not believe in it!

Time Zones of North America (E–W)

	Standard Time	Daylight Savings
Eastern	EST	EDT
Central	CST	CDT
Mountain	MST	MDT
Pacific	PST	PDT
Alaska	ALA	
Hawaii	HAW	

Conversion : Standard Time to GMT

GMT	ATL	EST	CST	MST	PST	ALA	HAW
Time Diff	-4	-5	-6	-7	-8	-9	-10
00 GMT	8 pm*	7 pm*	6 pm*	5 pm*	4 pm*	3 pm*	2 pm*
01 "	9 pm*	8 pm*	7 pm*	6 pm*	5 pm*	4 pm*	3 pm*
02 "	10 pm*	9 pm*	8 pm*	7 pm*	6 pm*	5 pm*	4 pm*
03 "	11 pm*	10 pm*	9 pm*	8 pm*	7 pm*	6 pm*	5 pm*
04 "	12 am	11 pm*	10 pm*	9 pm*	8 pm*	7 pm*	6 pm*
05 "	01 am	12 am	11 pm*	10 pm*	9 pm*	8 pm*	7 pm*
06 "	02 am	01 am	12 am	11 pm*	10 pm*	9 pm*	8 pm*
07 "	03 am	02 am	01 am	12 am	11 pm*	10 pm*	9 pm*
08 "	04 am	03 am	02 am	01 am	12 am	11 pm*	10 pm*
09 "	05 am	04 am	03 am	02 am	01 am	12 am	11 pm*
10 "	06 am	05 am	04 am	03 am	02 am	01 am	12 am
11 "	07 am	06 am	05 am	04 am	03 am	02 am	01 am
12 "	08 am	07 am	06 am	05 am	04 am	03 am	02 am

The pattern of time change is well established above, the reader can easily "fill in the blanks" for the remainder of the 24 hour day.

---

* Represents the previous day; i.e., 0300 GMT on January 23rd is equal to 8:00 p.m. MST on January 22nd.

Daylight Savings Time

This table is for those who observe the seasonal call of: "Fall back, Spring forward."

GMT	EDT	CDT	MDT	PDT
Hrs. Diff.	-4	-5	-6	-7
GMT Time				
0000	8 pm*	7 pm*	6 pm*	5 pm*
0100	9 pm*	8 pm*	7 pm*	6 pm*
0200	10 pm*	9 pm*	8 pm*	7 pm*
0300	11 pm*	10 pm*	9 pm*	8 pm*
0400	12 am	11 pm*	10 pm*	9 pm*
0500	01 am	12 am	11 pm*	10 pm*
0600	02 am	01 am	12 am	11 pm*
0700	03 am	02 am	01 am	12 am
0800	04 am	03 am	02 am	01 am
0900	05 am	04 am	03 am	02 am
1000	06 am	05 am	04 am	03 am
1100	07 am	06 am	05 am	04 am
1200	08 am	07 am	06 am	05 am
1300	09 am	08 am	07 am	06 am

* Represents the previous day. You can easily determine the times for 1400–2300.

U.S. and Canadian Station IDs (METAR/TAF)

ABI	ABILENE	TX	CLE	CLEVELAND	OH	EWC	ELLWOOD CITY	PA
ABQ	ALBUQUERQUE	NM	CLT	CHARLOTTE	NC	EYW	KEY WEST	FL
ABR	ABERDEEN	SD	CON	CONCORD	NH	FAM	FARMINGTON	MO
ABY	ALBANY	GA	COU	COLUMBIA	MO	FAR	FARGO	ND
ACK	NANTUCKET	MA	CRG	JACKSONVILLE	FL	FCA	KALISPELL	MT
ACT	WACO	TX	CRP	CORPUS CHRISTI	TX	FLO	FLORENCE	SC
ADM	ARDMORE	OK	CSN	CASSANOVA	VA	FMG	RENO	NV
AEX	ALEXANDRIA	LA	CTY	CROSS CITY	FL	FMN	FARMINGTON	NM
AIR	BELLAIRE	OH	CVG	COVINGTON	KY	FMY	FT MEYERS	FL
AKO	AKRON	CO	CYN	COYLE	NJ	FNT	FLINT	MI
ALB	ALBANY	NY	CYS	CHEYENNE	WY	FOD	FT DODGE	IA
ALS	ALAMOSA	CO	CZI	CRAZY WOMAN	WY	FOT	FORTUNA	CA
AMA	AMARILLO	TX	CZQ	FRESNO	CA	FSD	SIOUX FALLS	SD
AMG	ALMA	GA	DBL	EAGLE	CO	FSM	FT SMITH	AR
ANW	AINSWORTH	NE	DBQ	DUBUQUE	IA	FST	FT STOCKTON	TX
APE	APPLETON	OH	DBS	DUBOIS	ID	FWA	FT WAYNE	IN
ARG	WALNUT RIDGE	AR	DCA	WASHINGTON	DC	GAG	GAGE	OK
ASP	OSCODA	MI	DDY	CASPER	WY	GCK	GARDEN CITY	KS
ATL	ATLANTA	GA	DEC	DECATUR	IL	GEG	SPOKANE	WA
AUS	AUSTIN	TX	DEN	DENVER	CO	GFK	GRAND FORKS	ND
BAE	MILWAUKEE	WI	DFW	DALLAS FT WORTH	TX	GGG	LONGVIEW	TX
BAM	BATTLE MNTN	NV	DIK	DICKINSIN	ND	GGW	GLASGOW	MT
BCE	BRYCE CANYON	UT	DLF	LAUGHLIN AFB	TX	GIJ	NILES	MI
BDF	BRADFORD	IL	DLH	DULUTH	MN	GLD	GOODLAND	KS
BDL	WINSOR LOCKS	CT	DLL	DELLS	WI	GQO	CHATTANOOGA	TN
BFF	SCOTTSBLUFF	NE	DLN	DILLON	MT	GRB	GREEN BAY	WI
BGR	BANGOR	ME	DMN	DEMING	NM	GRR	GRAND RAPIDS	MI
BIL	BILLINGS	MT	DNJ	MC CALL	ID	GSO	GREENSBORO	NC
BIS	BISMARK	ND	DPR	DUPREE	SD	GTF	GREAT FALLS	MT
BJI	BEMIDJI	MN	DRK	PRESCOTT	AZ	HAR	HARRISBURG	PA
BKE	BAKER	OR	DSD	REDMOND	OR	HBU	GUNNISON	CO
BKW	BECKLEY	WV	DSM	DES MOINES	IA	HEC	HECTOR	CA
BLI	BELLINGHAM	WA	DTA	DELTA	UT	HLC	HILL CITY	KS
BNA	NASHVILLE	TN	DVC	DOVE CREEK	CO	HLN	HELENA	MT
BOI	BOISE	ID	DXO	DETROIT	MI	HMV	HOLSTON MNTN	TN
BOS	BOSTON	MA	DYR	DYERSBURG	TN	HNK	HANCOCK	NY
BOY	BOYSEN RESV.	WY	EAU	EAU CLAIRE	WI	HNN	HENDERSON	WV
BPI	BIG PINEY	WY	ECG	ELIZABETH CITY	NC	HQM	HOQUIAM	WA
BRD	BRAINERD	MN	ECK	PECK	MI	HTO	EAST HAMPTON	NY
BRO	BROWNSVILLE	TX	EED	NEEDLES	CA	HUL	HOULTON	ME
BTR	BATON ROUGE	LA	EHF	BAKERSFIELD	CA	HVE	HANKSVILLE	UT
BTY	BEATTY	NV	EIC	SHREVEPORT	LA	HVR	HAVRE	MT
BUF	BUFFALO	NY	EKN	ELKINS	WV	IAH	HOUSTON INTL	TX
BUM	BUTLER	MO	ELD	EL DORADO	AR	ICT	WICHITA	KS
BVL	BONNEVILLE	UT	ELP	EL PASO	TX	IGB	BIGBEE	MS
BVT	LAFAYETTE	IN	ELY	ELY	NV	ILC	WILSON CREEK	NV
BWG	BOWLING GREEN	KY	EMI	WESTMINSTER	MD	ILM	WILMINGTON	NC
BZA	YUMA	AZ	END	VANCE AFB	OK	IND	INDIANAPOLIS	IN
CAE	COLUMBIA	SC	ENE	KENNEBUNK	ME	INK	WINK	TX
CDS	CHILDRESS	TX	ENI	UKIAH	CA	INL	INTL FALLS	MN
CEW	CRESTVIEW	FL	EPH	EPHRATA	WA	INW	WINSLOW	AZ
CHE	HAYDEN	CO	ERI	ERIE	PA	IOW	IOWA CITY	IA
CHS	CHARLESTON	SC	ETX	EAST TEXAS	PA	IRK	KIRKSVILLE	MO
CIM	CIMARRON	NM	EUG	EUGENE	OR			

Continued

IRQ ...... COLLIERS .... SC	MSS ...... MASSENA .... NY	SBY ..... SALISBURY .... MD
ISN .... WILLISTON .... ND	MSY .... NEW ORLEANS .... LA	SEA ..... SEATTLE .... WA
JAC ...... JACKSON .... WY	MTU .... MYTON .... UT	SGF ..... SPRINGFIELD .... MO
JAN ...... JACKSON .... MS	MZB .... MISSION BAY .... CA	SHR ..... SHERIDAN .... WY
JCT ...... JUNCTION .... TX	OAK .... OAKLAND .... CA	SIE .... SEA ISLE .... NJ
JFK ...... NEW YORK/JFK .... NY	OAL .... COALDALE .... NV	SJI .... SEMMNES .... AL
JHW ..... JAMESTOWN .... NY	OBH .... WOLBACH .... NE	SJN ...... ST JOHNS .... AZ
JNC ...... GRAND JUNCTION ..... CO	OCS .... ROCKSPRINGS .... WY	SJT .... SAN ANGELO .... TX
JOT ...... JOLIET IL	ODF .... TOCCOA .... GA	SLC ...... SALT LAKE CITY ...... UT
JST .... JOHNSTOWN .... PA	ODI .... NODINE .... MN	SLN ..... SALINA .... KS
LAA ...... LAMAR .... CO	OED .... MEDFORD .... OR	SLT ...... SLATE RUN .... PA
LAR ..... LARAMIE .... WY	OKC ..... OKLAHOMA CITY ...... OK	SNS ..... SALINAS .... CA
LAS ...... LAS VEGAS .... NV	OMN ... ORMOND BCH .... FL	SNY ..... SIDNEY .... NE
LAX ..... LOS ANGELES .... CA	ONL .... ONEILL .... NE	SPA ..... SPARTANBURG .... SC
LBB ..... LUBBOCK INTL .... TX	ONP .... NEWPORT .... OR	SPS ..... WICHITA FALLS .... TX
LBF ...... NORTH PLATTE .... NE	ORD .... O'HARE INTL IL	SQS .... SIDON .... MS
LBL ..... LIBERAL .... KS	ORF .... NORFOLK .... VA	SRQ .... SARASOTA .... FL
LCH .... LAKE CHARLES .... LA	ORL .... ORLANDO .... FL	SSM ..... SAULT STE MARIE .... MI
LEV ..... GRAND ISLE .... LA	OSW ... OSWEGO .... KS	SSO ...... SAN SIMON .... AZ
LFK ..... LUFKIN .... TX	OVR .... OMAHA .... NE	STL ...... ST LOUIS .... MO
LGC ..... LA GRANGE .... GA	PBI .... WEST PALM BCH .... FL	SYR ..... SYRACUSE .... NY
LIT .... LITTLE ROCK .... AR	PDT ..... PENDLETON .... OR	TBC ..... TUBA CITY .... AZ
LKT ..... SALMON .... ID	PDX ..... PORTLAND .... OR	TBE ..... TOBE .... CO
LKV ..... LAKEVIEW .... OR	PGS .... PEACH SPRINGS .... AZ	TCC .... TUCUMCARI .... NM
LOU .... LOUISVILLE .... KY	PHX .... PHOENIX .... AZ	TCS ..... TRUTH OR CONS .... NM
LOZ .... LONDON .... KY	PIE .... ST PETERSBURG .... FL	TLH .... TALLAHASSEE .... FL
LRD ..... LAREDO .... TX	PIH ...... POCATELLO .... ID	TOU .... NEAH BAY .... WA
LVS ...... LAS VEGAS .... NM	PIR ...... PIERRE .... SD	TRM ... THERMAL .... CA
LWT .... LEWISTOWN .... MT	PLB ..... PLATTSBURGH .... NY	TTH .... TERRE HAUTE .... IN
LYH .... LYNCHBURG .... VA	PMM .... PULLMAN .... MI	TUL ..... TULSA .... OK
MAF ... MIDLAND .... TX	PQI ...... PRESQUE ISLE .... ME	TUS ..... TUCSON .... AZ
MBS ..... SAGINAW .... MI	PSB ..... PHILLIPSBURG .... PA	TVC .... TRAVERSE CITY .... MI
MCB .... MC COMB .... MS	PSK ..... DUBLIN .... VA	TWF..... TWIN FALLS .... ID
MCK .... MC COOK .... NE	PSX ...... PALACIOS .... TX	TXK ..... TEXARKANA .... AR
MCN ... MACON .... GA	PUB .... PUEBLO .... CO	TXO ..... TEXICO .... TX
MCW ... MASON CITY .... IA	PVD .... PROVIDENCE .... RI	UIN ...... QUINCY IL
MEI ...... MERIDIAN .... MS	PWE .... PAWNEE CITY .... NE	VRB ..... VERO BCH .... FL
MEM.... MEMPHIS .... TN	PXV .... POCKET CITY .... IN	VUZ .... VULCAN .... AL
MGM ... MONTGOMERY .... AL	PYE .... POINT REYES .... CA	VXV ..... KNOXVILLE .... TN
MIA ..... MIAMI .... FL	RAP .... RAPID CITY .... SD	YDC .... PRINCETON .... BC
MKC .... KANSAS CITY .... MO	RBL ..... RED BLUFF .... CA	YKM ... YAKIMA .... WA
MKG ... MUSKEGON .... MI	RDU .... RALEIGH-DURHAM ... NC	YOW ... OTTAWA .... ON
MLC .... MC CALESTER .... OK	REO ..... ROME .... OR	YQB .... QUEBEC .... QB
MLD .... MALAD CITY .... ID	RHI ...... RHINELANDER .... WI	YQL ..... LETHBRIDGE .... AB
MLP ..... MULLAN PASS .... ID	RIC ...... RICHMOND .... VA	YQT ..... THUNDER BAY .... ON
MLS ..... MILES CITY ....MT	ROD .... ROSEWOOD .... OH	YQV .... YORKTON .... SA
MLT .... MILLINOCKET .... ME	ROW ... ROSWELL .... NM	YSC ..... SHERBROOKE .... QB
MLU .... MONROE .... LA	RWF.... REDWWOD FALLS ..... MN	YSJ ...... ST JOHN .... NB
MOD .... MODESTO .... CA	RZC ...... RAZORBACK .... AR	YVV ... WIARTON .... ON
MOT .... MINOT .... ND	RZS ...... SANTA BARBARA .... CA	YWG... WINNIPEG .... MB
MPV .... MONTPELIER .... VT	SAC ..... SACRAMENTO .... CA	YXC ..... CRANBROOK .... BC
MQT ... MARQUETTE .... MI	SAT ...... SAN ANTONIO .... TX	YXH ..... MEDICINE HAT .... AB
MRF.... MARFA .... TX	SAV .... SAVANNAH .... GA	YYN ... SWIFT CURRENT .... SA
MSL ..... MUSCLE SHOALS .... AL	SAX ..... SPARTA .... NJ	YYZ ..... TORONTO .... ON
MSP ..... MINNEAPOLIS .... MN		

Alaskan Observation and TAF Station Identifiers

PADK.... ADAK	PANR ... FUNTER BAY	PAPO ... POINT HOPE
PAFM.... AMBLER	PAGB ... GALBRAITH LK	PPIZ ..... POINT LAY
PAKP .... ANAKTUVUK	PAGA ... GALENA ++	PAPC ... PORT CLARENCE
PANC.... ANCHORAGE ++	PAGM ... GAMBELL	PAPH ... PORT HEIDEN
PAGN .... ANGOON	PAGK ... GULKANA ++	PALJ .... PORT ALSWORTH
PANI ..... ANIAK	PAGS ... GUSTAVUS ++	PAAP ... PORT ALEXANDER
PANT .... ANNETTE	PAHN ... HAINES	PATO.... PORTAGE GLACIER
PANV.... ANVIK	PAHZ.... HAYES RIVER	PAPR ... PROSPECT CREEK
PARC .... ARCTIC VILLAGE	PAHV ... HEALY	PAUD ... PRUDHOE BAY
PATQ .... ATQASUK	PAHO ... HOMER++	PAPT .... PUNTILLA LK
PABR .... BARROW ++	PAOH ... HOONAH	PARD ... RED DOG MINE
PABA .... BARTER ISLAND	PAHP .... HOOPER BAY	PAPB ... SAINT GEORGE
PABE .... BETHEL ++	PAHS .... HUSLIA	PASN ... SAINT PAUL ++
PABT .... BETTLES ++	PAHY ... HYDABURG	PASM... SAINT MARY'S
PABI ..... BIG DELTA JCT. ++	PAIL ..... ILIAMNA ++	PASD ... SAND POINT
PALV .... BIG RIVER LK'S	PAIM .... INDIAN MTN	PASA ... SAVOONGA
PATW.... CANTWELL	PAJN .... JUNEAU ++	PASK ... SELAWIK
PALU .... CAPE LISBURNE	PAFE .... KAKE	PAWD .. SEWARD
PAEH .... CAPE NEWENHAM	PAEN.... KENAI ++	PASP .... SHEEP MTN
PACZ .... CAPE ROMANOFF	PAKT.... KETCHIKAN ++	PASY ... SHEMYA
PALR .... CHANDALAR LK	PAKN ... KING SALMON ++	PASH ... SHISHMAREF
PACK .... CHEFORNAK	PAKI ... KIPNUK	PASI ..... SITKA ++
PAEC .... CHULITNA LODGE	PADQ ... KODIAK ++	PAGY ... SKAGWAY ++
PACR .... CIRCLE CITY	PAOT .... KPTZEBUE ++	PASW .. SKWENTNA
PACD .... COLD BAY ++	PAKK ... KOYUK	PADT ... SLANA
PACV .... CORDOVA ++	PALH.... LAKE HOOD	PASL .... SLEETMUTE
PASC .... DEADHORSE ++	PAIZ ..... LAZY MTN	PALK ... SNOWSHOE LK
PADE .... DEERING	PALN.... LONELY	PASX ... SOLDOTNA
PAIN ..... DENALI NAT. PK	PAML ... MANLEY HOT SPGS	PASV ... SPARREEVOHN
PADL .... DILLINGHAM ++	PAMZ... MCCARTHY	PAJV .... SUTTON**
PADU.... DUTCH HARBOR ++	PAMC ... MCGRATH ++	PATK ... TALKEETNA ++
PAEG .... EAGLE	PAMY .. MEKORYUK	PATA .... TANANA ++
PABV .... EAGLE RIVER	PAMR ... MERRILL FIELD	PATL .... TATALINA
PAEH .... EGEGIK	PAER .... MERRILL PASS W.	PATC .... TIN CITY
PAEI ...... EIELSON AFB ++	PAMD .. MIDDLETON IS.	PATG ... TOGIAK
PAEL .... ELFIN COVE	PAMH .. MINCHUMINA	PAKU... UGNU KUPARUK
PAED .... EMENDORF AFB ++	PAGN ... NEBESNA	PAUM .. UMIAT
PAEM ... EMMONAK	PANN ... NENANA	PAUN ... UNALAKLEET ++
PAZK .... EUREKA	PAEQ.... NEWTOK	PAVW .. VALDEZ CITY
PAFA..... FAIRBANKS ++	PAWN ... NOATAK	PAVD ... VALDEZ AIRPORT ++
PAFL ..... FAREWELL LK	PAOM ... NOME ++	PAWI.... WAINWRIGHT
PAFV .... FIVE MILE	PAOR .... NORTHWAY ++	PAWS ... WASILLA
PAYU .... FORT YUKON	POLI ..... OLIKTOK	PAWR .. WHITTIER
PAFR .... FT RICHARDSON	PAAQ ... PALMER ++	[??] .... WILLOW
PABG .... FT GREELEY	PAXK ... PAXON	PAWG .. WRANGELL ++
PAFB .... FT WAINWRIGHT	PAPG .... PETERSBURG ++	PAYA ... YAKUTAT ++

++ Indicates those stations which have a TAF.

List current as of August, 2000

Current WSR-88 Radar Installations

Source:
http://www.nws.noaa.gov/pub/modernize/88d.txt

Check this website periodically for
updates and additions.

Agency: NWS

Equip ID	WFO/Radar Site
TLX	OKLAHOMA CITY, OK/Norman
AMA	AMARILLO, TX/Amarillo
HGX	HOUSTON/GALVESTON, TX/Dickins
MLB	MELBOURNE, FL/Melbourne
DDC	DODGE CITY, KS/Dodge City
ICT	WICHITA, KS/Wichita
IWA	PHOENIX, AZ/Phoenix
INX	TULSA, OK/Inola
LWX	BALTIMORE, MD/ WASHINGTON, DC
LZK	LITTLE ROCK, AR/North Little
FTG	DENVER/BOULDER, CO/Denver
LSX	ST. LOUIS, MO/St Charles
LVX	LOUISVILLE, KY/Fort Knox
DAX	SACRAMENTO, CA/Sacramento
BMX	BIRMINGHAM, AL/Alabaster
BOX	BOSTON, MA/Taunton
FWS	DALLAS/FORT WORTH, TX/Fort Worth
UEX	HASTINGS, NE/Webster County
VTX	LOS ANGELES, CA/Ventura Count
LOT	CHICAGO, IL/Romeoville
TWX	TOPEKA, KS/Alma
CBX	BOISE, ID/Ada County
EWX	AUSTIN/SAN ANTONIO, TX/New Br
NQA	MEMPHIS, TN/Millington
PBZ	PITTSBURGH, PA/Coraopolis
OKX	NEW YORK CITY, NY/Upton
JAN	JACKSON, MS/Jackson
CLE	CLEVELAND, OH/Cleveland
DIX	PHILADELPHIA, PA/Manchester
ATX	SEATTLE/TACOMA, WA/Camano Island
LIX	NEW ORLEANS/BATON ROUGE, LA/S
FFC	ATLANTA, GA/Atlanta
EAX	KANSAS CITY/PLEASANT HILL, MO
BGM	BINGHAMTON, NY/Binghamton
DTX	DETROIT, MI/White Lake
MOB	MOBILE, AL/Mobile
CCX	CENTRAL PENNSYLVANIA, PA/Rush
ENX	ALBANY, NY/East Berne
AMX	MIAMI, FL/Miami

Equip ID	WFO/Radar Site
GLD	GOODLAND, KS/Goodland
TFX	GREAT FALLS, MT/Great Falls
TBW	TAMPA BAY AREA, FL/Ruskin
MUX	SAN FRANCISCO BAY AREA, CA/Sa
GYX	PORTLAND, ME/Gray
MHX	MOREHEAD CITY, NC/Newport
LCH	LAKE CHARLES, LA/Lake Charles
IND	INDIANAPOLIS, IN/Indianapolis
CAE	COLUMBIA, SC/Columbia
MTX	SALT LAKE CITY, UT/Elder County
MSX	MISSOULA, MT/Missoula County
ILN	CINCINNATI, OH/Wilmington
DMX	DES MOINES, IA/Johnston
RGX	RENO, NV/Washoe County
MRX	KNOXVILLE/TRI-CITIES, TN/Morr
LTX	WILMINGTON, NC/Shallotte
RAX	RALEIGH/DURHAM, NC/Clayton
OHX	NASHVILLE, TN/Old Hickory
BHX	EUREKA, CA/Humboldt County
RTX	PORTLAND, OR/Scappoose
OAX	OMAHA, NE/Valley
GRB	GREEN BAY, WI/Ashwaubenon
JAX	JACKSONVILLE, FL/Jacksonville
TLH	TALLAHASSEE, FL/Tallahassee
ABX	ALBUQUERQUE, NM/Albuquerque
FCX	ROANOKE, VA/Floyd County
PUX	PUEBLO, CO/Pueblo County
AKQ	WAKEFIELD, VA/Wakefield
RLX	CHARLESTON, WV/Ruthdale
ABR	ABERDEEN, SD/Aberdeen
DVN	QUAD CITIES, IA/Davenport
PAH	PADUCAH, KY/Paducah
ESX	LAS VEGAS, NV/Nelson
LBB	LUBBOCK, TX/Lubbock
SGF	SPRINGFIELD, MO/Springfield
MAF	MIDLAND/ODESSA, TX/MidlandW
MKX	MILWAUKEE, WI/Dousman
HNX	SAN JOAQUIN VALLEY, CA/Hanfor
BRO	BROWNSVILLE, TX/Brownsville

Agency: NWS (continued)

Equip ID	WFO/Radar Site
SHV	SHREVEPORT, LA/Shreveport
BIS	BISMARCK, ND/Bismarck
FSD	SIOUX FALLS, SD/Sioux Falls
CYS	CHEYENNE, WY/Cheyenne
MPX	MINNEAPOLIS, MN/Chanhassen
EMX	TUCSON, AZ/Pima County
ILX	CENTRAL ILLINOIS, IL/Lincoln
GRR	GRAND RAPIDS, MI/Grand Rapids
MQT	MARQUETTE, MI/Negaunee
CBW	CARIBOU, ME/Houlton
SFX	POCATELLO/IDAHO FALLS, ID/Spr
GSP	GREENVILLE/SPARTANBURG, SC/Gr
BLX	BILLINGS, MT/Yellowstone County
BUF	BUFFALO, NY/Cheektowaga
RIW	RIVERTON, WY/Riverton
LRX	ELKO, NV/Lander County
MAX	MEDFORD, OR/Jackson County
DLH	DULUTH, MN/Duluth
FSX	FLAGSTAFF, AZ/Coconino
GJX	GRAND JUNCTION, CO/Mesa
CLX	CHARLESTON, SC/Grays
MVX	EASTERN NORTH DAKOTA, ND/Mayv
UDX	RAPID CITY, SD/New Underwood
OTX	SPOKANE, WA/Spokane
EPZ	EL PASO, TX/Santa Teresa
PDT	PENDLETON, OR/Pendleton
SJT	SAN ANGELO, TX/San Angelo
LNX	NORTH PLATTE, NE/Thedford
APX	NORTH CENTRAL LOWER MICHIGAN
GGW	GLASGOW, MT/Glasgow
ARX	LA CROSSE, WI/La Crosse
CRP	CORPUS CHRISTI, TX/Corpus Christi
NKX	SAN DIEGO, CA/San Diego
JKL	JACKSON, KY/Jackson
BYX	KEY WEST, FL/Boca Chica Key
YUX	PHOENIX, AZ/Yuma
SOX	SAN DIEGO, CA/Santa Ana Mount
ICX	SALT LAKE CITY, UT/Cedar City
CXX	BURLINGTON, VT/Colchester
SRX	TULSA, OK/Western Arkansas
HTX	BIRMINGHAM, AL/Northeastern A
IWX	NORTHERN INDIANA, IN/North We

Agency: FAA

Equip ID	WFO/Radar Site
APD	FAIRBANKS, AK/Pedro Dome
AEC	FAIRBANKS, AK/Nome
JUA	SAN JUAN, PR/Cayey
ACG	JUNEAU, AK/Sitka
AIH	ANCHORAGE, AK/Middleton Island
ABC	ANCHORAGE, AK/Bethel
HMO	HONOLULU, HI/Molokai
HKI	HONOLULU, HI/Kauai
AKC	ANCHORAGE, AK/King Salmon
AHG	ANCHORAGE, AK/Nikiski
HWA	HONOLULU, HI/Hawaii
HKM	HONOLULU, HI/Kohala

Agency: DOD

Equip ID	WFO/Radar Site
FDR	OKLAHOMA CITY, OK/Frederick M
EVX	TALLAHASSEE, FL/Northwest Florida
DOX	WAKEFIELD, VA/Ellendale State
GRK	DALLAS/FORT WORTH, TX/Robert
VBX	LOS ANGELES, CA/Orcutt Oil Field
GUA	GUAM, GU/Barrigada Communications
VNX	OKLAHOMA CITY, OK/Kegelman Au
DYX	SAN ANGELO, TX/Shackelford Co
JGX	ATLANTA, GA/State Hwy 96
MXX	BIRMINGHAM, AL/East Alabama
FDX	ALBUQUERQUE, NM/State Rd 89
HDX	EL PASO, TX/White Sands Missi
DFX	AUSTIN/SAN ANTONIO, TX/US Hwy
MBX	BISMARCK, ND/McHenry County
POE	LAKE CHARLES, LA/Ft. Polk
GWX	MEMPHIS, TN/MS Hwy 8 & US Hwy
EYX	LAS VEGAS, NV/Edwards AFB
VAX	TALLAHASSEE, FL/State Rd 129
BBX	SACRAMENTO, CA/Oro Dam Blvd W
TYX	BURLINGTON, VT/Ft. Drum
EOX	BIRMINGHAM, AL/Ft. Rucker
HPX	PADUCAH, KY/US Hwy 41 N

TOTAL: 154

NWS GPS Radiosonde Program

The NWS will be gradually replacing the current weather balloon (radiosonde) network in the U.S. with a new GPS radiosonde network. Currently the new network has almost 200 sites and is expected to be fully operational by 2005. The current radiosonde system consists of 102 weather balloon launch sites where balloons are launched twice daily (0000 and 1200Z) to sample the atmosphere. These are still labor intensive and prone to be error-laden. The new GPS-oriented system will be considerably more accurate but will still be balloon launched.

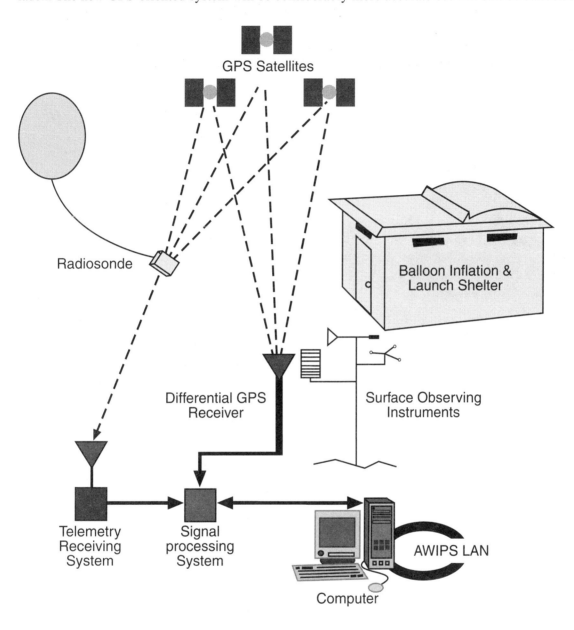

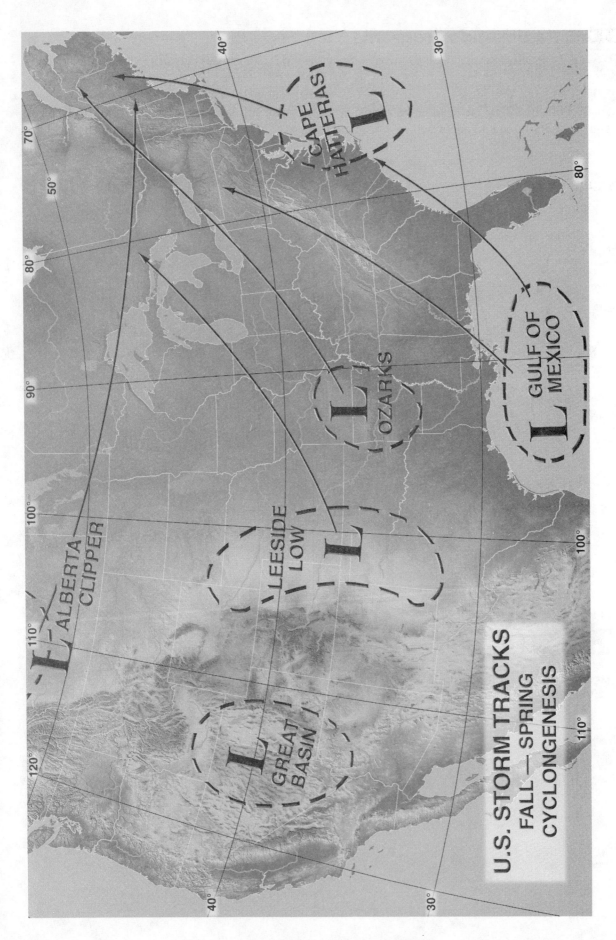

U.S. STORM TRACKS
FALL — SPRING
CYCLONGENESIS

GREAT
BASIN

ALBERTA
CLIPPER

LEESIDE
LOW

OZARKS

GULF OF
MEXICO

CAPE
HATTERAS

Appendix C: *Color Illustrations: Weather Maps and Analyses*

Descriptions of the charts

Page 169: Radar and WST messages charted on AWC "Product Overlay" webpage

This is really a cool weather product. AWC has set up a base map on their webpage upon which you can "overlay" different aviation weather data such as radar reflectivity, pilot reports on icing and turbulence, and much more. The example on Page 167 shows the base map displayed with terrain and states, over which is added: radar reflectivity (dark blue – yellow areas over Illinois, Indiana and Michigan—moderate to strong thunderstorm activity); turbulence (light blue symbols); icing (green symbols over Canada, northern Minnesota and eastern Iowa—symbol interpretations for these can be found on AC 00-45E Page 11-3); and finally, the green outlined areas are convective outlooks ("1E"), and two smaller red areas, convective SIGMETs 28E (east), and 28C (central). This webpage allows you to also call up visible satellite imagery, infrared imagery, AIRMETs, etc. …A good 3-D tool for the pilot to study weather products!

Pages 170–171: Plotted surface observation data (from the ADDS website)

Surface sea-level pressure changes are determined every 3 hours and coded as part of the Remarks section of the METAR, which indicates to pilots whether the pressure has been rising, falling, or steady in the last three hours at a station. These charts are a method to show this information *visually*. For example, in the 3-Hour Pressure Tendency chart (top left of the 4 charts), all the "plus" changes (tan to dark tan surrounding reddish hues) show where pressure is rising. Compare this to the Wind Speed/MSLP chart (lower right-hand chart): wind arrows are drawn on this chart, but also examine the pressure pattern (i.e., the isobars drawn for every 4 mb, just like on the surface analysis chart). This shows an area of high pressure over Oregon and eastwards into Utah. The pressure-tendency chart shows that area of high pressure will probably move eastward over the next 24 hours, with the highest pressure areas forming where the largest pressure rises are depicted (over the Great Plains) at 0100 UTC Wednesday January 31, 2001.

Now use the same type of reasoning for the low-pressure area shown over the Great Lakes to the New England region (0100 UTC, 01/31/01). According to the pressure "falls" (the large elongated oval shape off the eastern seaboard—the blue shades surrounding reddish hues), the low-pressure area will move offshore to this area of falls over the next 24 hours.

The bottom left chart is the Dewpoint-Temperature analysis: dew point is a measure of how much water vapor is in the air. The air's ability to hold moisture is a function of the air temperature—colder air cannot hold as much water vapor as warm air. For example, a station in California with a dew point of 45° and humidity of 90%, compared with a Gulf Coast station's dew point of 60° and humidity of 90%, has much less moisture than the Gulf station.

At top right, in the Temperature chart—compare the temperature and dew points over the Gulf of Mexico to those over coastal California. Stations along the Gulf Coast and adjacent waters have temperatures in the low-mid 60s (it is January!) with dewpoint values of high 50s to low 60s: very humid air with high moisture content. If dew points are over 70°, the air has enough moisture to create thunderstorms—providing that other atmospheric factors such as instability, etc., are present.

Can you locate the frontal zone on the Wind Speed chart? Notice the rapid change of temperature in a short horizontal distance occurring from pale green to the very dark green over central and northwest Texas. Actually, this "gradient" (change) is greater over central and northwest Arkansas, western Kentucky, and into southern Ohio, and marks the location of the front. Now can you explain why there are colder (light to medium green) temperatures extending almost north to south over western Virginia, North Carolina, into northwestern Georgia? If you think you can, email me the answer at darhol@bellsouth.net.

Further note about the Wind Speed/MSLP chart: this is nothing but a cleaned-up surface analysis chart with isobars and wind direction. Look closely and you can see a strong flow of winds from the south and southwest over the SE U.S., into east Texas. Over northwest Texas, Oklahoma, Missouri, and Arkansas, the winds are from the north or northwest and they appear to be pretty strong over Kansas and Nebraska. With a little effort you can draw a line from Lubbock, TX–southeast OK–northwest AR–southeast IL, to Chicago, IL, and come pretty close to the location of the surface cold front.

Pages 172–173: Jet stream analysis examples

This chart is an excellent example of how satellite imagery is helping to fill in "gaps" of the observational network. There are two jets shown on the chart: The meandering jet stream looping in a pronounced meridional pattern over the central and north Pacific, and then across the U.S. is the Polar Front Jet stream (PFJ). The 60-knot jet across the lower-latitude Pacific (east of Hawaii) is the Subtropical Jet (STJ), which shows a good cirrus-cirrostratus cloud shield mainly to the southeast of the jet. The **H's** and **L's** on the chart refer to high-speed and low-speed winds, respectively. The blue arrows show the overall flow of air at the 300 mb level.

The forecast chart on Page 173 is based on the data from the Page 172 chart. Compare the two charts and notice that the forecast calls for the major jet pattern of troughs and ridges to shift eastward. Also make note that the strong wind maxima of the jet over northern Oklahoma–southern Missouri has been forecast to shift eastward and northward into Kansas, to central Missouri, to southern Illinois and Indiana.

Page 174: "Hourly weather depiction" chart example from AAWU website

An excellent way to display surface weather observations (METARs). At a glance you can readily determine the areas of IFR, MVFR and VFR weather. The data is displayed in a modified format of the station model shown in Chapter 2 of this book and AC 00-45E Section 5. Notice the small black dots in British Columbia and the Yukon Territory of Canada—these are automated weather stations.

Page 175: Graphical area forecast chart examples from AAWU

These are excellent charts in that they give the pilot an overall view of several aspects of weather in "one look." The bottom panel is a surface forecast prog issued at 1200Z and valid for 1800Z, which shows the forecast position of a strong cold front type of occlusion moving to the northeast at 10 knots. Also shown are the clouds and weather that accompany the system. The top panel is valid 3 hours later (2100Z) and is a very nice display of forecast icing and freezing level information. (Now why can't the "lower 48" NWS do something like this?)

Page 176: Canadian graphical area forecast example

This is a colorful pictorial overview of the weather over a fairly large area. While the chart appears somewhat confusing at first, a closer look will reveal several patterns. The heavy black line delineates the forecast area—the maritime provinces of Canada. The large **H** and **L** show that the pressure systems dominate over the region. The lines—isobars—give the viewer a good indication of wind direction and speed. The brown scalloped lines denote areas of MVFR and IFR forecast weather conditions. No frontal systems are depicted, but it should be obvious to the viewer there is some kind of frontal system occurring between the north-northeast flow over the western half of the chart, and the south-southwest flow over the eastern half. Forecast conditions include visibility; for example, the "2-P6SM–SN" plotted on the chart over eastern Quebec is forecasting visibilities between 2–6+ statute miles in light snow. The small area outlined in red has forecast conditions of patchy 2–5 miles of freezing rain and drizzle; the cloud conditions are plotted over eastern Quebec. Notice the VFR conditions over southern Newfoundland just east of the low-pressure cell and the arrow with 20—this is the direction and movement of the cell.

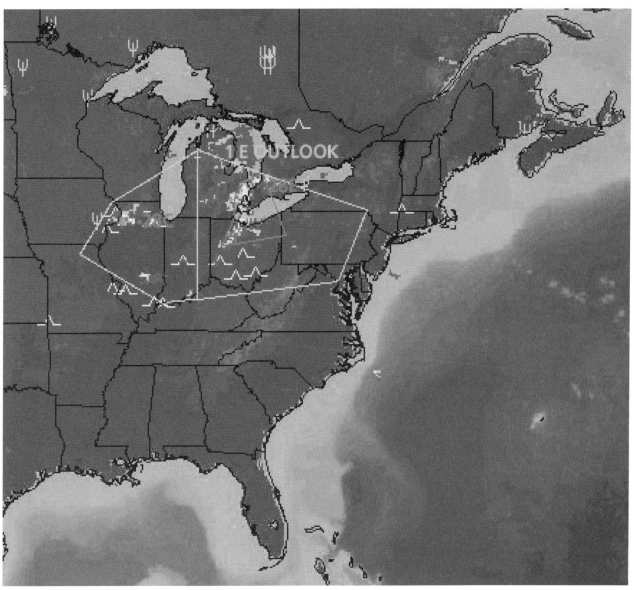

Courtesy NWS/AWC website (www.awc-kc.noaa.gov)

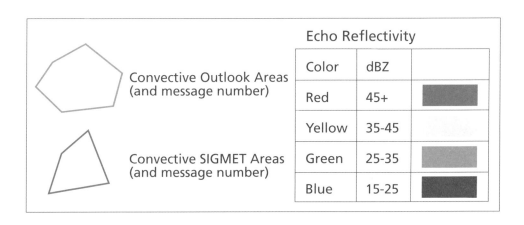

Convective Outlook Areas (and message number)	Echo Reflectivity		
	Color	dBZ	
	Red	45+	
	Yellow	35-45	
Convective SIGMET Areas (and message number)	Green	25-35	
	Blue	15-25	

3-Hour Pressure Tend. (mb/hr)

Source: Aviation Digital Data Service (http:adds.awc-kc.noaa.gov)

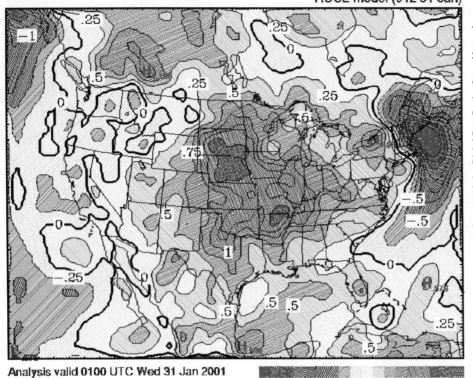

RUC2 model (01z 31 Jan)

Analysis valid 0100 UTC Wed 31 Jan 2001

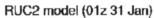

Dewpoint Temperature (F)

RUC2 model (01z 31 Jan)

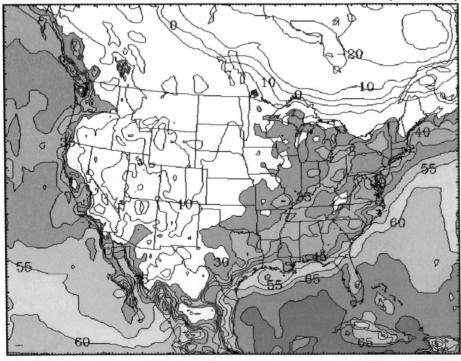

Analysis valid 0100 UTC Wed 31 Jan 2001

Temperature (F)

RUC2 model (01z 31 Jan)

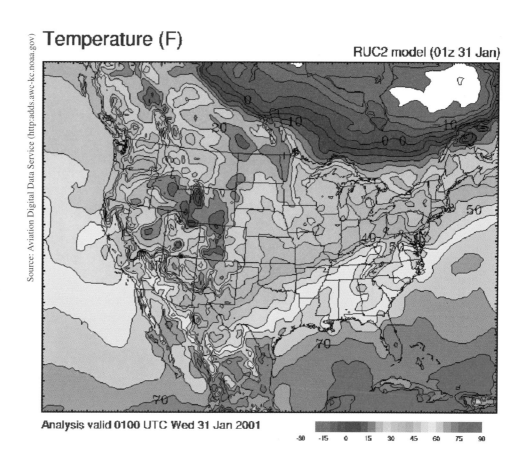

Analysis valid 0100 UTC Wed 31 Jan 2001

-30 -15 0 15 30 45 60 75 90

Wind Speed (kts) / MSLP (mb)

RUC2 model (01z 31 Jan)

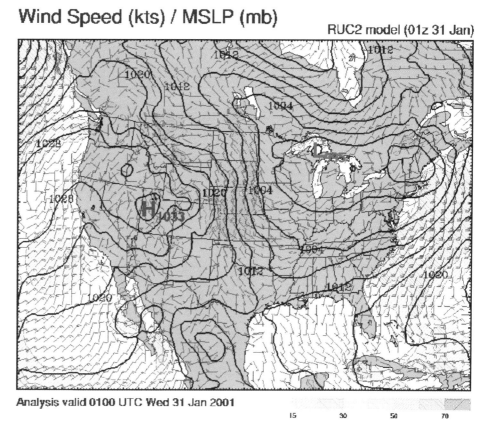

Analysis valid 0100 UTC Wed 31 Jan 2001

15   30   50   70

Appendix C: *Color Illustrations: Weather Maps and Analyses*   *171*

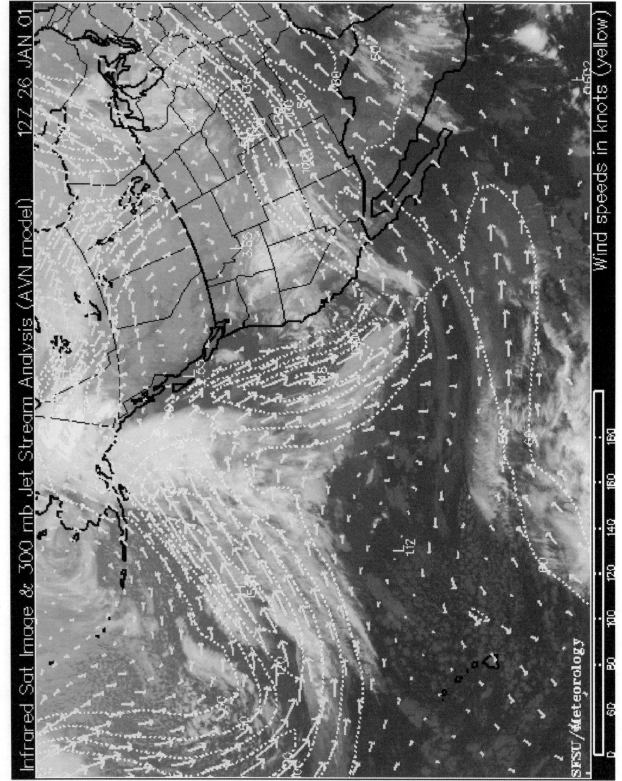

Courtesy Department of Geosciences, San Francisco State University

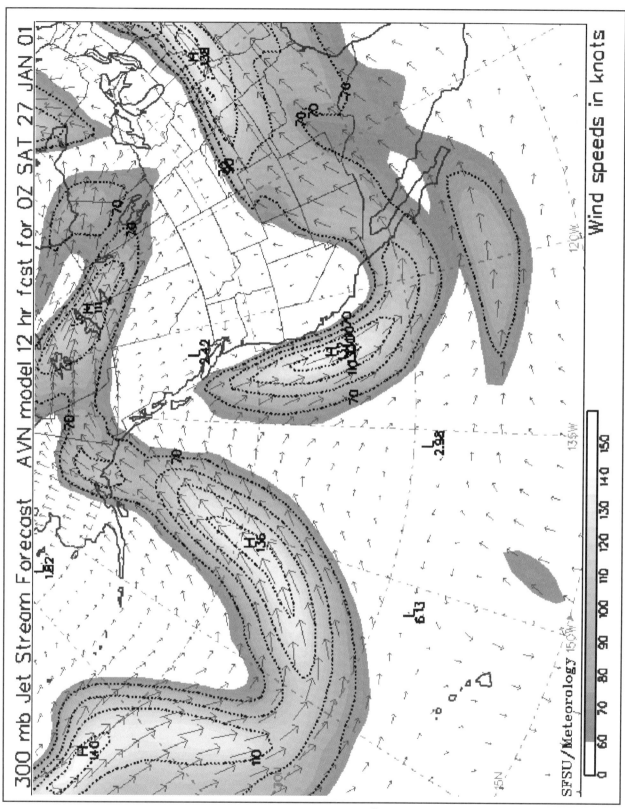

Courtesy Department of Geosciences, San Francisco State University

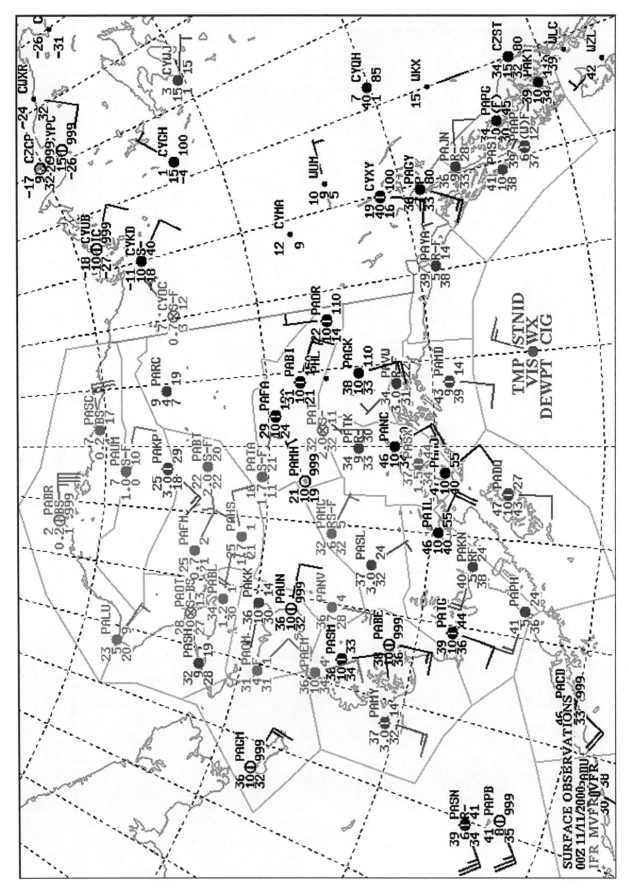

Courtesy Alaska Aviation Weather Unit website (www.alaska.net/~aawu)

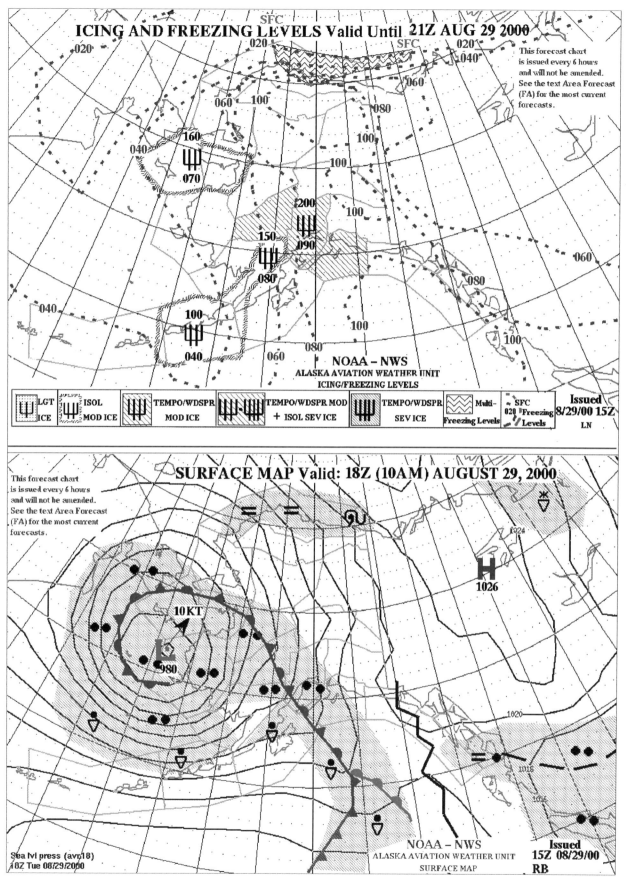

Courtesy Alaska Aviation Weather Unit website (www.alaska.net/~aawu)

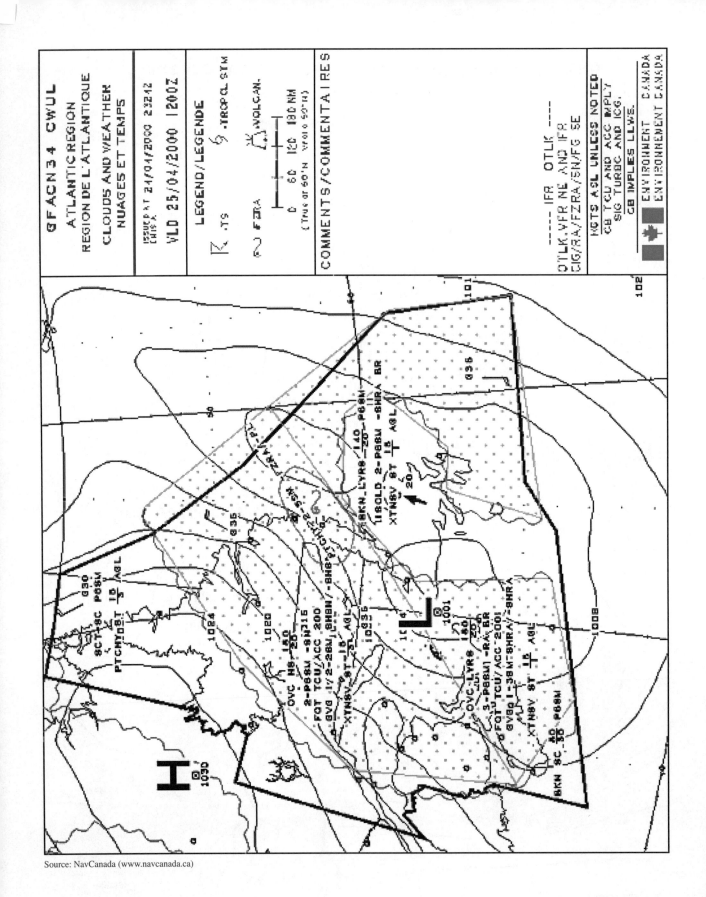

Source: NavCanada (www.navcanada.ca)

Appendix D: *Glossary*

absolute zero. A temperature reading of -273°C (-460°F); the temperature of free space.

adiabatic process. A process that takes place in the atmosphere with no transfer of heat between the rising or sinking of a mass of air. When a mass of air sinks, it warms by compression—the temperature of the air goes up and the humidity drops. Inversely, a rising air mass is cooled by expansion and the humidity rises.

advection. The horizontal movement of air (wind). Advection may move colder air into a warmer area (cold air advection), or move warmer air into a colder area (warm air advection).

advection fog. Warm moist air moves over a colder surface; the air cools to its dewpoint temperature, and fog forms. Very common along the coast of California and Oregon.

albedo. The percentage of solar radiation *reflected* by a surface compared to the amount of radiation striking and being *absorbed* by the surface.

Aleutian low. The subpolar low-pressure system usually located over or near the Aleutian Islands and the Bering Strait.

anabatic wind. An upslope wind.

arcus cloud. A type of roll cloud associated with thunderstorm gust fronts. The cloud forms when warm, moisture-laden air is forced upward over the leading edge of the thunderstorm's cold air outflow. It is sometimes called a shelf cloud.

atmospheric boundary layer. The layer of air from the surface upwards to about 3,000–4,000 feet AGL where the wind speed and direction is changed by the frictional effects of the surface over which the air is passing. Sometimes referred to as the friction layer.

backdoor cold front. This type of cold front is typical of the northeastern U.S. Here, colder Canadian air moves from the northeast towards the southwest—its leading edge is called the backdoor front. Most cold fronts move from the northwest or north towards the southeast or south.

backing wind. A wind that changes direction in a counterclockwise direction with increasing height. *See also* warm and cold air advection.

baroclinic atmosphere. On an upper-air constant pressure chart (e.g. the 500-mb chart), if the isotherms and contour lines are drawn so that the contours cross the isotherms (lines of equal temperature), this atmosphere is described as baroclinic, associated with developing storm systems and variable weather conditions.

baroclinic instability. (Related to the above definition.) Strong cold and warm air advection, along with pronounced vertical wind shear and the flow pattern aloft, shows a diverging or diffluent pattern: this is a very unstable atmosphere.

barotropic atmosphere. A stable atmosphere; on the constant pressure charts, the contour lines of pressure are parallel to the isotherms—no advection is occurring and no storms can develop.

billow clouds. Rows or lines of clouds oriented at right angles to the wind. There is also a stable layer of air (inversion) at the top of these clouds. They usually only last for a few minutes or so.

blizzard. Heavy falling snow and low temperatures with strong winds in excess of 35 mph; if these conditions persist after the snow has stopped falling, it is called a ground blizzard.

Boulder winds. Locally strong downslope winds along the eastern slopes of the Rockies near Boulder, Colorado. These occur most frequently in the late winter into spring.

bow echo. Radar echo shaped like an archer's bow. This is a radar "bulge" on a squall line, where severe convective activity is most likely to develop.

Buys Ballot's Law. A handy rule for determining where low pressure is with respect to your location. With your back to the surface wind, you extend your left arm and then turn your body 20–30 degrees to the right; your left hand is now pointing towards low pressure. For example: The surface wind is blowing from the southwest (240 degrees). You put your back to the wind and then turn your body 20 degrees. Your left hand is now pointing towards the north-northwest (350 degrees). Over the ocean, since the effect of friction is minimal (except in a hurricane!), you would not turn your body more than 5 degrees. If you use the upper-level winds (above the friction or boundary layer) you do not turn your body to the right at all.

California norther. Strong cold dry northerly winds in north central California. Much like the Chinook in that downslope heating warms the air—but the air is still cold.

CAPE. Convectively available potential energy. Used by the Storm Prediction Center (SPC) at Norman, OK.

Chinook wind. A strong, warm downslope wind that flows downward over the eastern slopes of the Rockies. Particularly active in eastern Colorado and northeastern New Mexico in late winter and spring.

cloudburst. A sudden heavy rain shower.

cold air advection. When the wind direction changes counterclockwise (i.e., south to southeast, east) with increasing height above the surface, cold advection is occurring (also called a backing wind).

cold core low. A deep low-pressure cell found on the upper-level constant pressure charts. The coldest air on any particular upper-air chart is found in the trough of low pressure where this low is located. One example is the Icelandic Low. Associated with strong mid-latitude wave (frontal) cyclones.

Columbia Gorge wind. Occurs in Washington State over the Columbia River Gorge area. Cold high pressure air accumulates over the Columbia Plateau and then flows westward in response to a pressure gradient (high to low) between the cold high pressure and warmer low pressure offshore from Washington. These winds, channeled by the river gorge, are often blustery, cold, and gale force.

comma cloud. As viewed from a satellite, the shape of clouds associated with a mid-latitude wave cyclone as it starts to "occlude."

condensation. When air is cooled to its dew point the air is said to be saturated. Any further cooling will produce condensation either as dew, fog or cloud droplets.

conditionally unstable air. A state of the atmosphere brought about when the radiosonde (balloon data) indicates that the temperature of the air is less than 10°C/km, but greater than 6°C/km. This is a common atmospheric condition when the air is stable in the morning but becomes unstable in the afternoon. Associated with stratocumulus clouds (mildly unstable). *See also* dry adiabatic lapse rate, and moist adiabatic lapse rate.

constant pressure charts. (Also called isobaric charts.) These charts are prepared for standard atmospheric levels (850 mb, 700 mb, 500 mb, 300 mb, 250 mb and 200 mb; for 5,000', 10,000', 18,000', 30,000', 34,000' and 39,000'). *See* AC 00-45E Section 8 as well as Chapter 15 in this book.

convectively unstable. This atmospheric condition occurs when the lower layers of the atmosphere consist of warm moist air with a layer of drier colder air above the warm moist air. As the lower layer of air becomes heated (solar heating) or is forced to rise (terrain features), the layers of air being lifted will become unstable. This leads us to an old rule: "If you want the atmosphere to become unstable, lift it."

convergence. This process can occur at or near the surface or aloft. This refers to the mass movement of air where faster-moving air overtakes slower-moving air. If this process occurs aloft, the pressure at and near the surface will rise (increased mass). Where lower-level winds are moving air towards the center of a low-pressure cell (mass convergence) this air will then rise, cool adiabatically, and eventually clouds will form.

cutoff low. A cold-core low that has been "cut off" or separated from the main trough of low pressure and exists as a cool or cold area of colder/cooler air. This low cell will now slowly drift eastward causing cloudiness and precipitation and will eventually "fill" (pressure rises) and will then cease to exist. This type of system is common in the winter or early spring over the Pacific coastal areas of southern California, and over southern Nevada-Arizona.

cyclogenesis. The process by which a low-pressure system undergoes intensification (deepening). If a surface low-pressure system intensifies within a relative short period of time, you can be sure there is significant divergence going on aloft over this area of low pressure.

deposition. At subfreezing temperatures, ice will often form as water vapor changes directly into ice without going through the liquid stage. Frost is a good example of deposition.

derecho. A rare severe thunderstorm known for its straight-line damaging winds; sometimes occurring over Minnesota. Derechoes have strong winds that may be enhanced by microburst activity; they can cause widespread damage over hundreds of square miles.

dewpoint temperature. The temperature at which condensation will start to occur if further cooling takes place.

dissipation stage. The dying stage of a thunderstorm; characterized by downdrafts predominant throughout the main body of the storm.

divergence. Just like convergence, divergence can have speed as well as directional divergence. A flow of slow-moving air suddenly shows an increase in speed aloft—at the surface the pressure will show a decrease. Directional divergence is very similar to what happens when a stream of water suddenly flows into an area where its banks are further apart.

Doppler radar. This radar calculates the velocity of falling precipitation either away or towards the radar set by using the Doppler shift effect. See the following address for radar information: www-empo.mit.edu/Radar_lab/FAQ.html.

downburst. A very strong but localized downdraft of air that occurs with a severe thunderstorm. This will often spread out rapidly in advance of the storm system. *See* gust front.

dry adiabatic lapse rate. Air that is not saturated—its humidity is less then 100%. When this air is lifted by a frontal surface, convergent winds, or terrain, it will cool at the rate of 10°C/km (5.5°F/1,000 feet).

dryline. A moisture boundary that separates warm moist air from hot dry air in west central or western Texas. Represents a zone of instability where severe thunderstorms may occur. Also called the Marfa or dewpoint front.

easterly wave. A relatively shallow disturbance in the Trade Wind regions of the tropics which migrates from east to west. This is a north-south line of thunderstorms and rain showers which may occasionally develop into a tropical depression or storm.

entrainment. As a thunderstorm starts to build, it will "entrain" or pull-in the outside air into the storm cell. This is similar to the principle of "drafting" as practiced by professional racing drivers at places like Daytona Beach Speedway.

environmental lapse rate. The rate of temperature decrease in the atmosphere as a weather balloon rises.

extratropical cyclone. Another name for a mid-latitude, low-pressure system and its associated frontal systems.

eye wall. The rather dense area of clouds surrounding the eye of a hurricane/typhoon.

fall streaks. Heavier ice crystals that fall from cirrus clouds and then evaporate in the drier air below the clouds.

fall wind. (Also called a *katabatic* wind.) Strong winds, usually cold, that blow downslope from areas of cold, high-pressure air.

freezing rain. Warm air or drizzle that falls through a layer of subfreezing air and turns into ice upon impact with an object—such as an aircraft! (This forms clear ice—FZRA or FZDZ.)

flanking line. A line of cumulus and cumulus congestus connected to and extending outward from the most active part of a severe thunderstorm. The line is usually located on the south or southwest side of the parent storm and has a stair-step appearance in that the cumulus gets progressively larger and higher, closer to the parent thunderstorm.

frontal wave. A wave-like deformation that forms along a frontal zone, usually a cold front. These may develop into an "open wave" and then into an occluded frontal system.

frontogenesis. The forming and strengthening of a frontal system.

frontolysis. The weakening and dissipation of a frontal system.

graupel. Small granular pieces of ice, a form of precipitation—sometimes referred to as "soft hail."

ground fog. Also known as radiation fog. Fog that forms over land surfaces during a clear night with light winds.

gust front. The leading edge of the cold air moving rapidly outward from a thunderstorm's downburst of precipitation and cold air. This is a boundary between the cold air and warm moist unstable air. Also referred to as an outflow boundary.

gustnado. A vertical spinning circulation that often forms along a thunderstorm's outflow boundary/gust front. A non-tornadic circulation, it is still capable of causing a lot of damage.

haze. Dry or wet — dry haze is formed from very small dust or dirt particles and can reduce visibility to 5 or 6 miles. Usually occurs in the drier western states and has a violet or purplish color due to light refraction by the haze particles. Wet haze forms near the coast and appears white, but it is not fog since the temperature/ dew point is some value (i.e., not 100% humidity). Condensation of water on very small salt particles forms the wet haze when the relative humidity is as low as 75% or higher.

heat lightning. Distant lightning that is occurring but is too far away for one to hear the thunder.

high inversion fog. A layer of fog that lifts away from the surface of the earth because of surface heating in the morning. The fog doesn't dissipate because of a strong inversion above the fog layer. Common over the Sacramento and San Joaquin Rivers (California) in winter.

hook-shaped echo. An echo on the radar scope in the shape of a hook or curve on the south side of a thunderstorm which often denotes the formation or occurrence of a tornado.

Icelandic low. A deep subpolar low-pressure system usually situated near Iceland. Can be located on the surface analysis chart as well as the upper-level charts. Also called a wave cyclone.

isobars. Lines of equal pressure drawn on the surface analysis chart to determine the pattern of high- and low-pressure systems.

isotachs. Lines of equal wind speed drawn on the 300, 250, and 200 mb charts. (AC 00-45E, Section 8.)

jet streak. The elongated relatively narrow band of the winds at and above 70 knots drawn on the 300, 250, and 200 Mb charts. Also called the jet maxima.

Joules/kg. The amount of work done by lifting a force of one Newton by one meter.

katabatic wind. Any strong downslope wind; usually cold.

lake effect snows. Snow showers that form on the downwind side of a large body of water; i.e., the great Salt Lake or Great Lakes. Cold dry air from Canada is rapidly modified into a moist unstable air mass on the downwind side of the lake, and snow showers occur.

land breeze. A coastal or lake breeze that flows from land to water. Usually weak and occurs at night. One half of the land-sea breeze couplet.

LCL. Lifting condensation level. The level at which the cloud base formed when air is lifted to condensation. You will often find this term in the convective outlook (AC) message.

lee-side low. An area of low pressure that forms and develops on the lee (downwind) side of a mountain range. Common in the colder half of the year on the eastern flanks of the Rockies and to a lesser extent the Sierra Nevada mountains. A famous example is the storm system that forms to the lee of the Canadian Rockies — the "Alberta Clipper."

lifted index (LI). *See* AC 00-45E Section 9 and Chapter 14 in this book.

long waves. Also called Rossby waves. The wave-like pattern of the upper-level winds in the prevailing mid-latitude westerlies.

low-level jet stream. These form in the lower 1,000–6,000 feet of the atmosphere with speeds of 35–50 knots, appearing most often over Texas and northward into Oklahoma. They are instrumental in the development of the vertical wind shear that is necessary for a severe thunderstorm to develop.

macroburst. A strong thunderstorm down burst of cool moist air larger than two miles. Smaller bursts are called microbursts.

mammatus clouds. These are associated with thunderstorm activity and are usually formed on the underside of the thunderstorm anvil; they resemble sagging pouches. They do not signify a tornado's occurrence.

meridional flow. An atmospheric circulation in the middle latitudes (westerlies) that has a strong looping pattern of ridges and troughs. *See* Chapter 15.

mesoscale convective complex (MCC). This is a large area of thunderstorm activity which can cover an area as widespread as, for example, the size of the state of Iowa.

mesocyclone. A strongly sheared thunderstorm may produce a strong column of cyclonically rotating air within the storm which may then produce a tornado.

moist adiabatic lapse rate. When saturated air (100% relative humidity) is lifted, it cools at an average rate of 6°C/km (3.3°F/1,000') and will produce clouds.

multi-cell storm(s). Thunderstorms organized in a line or cluster, with each cell in a different stage of growth and development.

north-easter (nor'easter). Winds associated with a strong Cape Hatteras storm which sets up strong, persistent northeasterly winds and inclement weather over the New England states and as far south as New Jersey and Delaware. May also develop as a backdoor cold-frontal system moves southwest over New England.

occluded frontal system. Two variations of the occluded front—

cold frontal occlusion. Common in the central plains and eastward where cold, continental polar air pushes into the U.S. behind an active cold front. East of the frontal wave, cool, somewhat moist air from the Atlantic, or colder air from Canada, is dominant. The cold front pushes under warmer air from the Gulf, as well as the cool air east and north of the warm frontal system. The occluded front that forms is a continuation of the warm front that was forced aloft by the colder dense air from Canada.

warm frontal occlusion. Common along the Pacific Northwest coastal region into California, Oregon and Washington States. Cool, moist Pacific air (that originally came from Siberia) pushes in behind the cold front and moves onshore. Cold, dry Canadian polar air lies northeast of the warm frontal system and the cool Pacific air is lifted up over the colder denser air.

omega high. (Also called a blocking high.) A ridge of high pressure, found in the middle and upper levels of the atmosphere, that has the shape of the Greek letter "omega" (Ω). This pressure system will persist over the same region for many days. With this situation, the storm track will be pushed north of its usual position, bringing abnormally dry conditions across a broad area.

overrunning. This occurs when warm moist air is either forced aloft by colder denser air (cold front), or when retreating cold air is overtaken by warm moist air (warm front).

pileus cloud. A smooth arcuate-shaped cloud that forms above a growing thunderstorm or over the crests of a mountain range. Also called a cap cloud.

polar easterlies. In the lower atmosphere over the polar regions, we find cold high-pressure air. To the south we find the polar front. The predominant wind pattern is that of air flowing from the north towards the lower pressure zone of the front; polar easterlies or north-easterlies.

polar front. This is an almost continuous frontal zone around the world in the higher latitudes, which separates colder, denser air masses from warmer, usually moist, lower latitude air masses.

polar front jet. At the 300-mb level, this jet is the boundary between colder low-pressure air to the north and warmer higher-pressure air to the south. The surface boundary between cold polar air and warmer subtropical air is the polar front; this front slopes back over the colder air aloft.

prevailing westerlies. Also called the "westerly wind belt"; it is strongest and more persistent in the southern hemisphere (which is predominantly ocean).

pulse thunderstorm. Some single-cell thunderstorms (LI-1 or -2) may produce brief severe weather events (strong winds, precipitation, small hail). These thunderstorms tend to form in a more unstable environment (LI-3 or -4).

radiosonde. An instrument package that is borne aloft by balloon twice daily. Measurements of pressure, humidity and temperature are transmitted to a ground receiving station. Wind measurements are obtained by the balloon with radar. The radiosonde was first developed and used in the USSR in the late 1920s.

rain-free base. The dark base of the cumulonimbus that has no precipitation. Usually observed to the south or southwest of the precipitation shaft. The wall cloud usually forms on the rain-free base.

rain shadow. The area downwind (lee) of a mountain range. These areas are quite drier then the upwind slopes. Area west of the Andes and the Cascade Mountains are two good examples.

relative humidity. The ratio between the amount of water vapor in the air, to the amount of water vapor the air *could* contain at a particular temperature. A common measurement, but it doesn't give you an idea of how much vapor is actually in the air.

return stroke. This is the stroke of lightning that we *see* as lightning—the luminous stroke that propagates upward from the surface to the cloud.

ridge. An area of high pressure where the air flow aloft has a pronounced looping, with the winds (west to east) moving to the northeast, then east and then southeast, as the air passes over the ridge.

roll cloud. Tubular-shaped, horizontally-oriented cloud forming above and behind the leading edge of the cold, outward-moving air (gust front). These have a very visible and pronounced spinning motion.

rotor cloud. These cumuliform clouds are located on the leeward side of mountain ranges that have strong updrafts on the upwind side of the cloud and strong downdrafts on the downwind side of the cloud. If sufficient moisture is not available, these rotors can then become invisible and be quite hazardous to flight.

Santa Ana wind. A cousin of the Chinook, in that it is a very dry, warm downslope wind that blows in southern California. Strong high pressure over the Basin and Range mountain complexes of Nevada, coupled with low pressure offshore of California will establish these winds.

sea breeze. Found along coastal regions of lakes or oceans, this is part of the land-sea breeze couplet. The sea breeze, with its lower pressure, blows from the higher pressure offshore towards the land. The leading edge of this cooler moist air is also called a sea breeze front.

semi-permanent highs and lows. The high-pressure regions are more popularly known in the U.S. as the "Bermuda" or "Azores high." Other large high-pressure areas are located over every major ocean in the subtropical regions. The lows, or cyclones—which are found in the higher, colder latitudes—are known as the Icelandic and Aleutian lows. These systems tend to persist over their respective latitudes, although the low-pressure systems show greater latitudinal movement.

"scotch mist." (No, it's not an alcoholic beverage!) This is an IFR combination of drizzle and mist, what is now reported on METARs as BR. In Cornwall and Devonshire, UK, this phenomenon is known as "Mizzle."

scud. A pilot should never "scud" run. These are ragged fragments of stratus or fractus that often move fairly rapidly under the main deck of clouds; drizzle is also usually present (or is a distinct possibility). These fragments can quickly increase from a scattered to an overcast condition.

sheet lightning. This is nothing more than in-cloud lightning, in which the lightning stroke(s) are diffused by the cloud mass.

shelf cloud. This cloud is attached to the leading edge of a thunderstorm; it is formed when warm moist air is "scooped" or forced to rise over the colder air of the thunderstorm's gust front.

Siberian high. A cold, shallow high-pressure system that forms over the cold elevated terrain of Mongolia and Siberia—only found in the winter half of the year.

snow flurries. Light intermittent showers of snow.

snow pellets. Small round ice particles about 2–4 mm in diameter. These pellets are brittle and bounce upon striking the surface. They only form and fall from cumulus congestus clouds and are also called *graupel*.

squall line. A line of strong-to-severe thunderstorms that form in advance of a cold front as an instability line, and often move faster then the front itself.

stratosphere. The layer of the atmosphere from about 12 km to 50 km. In this layer, the air temperature increases (an inversion) and the layer is stable. This layer of the atmosphere also has a relatively high concentration of ozone.

subpolar low. This is a generalized zone of low pressure girdling the globe between 50–70 degrees North and South. The Aleutian and Icelandic lows are a part of this larger zone of low pressure.

subsidence inversion. A temperature inversion aloft formed by the sinking of massive amounts of air warmed by compression. These inversions are particularly strong and persistent in the eastern ends of the large high-pressure regions of the Hawaiian and Azores highs.

super-cell thunderstorm. A very large severe thunderstorm whose updrafts and downdrafts are dynamically coupled together—this allows the storm to persist for several hours. Sometimes referred in the convective outlook as an LP or HP supercell (LP is low precipitation, HP is high precipitation).

Texas norther. A strong, fast-moving cold front that sweeps down from Canada to Texas in 24 hours or less. Behind this front are strong, cold northerly or northeasterly winds. Known in Texas as a "Blue Norther."

thermal highs/lows. Thermal high and low pressure that forms over land areas only. The Siberian high is one example; a thermal low over the hot Sahara or Sonora deserts is another. These are shallow systems that weaken with height.

tropopause. The boundary between the troposphere and the higher layer of the atmosphere, the stratosphere. It is normally marked by a layer in which the temperature does *not* increase *nor* decrease with height (isothermal). The polar front jet (PFJ) and the subtropical jet (STJ) streams occur in this layer.

troposphere. The lowest region of the atmosphere from the surface upwards to an average height of 12 km. The actual height varies from 9 km over the polar regions to 16 km over the equatorial regions. Temperature normally decreases with height upward through this layer; moreover, much of the world's weather occurs within this layer.

TVS (tornado vortex signature). This is a small area of rapidly changing wind directions inside a mesocyclone. This signifies that a tornado is forming and gives the forecaster some 25–30 minutes of precious lead time to issue a Tornado Warning.

veering wind. A wind that changes circulation in a clockwise direction (south to west to north) and implies that warm air advection is occurring.

virga. Precipitation that falls from a cloud but evaporates before reaching the ground. Seldom seen in the humid south or southeast U.S., virga is common in the semi-arid and arid western U.S.

vorticity. This is a measure of the "spin" of fluids (air and water). For our planet and its atmosphere, we consider the vorticity of the spinning earth itself, plus the vorticity of the air moving over the surfaces of the planet. This is a useful concept in understanding the difficult-to-measure *vertical* motion in the atmosphere.

wall cloud. The bottom of the mesocyclone which protrudes below the rain-free base of a severe thunderstorm. A funnel cloud may form within the mesocyclone, lower, and then strengthen into a tornado.

warm nose. A layer of warm air aloft, overlying a layer of subfreezing air and below freezing temperatures above the warm air. This condition might produce a freezing rain or drizzle condition.

zonal winds. Winds aloft in the westerly wind belt that have a pronounced west-to-east movement—or, a barotropic atmosphere.

Appendix E: *Weather Websites*

www.landings.com

One of the best general aviation websites is Landings.com. This site offers the pilot everything from some excellent online flight planning services to several weather links. Their section on satellite imagery has a fantastic array of satellite picture links from many different sources.

http://www.nws.noaa.gov/

The National Weather Service home page—this is the "supermarket" of weather products. Linked to this site, for several examples, are: national and regional weather, radar and satellite imagery, current weather products such as METARs and TAFs (via the Internet Weather Source, IWS), the Storm Prediction Center (at Norman, OK), the Interactive Weather Information Network (IWIN), international weather services, and specialized centers such as the Aviation Weather Center (AWC), and the Climate, Tropical, and Marine Prediction Centers.

Go to "Current Conditions" for METARs and TAFs with an interactive menu system and maps (as shown in Chapter 2). At the Storm Prediction Center (SPC), get convective outlooks, watch and warning displays, experimental probability severe weather forecasts, and a lot of neat imagery on severe weather. International weather services can be found at the IWS link; you can call up current weather conditions for almost every country in the world. Select a country, and you will receive a menu of every weather station in that country. A click on each one gives you the current plain English weather report, the conditions for the past 24 hours and the METAR format of the report.

The Interactive Weather Information Network is a great site where you can click on a U.S. map to get weather data for certain geographical areas, that leads you to:

- a state map showing all weather locations including military (in blue letters). Click on a location ID and you will receive the latest plain language weather report, the METAR form, and what has happened over the last 24 hours.

- forecast discussions that tell you what was the weather forecasters' thinking behind a particular forecast.

- current severe weather watches and warnings by state or geographic area.

The Aviation Weather Center (AWC) is a major link from the NWS site that gives you the following menu items:

- "Official Forecast Products" in the form of a Standard Weather Briefing (*see* Chapter 19 for a detailed look at this briefing).

- "Test Products" such as the convection forecast (VVSTORM), mountain wave turbulence (MWAVE), and icing forecasts (Neural Icing and VVICE).

- Aviation Digital Data Service (ADDS):

- Central Weather Service Unit (CWSU) Corner: MIS and CWA messages and area of responsibility of ARTCCs in U.S.

- Collaborative Convection Forecast: This is now an online product and should be mentioned in weather briefings where applicable.

- "International Flight Folder" program: Gives weather information organized into a route format for a wide variety of international flight destinations.

Web addresses for some of the main links under the NWS website are:

http://www.awc-kc.noaa.gov   (Aviation Weather Center)

http://weather.noaa.gov/   (NWS Internet Weather Source)

http://iwin.nws.noaa.gov/   (IWIN's Weather Links main page)

http://adds.awc-kc.noaa.gov/   (Aviation Digital Data Service)

http://www.goes.noaa.gov   (Geostationary Satellite Server, "U.S. Satellite Sectors" link)

http://weather.noaa.gov/radar/radinfo/about.html

("About this Mosaic" under the "Latest Radar Image" link; contains a tutorial on the new WSR-88 Doppler radar imagery.)

http://www.nhc.noaa.gov/   (National Hurricane Center)

http://www.spc.noaa.gov/   (Storm Prediction Center)

http://weather.noaa.gov/fax/nwsfax.shtml   (NWS fax charts)

(*Note:* The NWS has announced that their "Difax" chart service will unavailable soon, but their webpage that contains the same charts will stay indefinitely. Keep checking the NWS site for more information on the availability of these clean-printing, black-and-white weather charts on the internet.)

http://www.faa.gov/asos/asos.htm

The FAA's Automated Weather Sensors homepage, where you can get information about AWOS and ASOS installations. Click on "Map of Sites" to find the automated stations in each state, on their Automated Weather Observing Site Map.

http://www-das.uwyo.edu/upperair/

The "Upper Air Observations" link leads to either raw or plotted radiosonde balloon data as well as constant pressure (upper air) charts, and the wind profiler time series.

An additional source for upper-air data: **http://weather.unisys.com/upper_air/index.html**

http://www.rap.ucar.edu/weather/upper/ and
http://www.rap.ucar.edu/weather/surface/

Beautiful graphical charts in vibrant colors for the upper-air and surface data offered by the folks at the National Center for Atmospheric Research (NCAR) as part of their "Real-Time Weather Data" pages. Weather plots are clear and easy to read on these well-drawn charts.

http://weather.cod.edu/nexlab.frames.html

College of DuPage "NexLab" weather pages—current weather analysis, satellite, radar, upper air data, in very clearly-drawn charts (some with white backgrounds, and some have black backgrounds with color plots and contours).

http://ww2010.atmos.uiuc.edu/(Gh)/home.rxml

At the University of Illinois Dept. of Atmospheric Science, the "Weather World 2010 Project" is a great "F.Y.I." website for all pilots, with meteorological guides, current weather, and excellent printable weather maps.

http://www.alaska.net/~aawu/

The Alaska Aviation Weather Unit, as described in Chapter 18, has the full range of weather charts and data for this flight region.

http://www.navcanada.ca/

Canadian weather services are available at the NavCanada site: click through from this address (through flight planning, aviation weather services, etc.) to a page that has various "folders" in a list shown at the left. Click on a folder to get more choices.

http://www.cmc.ec.gc.ca/cmc/

Canadian Meteorological Center: This site brings you all operational and forecast charts and bulletins as well as excellent quick-loading radar snapshots with some animation. If you click on "Forecasts" from this page, it leads to an "Aviation Products" link.

http://squall.sfsu.edu/crws/jetstream.html

The California Regional Weather Service has this page dedicated to jet stream charts, in full color.

Appendix F: *Answers to Practice Questions*

For Chapters 2 through 16 in this book: Following are answers for the practice questions and exercises at the end of these chapters. Also included are some references (where appropriate) to the AC 00-45E sections, as well as other books or sources for further study. For some questions, a specific page reference is given for you to look up in the source material, in order to find the answer.

Chapter 2

1. c. METAR KXYZ (AC 00-45E p.2-1)

2. c. AUTO

3. 06014KT, 24035KTG52, 00000KT (AC 00-45E p.2-4)

4. 36012G24KT

5. a. (*See* AC 00-45E p.2-9)

    b. Temp. = -4.4°C, dew point = -5.6°C, pressure change of .1, decreasing steadily in last 3 hours.

    Note: AC 00-45E Page 2-23 has a METAR for Jackson, TN, with a temperature and dew point. However, they do not explain the use of **0** and **1** to indicate when the temperature or dew point is above or below freezing: **T1XXX1XXX** (below freezing) **T0XXX0XXX** (above freezing). *Also: See* Appendix A for explanation of the pressure tendency codes.

6. (*See* AC 00-45E p.2-8)

7. **KSZL 18th 0255Z** Winds variable at 6 knots. **VSBY** 3 miles with a thunderstorm, light rain and mist. Overcast of cumulonimbus with a ceiling at 500 feet AGL. Temperature and dew point are 2°C and 1°C. Altimeter is 29.86 inches. Remarks: Tower visibility is 2 miles. Occasional lightning in-cloud and cloud-to-ground. Thunderstorm overhead and eight miles west, moving to the northeast. Sea level pressure is 1011.9 mb. The **6** identifier is rainfall amount for the last 3 to 6 hours: 0.12 inches. The **8** is the group number that identifies cloud types: **9** is cumulonimbus. Page 5-10, AC 00-45E, has a table that defines the different cloud types, and Appendix A also has a version of this table on Pages 150–152. (Hint: *see* Page 197, "Suggested Reading" for more good references on cloud types, such as C. Donald Ahrens' *Meteorology Today*.) U.S. stations will only identify certain cloud types (AC 00-45E p.2-17), but the Canadian stations identify all cloud types—and even tell you how much of the sky is covered by the different cloud types.

8. R060/700FT, R12L/1200FT, R24R/2400FT (AC 00-45E p.2-6)

9. d. (AC 00-45E p.2-20)

10. c. 7 miles (AC 00-45E p.2-5)

11. MI = shallow, BC = patches (AC 00-45E p.2-8)

12. False, only the **RA** has the + sign—heavy rain showers and snow.

13. b. (AC 00-45E p.2-21)

14. TORNADO B52 E10 MVG SW

15. PK WND 28046/22 (AC 00-45E p.2-4, 2-5)

16. TCU, CB (AC 00-45E p.2-13)

17. 12,000 feet (AC 00-45E p.2-11)

18. False.

19. b. or e. are both good candidates for the correct answer.

Here's why: First mark the location of the four METARs on the Inflight Advisory Plotting Chart. Pencil-in the temperatures of the four airports and the wind directions. Locate the low pressure (using "Buys Ballot's Law"—*see* Appendix D, Glossary); Omaha (Offutt) has a northeast wind, Whiteman is light and variable, and Iowa has easterly winds. Therefore if we put our back to the winds (forget about Whiteman's LV winds for the moment), it appears that the low pressure is somewhere to the northwest of Whiteman AFB. Let's nail it down by looking at the sea-level pressure readings: Offutt AFB has no SLP, so let's use the QNH (altimeter) values—the terrain is roughly the same elevation over this region. Lowest QNH setting is Whiteman AFB and Whiteman doesn't have any winds...or, perhaps it does. Check out the remarks at SZL: CB moving NE? Thunderstorms don't just amble along, they are moved by the average winds aloft. Using this wind from the southwest as an indicator, it appears that somewhere very close to SZL is the center of low pressure which can also explain the light and variable winds at SZL. But where is the front? Probably to the north of SZL along the Iowa/Missouri border area, helping to separate two separate air masses: Colder with snow north of the warm (or occluded) front and warmer unstable air (TSRA) to the south.

Chapter 3

1. Urgent Pilot Report: location 45 NM from SEA (Seattle) on a heading of 060 degrees; time 2018 UTC; flight level 14,000' MSL. Aircraft type, Beachcraft Baron. Sky condition, broken layer with bases at 8,000' MSL, tops at 13,200' MSL. OAT -4°C. Turbulence, severe clear air turbulence. Icing, light rime encountered between 8,000 and 12,000' upon climb out. ARTCC center Seattle.

2. *See figure at right.*

3. UUA /OV KOKC 270040/TM ??/ FL095/TP C172/TA 01/TB LGT-MDT/ IC LGT MXD ON STRUTS.... (Remember to give the *time* this happened, in your report.)

4. 1st PIREP: "Urgent PIREP from DC-9 over Great Falls, MT at 1705 UTC during descent. Low-level wind shear encountered at 200 feet AGL on approach runway; ±21 – 15 knots."

2nd PIREP: "Report transmitted by SEE (San Diego, Gillespie airport). Location: 40 nautical miles ENE (060°) of Oceanside, CA. Time of report is 1727 UTC at flight level 6,000' MSL. Aircraft is a Cessna 152. Sky condition is scattered clouds with bases at 3,500' and tops at 6,000 feet (MSL). Weather: Flight Visibility is 6 miles in haze from surface to 3,500 feet. Turbulence was occasional light at 6,000 feet."

Note: This type of PIREP is typical in the summer over southern and central California. Why? Strong and pronounced subsiding, warming air creates a strong marine layer inversion that results in reduced in-flight and slant-range visibilities."

3rd PIREP: "Report transmitted by Lake Tahoe airport (KTVL). Aircraft is enroute from Lake Tahoe to Stockton (SCK) at 12,500 feet MSL. Aircraft is a Cessna 210; flight in clouds. OAT is minus 1°C. Light rime icing was encountered. On climb out at Lake Tahoe, moderate to strong up/downdrafts were encountered."

4th: "Detroit (KDTW) transmitted the report. Aircraft was 30 NM SSW (210°) of Detroit. Time of report was 1901 UTC. Flight level was during climb out and aircraft is a Boeing 727. Sky condition: overcast condition with bases at 7,000' MSL and tops at 15,000' MSL, higher broken layer at 21,000' MSL. Light turbulence, occasionally moderate, on climb out between 10,000 and 15,000 feet MSL."

5th: "Urgent PIREP transmitted by Denver ARTCC. Aircraft was 35 NM south-southwest (200°) of Pueblo, CO at 2219 UTC. Aircraft type is a Cessna 182. Sky condition: altocumulus standing lenticular clouds northwest. Turbulence encountered was moderate, occasional severe. Remarks: Strong up and down-drafts of ±900 feet encountered. ZDV = Denver ARTCC."

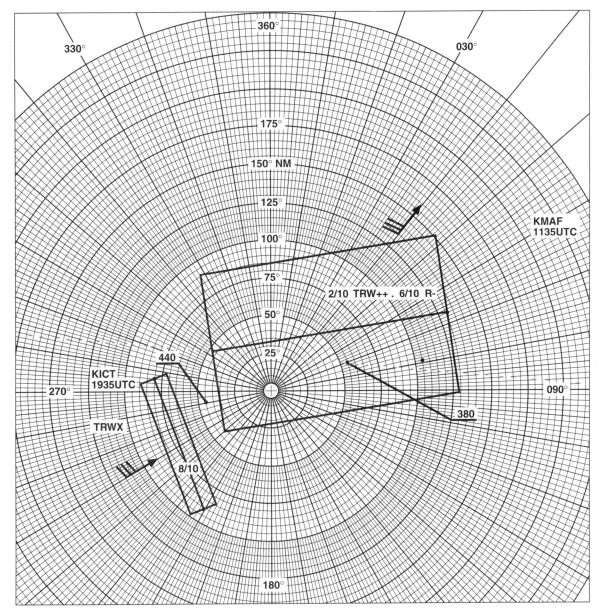

Answer to Chapter 3, question #2.

Chapter 4

1. KMSP 140/15 knots, gusts 25; 5 miles VSBY in mist; 1,500' broken and 4,000' overcast; 40% probability of 3 miles in mist and 1,500' overcast.

2. From 1600Z on the 25th to 1200Z on the 26th.

3. NWS/FAA site; no military installation at MSP, according to information in Table 2-2 (Page 17).

4. Temporary conditions 0000Z–0400Z; winds about the same as start of forecast (350/12 kts) with 4 miles in light rain and mist with 500' overcast (probably nimbostratus, NS).

5. e. (*See bottom* of Page 4-4 in AC 00-45E.)

6. P6SM: visibility greater than 6 miles.

7. No TAF available; go to area forecast (FA) that covers the flight destination.

Chapter 5

1. Estimated time of takeoff 1245Z. Light rain, 1,000–2,000' overcast, tops 30,000'. Visibility not given (unrestricted, P6SM). Widely scattered light thunderstorms/rain showers, cloud tops to 40,000'. No winds given, but synopsis states that a low pressure area is moving into west-central Minnesota, so winds at Devils Lake should be from the northeast at about 10–15 kts.

2. 3 times daily.

3. c. 20 knots. (AC 00-45E p.4-20)

4. Western Texas, north of a Marfa-San Angelo line. Ceilings 1,500 to 2,500' broken to overcast, 15,000' scattered. Light rain showers. 0300Z 3,000 to 5,000 scattered, 12,000' scattered. Outlook: VFR.

5. Always MSL. (AC 00-45E p.4-18)

6. Surface frontal boundary from Great Lakes, southwestward into southwestern Texas, will move southeastward to southeastern Ontario Province to lower Mississippi River Valley by 1500Z.

7. If no TAF is issued for the destination airport.

8. (*See* AC 00-45E p.4-19)

Chapter 6

1. Infrared satellite imagery shows convective cloud top temperatures over southern Wisconsin have been warming steadily, indicating a weakening trend. This also reflected by latest radar and lightning data. Weakening trend of present line may continue—however, new development is possible along outflow boundary [*see* Appendix D, Glossary] and over Nebraska, Iowa, and southwest Wisconsin behind current activity.

   A second thunderstorm is continuing to move eastward through eastern Montana. New development occurring over central North Dakota. Montana activity is moving toward more favorable airmass over western Dakotas, where dew points are in the upper 60s with Lifted Index values to -6. Thunderstorm activity expected to increase in coverage and intensity during afternoon hours.

2. 2 hours

3. *See* AC 00-45E Page 4-26.

4. a.

5. *See* AC 00-45E Page 4-26.

6. Isolated severe thunderstorms diameter 30 miles is moving from 240 degrees at 20 kts. Tops above 50,000'. Wind gusts of 65 kts possible.

7. Aviation Weather Center (AWC). Note that the Storm Prediction Center (SPC) also has good information on forecast storm activity (link to their website from the NWS webpage).

8. Aviation Weather Center.

9. Seattle to Pendleton to Eugene to Seattle. Occasional moderate or greater CAT between 28,000'–35,000' expected due to jet stream conditions beginning after 0200Z continuing beyond 0530Z and spreading over central Oregon by 0400Z.

10. Memphis to Meridian, Mississippi to Baton Rouge, LA to Memphis, TN. Moderate to occasional severe icing between the freezing level and 15,000'. Freezing level is 8,000' MSL in the east to 12,000' in the west.

11. 2 hours

12. 6 hours

13. b.

14. 6 hours

Chapter 7

1. Cheyenne, WY, synopsis valid time 1400 on the 10th to 0200Z on the 11th. Strong upslope winds over Wyoming until 0100Z with widespread IFR conditions in light snow and blowing snow. Conditions will improve from north to south across WY after 0100Z with decreasing clouds.

2. TWEBs are valid for 12 hours. (AC 00-45E p.4-31)

3. 50 NM-wide corridor.

4. MIA-FMY: Clear 5 miles in mist (BR), no winds given. FMY-TPA: 3,000' scattered to broken. Visibility probably better than 5 miles as mist should be broken up by 1900–2000Z. No TS in vicinity this early.

Chapter 8

1. Leg 1, ABQ–midpoint: 260/20, -4°C.

   Leg 2, midpoint–MKC: 270/20, -9°C.

   Typically, temperatures are colder east of a ridge of high pressure, where cold air masses move southward. Leg 2 is probably on the eastern side of a ridge, and the northwesterly flow of air is typically colder than the air to the west of the ridge.

2. 300 degrees at 125 kts, -51°C.

3. b. (*See* AC 00-45E p.4-35)

4. 9900 light and variable.

5. No (*see* AC 00-45E p.4-35).

6. 240/30, +8°C.

Chapter 9

1. b. CWA; because it can be issued faster and is a 2-hour forecast reflecting current conditions.

2. Area of heavy rainshowers/thunderstorms moving northeast at 40 knots and will affect southeast Maine and Cape Cod area next 1 to 2 hours.

3. St. Louis, Missouri: Scattered occasional broken layer 1,500 to 2,000' AGL. Broken layer occasionally overcast with chance of Level 3–4 thunderstorms widely scattered and moving east at 20 knots. 2200Z: MVFR conditions with broken to overcast layer 800 to 1,500 feet AGL. Chance visibilities 3–4 miles in fog and haze. Winds 250 to 280 at 10 to 15 knots. Shifting to 280 to 310 degrees after 2200Z.

4. *See* AC 00-45E p.4-38.

5. Yes. *See* AC 00-45E p.4-39.

Chapter 10

1. Strong cold front currently along line from Erie, PA to Zaneville, OH to Bowling Green, KY to Memphis, TN, 60 NM north of Texarkana, TX to Dallas/Fort Worth. Strong upper-level low centered at 1200Z over Lake Erie moving slowly northeastward at 10 knots. Strong jet stream will provide strong divergence pattern aloft. Narrow zone of instability ranges from -7 to -5 with good moisture available along and ahead of frontal zone. (*Note:* Remember that "minus" lifted-index stability values are unstable.)

2. (*See* AC 00-45E p.12-2, Table 12-1)

3. (*See* AC 00-45E p.4-26)

4. *See* Glossary (Appendix D)… and may you never encounter one!

5. Day 1 chart: Issued 5 times a day, first issued at 0600Z.

   Day 2 chart: Issued 2 times daily, first issued at 0830Z.

   (Standard time)

Chapter 11

1. 39,000 feet;

    a. MSL

2. Located in NW corner of South Carolina; NE movement. (*See* forecast winds aloft, AC 00-45E Page 10-5.)

3. The low pressure cells are associated with a frontal system, and short-wave trough which is probably moving eastwards along the front—these features can also be seen on the constant pressure charts (in AC 00-45 Section 8).

4. c.

5. A TROF, moving eastward.

6. TSHRA over Virginia and the Carolinas (particularly the western areas) caused by the following factors: Deep, warm, moist airflow over the region from Gulf of Mexico. Composite moisture/stability chart (1200Z) doesn't show much instability (0, -1; high K-index numbers, 29). But 1200Z is the morning balloon-run; with time and heating, the air mass over the southeast U.S. ahead of the frontal zone has become more unstable, with lifted-index values probably running -4 to -5 by 0000Z. Activity is being triggered by TROF.

7. Tops 25,000' MSL. Rain and rainshowers. Moderate steady rain is reported on weather depiction chart. Activity probably moving towards the WSW or SW (according to the forecast winds aloft, AC 00-45E Page 10-5).

Chapter 12

1. Just north of front, temps are +5 to +6°F, but drop to -7°F about 300 NM north of the front. Winds north of the front are from the NW to N, 5-10 knots.

    South of the front, temps are mid-high 30s dropping to high 20s over Wyoming. Winds S-SW at about 5 knots.

    The front coded as 027 is a quasi-stationary weak front with waves. Further west, the front is coded as 450, a cold front of moderate intensity with little change.

2. Temperature in low to high 30s (F). Pressure is approximately 1016.2 to 1004.0 mb. Wind is from N-NE 10–15 knots. Pressure has fallen, but is now steady.

3. TX–LA area: winds from W-NW, at 10-15 knots. Temps low to mid-40s in TX and low to mid 50s in LA, dew points are low 30s to mid-40s.

4. Front type is 420, a cold weak front.

5. b.

6. Temperature and dew point are 35° and 19°F, winds N-NE at 10 knots. Pressure has fallen 3 mb in the last 3 hours. Sky cover is 5/8 to 7/8 coverage (broken).

7. b.

Chapter 13

1. Height of the base of the lowest scattered layer. *See* AC 00-45E Pages 6-2, 6-3.

2. This is new! See "Cloud Height," AC 00-45E Page 6-2. A partially obscured sky cannot be recognized by auto-station's optical scanner, so the sky-cover circle will have an "M" inside it.

3. A thin layer at 1,000 feet cannot be recognized by the automated optical sky scanners. If there are no other cloud layers, an "M" will be entered in the sky-cover circle.

4. a. IFR

    b. VFR

    c. LIFR

    d. LIFR

    e. VFR

    f. MVFR

5. A trough of low pressure, which can also act as an instigator of convective activity.

6. Thunderstorm activity with rain and snow; heavy continuous rain at Tallahassee, FL.

7. Stay-on-the-ground weather! Freezing rain and drizzle.

8. b. You can get a clue to this by examining the airflow pattern on the 700 and/or 500 mb charts. The alignment of the surface isobars on the surface analysis chart are roughly the same as the contour lines on the 700/500 mb charts. Activity is moving roughly from the southwest toward the northeast.

    More hints about determining wind direction and speed: sometimes there might not be a TAF available, and the METAR or TWEB doesn't give wind information, etc., so you need other ways to deduce wind conditions. Try to find a reporting station with a TAF in the area near your flight path, and note the wind report/forecast. If the terrain is relatively smooth over this region, you can use that TAF's wind information for your flight. Also, the isobars drawn on latest surface analysis chart can help, because winds flow roughly parallel to the isobars, counterclockwise around lows, and clockwise around highs. Many times these isobars will be drawn for every 2 mb of pressure; the rule for speed is: "the closer together the isobars, the stronger the wind speed."

    Generally, the winds east and northeast of a low-pressure system, north of a surface warm front, are from the east-northeast to east-southeast and fairly light (5-10 kts). The closer you get to the low, wind speeds will pick up to 10–15 kts.

    West and west-northwest of a low-pressure cell, behind a cold front with increasing pressure, winds are north to northwest at possible speeds of 15–20 kts (or even higher depending on the distance from the low center).

    East and southeast of a low, ahead of a cold front and south of a warm front, winds generally come from the southwest and southeast. Speeds can vary considerably with the stronger winds just ahead of the cold front (15–20 kts), and weaker further to the east around 10-15 kts.

    But always pay attention to topography when determining winds—hills and valleys can cause variation in direction and speed.

Chapter 14

1. a.

2. d.

3. b.

4. d.

5. a.

6. c.

7. Most unstable, c.

    Most stable, b.

    Air mass, a.

    Driest, c.

8. b.

9. a. (*See* AC 00-45E p.9-4.)

Chapter 15

1. 30; 60 (*see* AC 00-45E Table 8-1).

2. Yes; if temperature is colder than -41°C (*see* AC 00-45E Table 8-1).

3. 300 mb level and up; starts at 10 kts with 20-knot increments.

4. Zonal.

5. c.

Chapter 16

1. 8,000' at KSTL, rising to 10,000' at KBNA, and about 12,000' MSL at KATL.

2. Level drops from about 8,000' MSL to 4,000' MSL on the 1800Z panel. Yes, icing is a real possibility judging from the MVFR/IFR weather expected over the area, and the low freezing levels.

3. Yes—moderate up to 18,000 feet MSL.

4. Yes—moderate to severe, up to 24,000 feet, probably because of forecast convective activity.

5. IFR conditions (less then 1,000' and less then 3 miles).

6. Cold front (450), moderate with little or no change, and no specifications given.

7. Continuous rain; changing to showery continuous TSHRA between KBNA and KATL.

8. Cold front (moderate, increasing with waves) is expected to move through KSTL (moving to the east-southeast) at 0000Z. Skies will probably be clear, or scattered clouds at worse. Temperatures colder and winds from the north or northwest.

9. Warm front (257). Moderate with little or no change; front with waves.

10. Freezing rain and ice pellets (*see* AC 00-45E Page 5-9; these are symbol numbers 66 and 79 on the symbols table) for the 0000Z panel. 1200Z panel shows continuous slight rain in this area (symbol number 62 on the Page 5-9 table).

11. Jet is indicated by the heavy line. Starting over Pacific and moving eastward: 80 knots at start of jet line. First double line = 100 kts; second double line = 120 kts; third double line, just offshore of southern California is 140 kts. Strongest winds are at FL350 over central Arizona (150 kts). Double line over New Mexico is for 120 kts. Last double line over Illinois/Iowa border = 100 kts, and end of jet line = 80 kts.

12. Moderate turbulence from 28,000 to 38,000 feet over an area that covers much of Utah, Colorado, Arizona and the northern half of New Mexico.

13. Lowest tropopause height of FL 27,000' is at 44N, 40W. Highest tropopause height of 52,000 feet is at 18N, 115W.

14. Higher tropopause heights are usually found in the low latitudes (subtropical jet stream), and lower tropopause heights are found at higher latitudes (polar front jet stream).

15. Front moving to southeast at 15 knots.

16. Occasional embedded cumulonimbus (CB) with tops to 36,000 feet.

Suggested Reading

In addition to the textbooks listed here, there are pamphlets and guides available through the NWS "METAR/TAF Information" page at **www.nws.noaa.gov/oso/oso1/oso12/metar.htm**, as well as through other NWS webpages mentioned throughout this book.

Ahrens, C. Donald *Meteorology Today: An Introduction to Weather, Climate, and the Environment.* 6th ed. Florence, Kentucky: Brooks/Cole Publishing, 1999.

Buck, R. N. *Weather Flying.* 3rd ed. New York: MacMillan, 1988.

Heldref Publications *Weatherwise* magazine. Bimonthly. See their website for subscription information: **http://www.heldref.org** or go directly to *Weatherwise* online at **http://www.weatherwise.org/**.

Lester, Peter *Turbulence.* Englewood, Colorado: Jeppesen-Sanderson, Inc., 1994.

Newton, Dennis *Severe Weather Flying.* 2nd ed. Newcastle, Washington: Aviation Supplies & Academics, Inc., 1991.

Taylor, Richard L. *Aviation Weather.* Greenwich, Connecticut: Belvoir Publications, Inc., 1991.

U.S. Dept. of Transportation, F.A.A.; U.S. Dept. of Commerce, N.O.A.A., N.W.S. *Advisory Circular 00-30A, "Rules of Thumb for Avoiding or Minimizing Encounters with Clear Air Turbulence."* AC 00-30A, AFS-400. Washington, DC: November 21, 1988.

Notes

Notes